REX DEUS
THE FAMILIES OF THE GRAIL

CYNDI AND TIM WALLACE-MURPHY

Grave Distractions Publications
Nashville, Tennessee

REX DEUS
THE FAMILIES OF THE GRAIL

ISBN-13: 9781944066116

In Publication Data
Wallace-Murphy Cyndi and Wallace-Murphy, Tim
BISAC Category: OCC031000
Body, Mind, and Spirit / Ancient Mysteries & Controversial Knowledge

Find out more about that authors at: www.timwallace-murphy.com

Printed in the United States

DEDICATION

To all our brothers and sisters worldwide who follow
'The Way' of Love, Compassion and Service.'

PREVIOUS WORKS BY TIM WALLACE-MURPHY

The Mark of the Beast
A collaboration with Trevor Ravenscroft

An Illustrated Guidebook to Rosslyn Chapel

The Templar Legacy and Masonic Inheritance within Rosslyn Chapel

Rosslyn, Guardian of the Secrets of the Holy Grail
A collaboration with Marilyn Hopkins

Rex Deus
A collaboration with Marilyn Hopkins and Graham Simmans

Templars in America
A collaboration with Marilyn Hopkins

Custodians of Truth
A collaboration with Marilyn Hopkins

Cracking the Symbol Code

The Enigma of Freemasonry

What Islam Did For Us.

The Knights of the Holy Grail

Hidden Wisdom

The Genesis of a Tragedy: A Brief History of the Palestinian People

TABLE OF CONTENTS

Acknowledgments

While all responsibility for the contents of this book and the opinions expressed therein rests entirely with the authors Cyndi and Tim Wallace-Murphy, we would, nonetheless like to express our thanks to all who have contributed material, ideas and other practical forms of help to this project. Firstly we list those who are, sadly, no longer with us: Trevor Ravenscroft; Michael Monkton; Andy Pattison of Edinburgh; Robert Brydon of Edinburgh; Frederick Lionel of Paris; Guy Jordan of Provence; Colin Wilson of Cornwall; Michael Bentine; Professor Yun Lin of California; Andy Boracci of Sag Harbor and Laurence Gardner. Those who, thank God are still with us: Richard Beaumont; Jean-Michel Garnier of Chartres; Georges Keiss of Fa; Dr Hugh Montgomery; James McKay Munro of Edinburgh; Stella Pates of Ottery St Mary; Alan and Fran Pearson of Rennes-les-Bains; David Pykett; Amy Ralston; Vic Rosati of Totnes; Pat Sibille of Aberdeen; Laurence Bloom of London; Patrick Tresise of Quillan; Gloria Amendola of CT; our publisher, Brian Kannard of Grave Distractions Publications and last, and most certainly not least, our spiritual brother, Niven Sinclair of Haslemere .

Introduction

Rennes-le-Château is a small commune perched on a hilltop in South-western France that was virtually unknown until a documentary presented by Henry Lincoln[1] was aired on BBC television in 1972 bringing it to the attention of the British public. This gifted storyteller related a series of interlinked mysteries[2] presented in three programmes shown over several years.

After these, a book followed entitled, *The Holy Blood and the Holy Grail*,[3] written by Michael Baigent, Richard Leigh and Henry Lincoln. This book was phenomenal, a huge sensation. It was described as a 'brilliant piece of detective work,'[4] as a work 'that will infuriate many ecclesiastical authorities'[5] and, more simply as blasphemous. It rapidly attained bestseller status and was translated into most European languages. It made an astounding announcement viewed by many to be the most shattering secret of the past 2,000 years. A secret which could shake the Christian Church to its foundations-the marriage of Jesus and his founding of a dynasty that is still with us today.

Lincoln began his investigation by researching the strange story of a highly gifted parish priest, Bèrenger Saunière, who was banished to Rennes-le-Château for some unnamed misdemeanour in the late 19th century.[6] When the priest arrived to the village, he lived in utter poverty but it seems fortune smiled on him because he suddenly started spending millions of francs. Where did this money come from? The story continued with suggestions of buried treasure and then turned into a profound historical investigation, a modern Grail quest with aspects of mystery, cryptically coded documents, political intrigue, secret societies, a conspiracy that spans the centuries, the activities of the Knights Templar, the Cathars, and the Inquisition.

In consequence, Rennes-le-Chatèau had been "put on the map" and it was estimated in 1999 that more than 20,000 people visit this village every year from all over the world—since then the numbers have steadily increased. The same authors would follow-up *The Holy Blood and the Holy Grail* with *The Messianic Legacy*.[7] There are a plethora of other works, all more or less based on the foundation laid down by Baigent, Leigh, and Lincoln. The continuing international fascination with Rennes-le-Château is sustained by various clubs and associations devoted to further investigation of its mysteries. For example, by 2015 there were over 600,000 webpages on the Internet which focus on the enigma first brought to our attention by Henry Lincoln.

Adding another twist to the tales of buried treasures, sacred bloodlines, historical conspiracy, persecution and genocide, we must now add forgery, fantasy and complete fiction. A prestigious BBC television programme[8] made this startling assertion when it refuted yet another well-publicized book, *The Tomb of God*,[9] which claimed that Jesus was buried on a mountainside near Rennes-le-Château. More recently, another fraudster, who calls himself Ben Hammot, claimed to have to discovered the tomb of the Magdalene in the vicinity of Rennes-le-Chateau. This claim was on a par with his earlier photographic hoax of the Loch Ness monster, and his recent more nonsensical claim to have discovered the Ark of the Covenant.

As strange as it may seem, when the layers of invention are peeled off and the clouds of fabrication and questionable research are lifted away from the works centred on Rennes-le-Château, several very real mysteries remain. Once all the extraneous material is removed, we discover an historical basis for the most improbable claim of them all, the dynasty of Jesus, as part of a group of interlinked families who have continuously conspired together in an attempt to change the course of European History. These families all claim to be descendants of the 24 high Priests of the Temple in Jerusalem. The story unfolding in this book is the true mystery that surrounds Rennes-le-Château.

SECTION I

THE MASTERLY STORYTELLER
HENRY LINCOLN
AND RENNES-LE-CHÂTEAU

CHAPTER 1
THE MYTHOLOGY OF
RENNES-LE-CHÂTEAU

Each year thousands of tourists make their way up the scenic, twisting road to Rennes-le-Château either by foot, bicycle, car, horse back, or by coach.[1] These visitors arrive and depart by the same narrow road that climbs up from the town of Couiza, traverses the northern face of the mountain for the first few kilometres before turning to the west for the final and most precipitous part of the journey. The scene from this point is breath-taking with views of rolling landscape that is punctuated here and there with reminders of the turbulent history of this area. There is a shell of a château on a small hillside to north of Coustaussa dating from the 12th century.[2] There is also an equally impressive 16th century castle ruin in the village of Cassagnes and a 12th century Romanesque church. Looking due east of the road at this point you can see the remnants of the medieval Château de Blanchfort. Ascending the last kilometres of the twisting serpentine road, the village finally becomes visible. The short distance from the first house to the car park, which occupies a considerable portion of the village, is a clear reminder that this small hamlet and its mere existence and excellent location, cannot explain of itself, why it has such a worldwide attraction

Located in the middle of the car park is a strange water tower, and to the right, facing the precipice at the edge of the area, is an architectural oddity, a rectangular structure with a turreted tower, overhanging the cliff at one corner. Visible to the southeast is a peak, which is surmounted by the ruins of the

Château of Bèzu, and beyond that are the purple foothills of the Pyrenees. Facing the distant horizon, are the outlines of the jagged mountain terrain that separates France from Spain, its rough snow-capped peaks are visible even in the month of May.

The Celts and Cathars

In the surrounding countryside are megalithic remains providing evidence this area has been inhabited for at least 4,500 years,[3] and a Neolithic cemetery near the village dating back over 3,000 years. The Celts regarded this site as a sacred place and named it Rhedae after their principal local tribe.[4] Districts located near natural borders such as the Pyrenees have been fought over many times by successive waves of invaders from other cultures. After the Greeks colonized the port of Agde and subsequently founded the port of Marseilles in 639 BCE, it was suggested that they settled here. During the Roman occupation, the area of Rennes-le-Château increased in its importance. The large and beautiful mountain of Bugarach[5] was mined for gold and they also exploited Campagne-sur-Aude and Rennes-les Bains;[6] Rennes-le-Château is situated midway between these three points.

Before the collapse of the Roman Empire, it is alleged that Rhedae was a large town of nearly 30,000 inhabitants. During the time of the Merovingian King of France, Dagobert II (died 679) who married a Visigoth princess,[7] it was reputed to have been an important city and centre of power of the Visigoth Empire founded in 418 CE which straddled the Pyrenees and encompassed a vast tract of what is now present-day Spain.[8] Sweeping from central Europe westward, the Visigoths, a Teutonic warlike tribe, devastated everything in their path. In 410 CE, they besieged and conquered Rome, stripping it of its accumulated treasures, and toppling the Roman Empire before creating one of their own, which included Rhedae.[9]

Subsequently, the Visigoth Empire would also face collapse and the village became the seat of an important county, that of Razès.[10] At the onset of the 13th century this area was part of the Languedoc, the western part of greater Provence. Inspired by the Cathars, a religious group, this entire area developed in a way that its culture was so prosperous that many historians believe that, had the Catholic Church not instigated a brutal crusade against the 'Cathar heresy,' the Renaissance might well have occurred 200 years earlier and in the Languedoc rather than in northern Italy.[11]

The Albigensian Crusade and the Knights Templar

The word crusade brings to mind memories from school days, recalling the many wars that were fought against the infidel to liberate the Holy Land. The idea of a crusade against fellow Christians in Europe seems unthinkable, yet early in the summer of 1209, at the behest of the Pope, an army of northern knights descended upon the tolerant and peaceful people of the Languedoc to weed out and destroy the Cathar heresy.[12] The same ecclesiastical rights and privileges that were granted to the crusaders in the Holy Land were also granted to these knights; absolution for all the sins they had committed or might commit; and the right to confiscate all land and property belonging to those deemed heretics by Holy Mother the Church.[13] For more than twenty years the Cathar, or Albigensian, Crusade waged a bloody and brutal campaign in the Languedoc. This genocidal nature would not be matched again until the Holocaust against the Jews during the Second World War.[14] It is claimed that in the course of this crusade that ended with the fall of Montségur in 1244, the village of Rennes-le-Château was captured and recaptured many times.

A fact that has puzzled many historians over the years is that neither of the two knightly crusading Orders, the Knights Templar or the Knights Hospitaller took any military part in this vicious movement.[15] Both Orders owed the gift of their land in many cases to the Cathars or to nobles who were Cathar sympathizers so it would be a reasonable explanation that they would not want to repay their support with warfare.[16] The Templars held immense amounts of properties throughout the Languedoc, Roussillon and in the eastern part of the Provence proper. The vast majority of Templar holdings in mainland Europe lay within these districts.[17] In the swathe of countryside ranging from the commanderie at Campagne-sur-Aude, nearly 10 kilometres from Rennes-le-Château, to the coast at Baccares one is never out sight of Templar holdings, commanderies, castles, and fortified farms.[18] Thousand of pilgrims from the Mediterranean coast, Italy and beyond, followed the southern route to the medieval centre of pilgrimage at St James of Compostela, which passed nearby.[19] Here, as elsewhere in Europe, the Templars policed the pilgrimage routes. While their principal role was to protect the pilgrims, they also acted as bankers to both the pilgrims and the Church. With its holdings in farming, vineyards, quarrying, banking and the pilgrimage business, the order became immensely rich, and its activities spanned all of Christian Europe and the Holy Land.[20]

Following the Albigensian Crusade, Rennes-le-Château, along with all of the Cathar country, was subjected to the unwelcome attention of the Inquisition. During the 1360s, an outbreak of plaque, or the Black Death decimated the local population. Adding to its troubles, the hilltop town, despite its superb defensive location, was virtually destroyed by Catalan bandits.[21] A major political consequence that flowed from the crusade against the Cathars placed all the provinces of the Languedoc and Roussillon, which had been previously independent counties of considerable power and autonomy, under the rule of the king of France, administered by his feudal lords.[22] The main building within Rennes-le-Château, the Château d'Hautpoul, the one-time residence of the family d'Hautpoul who lived there for centuries, reflects this change in feudal administration. Following the crusade and up to the middle of the 20th century, Rennes-le-Château steadily declined in importance until it became yet another insignificant hilltop village solely dependant on eking out a living from the surrounding land. This small hamlet would see a renewal of interest and its modern revival centres around the strange events that began with the installation of a certain parish priest, Bérenger Saunière, on 1 June 1885.[23]

The Hilltop Parish Priest Saunière

The parish priest, Bérenger Saunière would have known Rennes-le-Château extremely well as he had been born and raised in the village of Montazels only a few kilometres away.[24] Saunière was an extremely intelligent, active, handsome and scholarly man who at first seemed destined for a promising career in the Church but, for reasons that have never been explained, seems to have lost the confidence of the hierarchy. To all outward appearances it would seem that his appointment to an insignificant and poverty stricken parish of Rennes-le-Château was some form of punishment or banishment.[25]

Bérenger Saunière

Between 1885 and 1891 parish records show that Saunière's stipend averaged the equivalent of about £6 sterling per year; hardly a lavish income for a priest who had once been thought of as being extremely bright. He used his

An aerial photo of Rennes-le-Château.
Photo by: G. Simmans

hunting and fishing skills to supplement his diet, and with his small income and the meagre gratuities provided by his parishioners he seemed to have led a pleasant and productive life.[26] He engaged Marie Dernarnaud, an 18-year-old peasant girl, as his housekeeper, and she became his lifelong companion and confidante.[27] He spent his evenings industriously improving his Latin and reading insatiably. Saunière also studied ancient Greek and Hebrew in order to increase his understanding of the Scriptures.[28] Abbé Henri Boudet, a parish priest in the nearby village of Rennes-les-Bains, was his nearest friend whom he visited frequently. Boudet was not only Saunière's friend but also his tutor; and he began to gain a profound knowledge of the complex and turbulent history of this region of France.[29]

Like so many other churches in the area, the ancient and dilapidated village church of Rennes-le-Château was built on the foundation of a far older place of worship. It is claimed that the Visigoths, dating from 6th century, built an early church on this site.[30] By this time Saunière was established as priest of the village, the church, which was dedicated to Mary Magdalene in 1059, was in poor condition almost beyond repair, for the roof leaked to such an extent that it rained on the heads of priest and parishioner alike.[31] It is not surprising that he wanted to restore it, so with the help and encouragement of his friend Abbé Boudet, he borrowed a small amount of money and, in 1891, a modest restoration began. While the renovation was in progress, it is claimed that he removed the altar corner stone that was supported by two Visigoth columns. One of the columns was hollow and inside of it were four parchments that had been rolled up and inserted into sealed wooden tubes. There were two documents said to have comprised genealogies, one dating from 1644 and the other from 400 years earlier. Two other documents in the wooden tubes are said to have been the work of one of Saunière's predecessors, the Abbé Antoine Bigou, who had been the priest here in the 1780s.[32] Saunière notified his immediate superior, Mgr Felix-Arsene Billard, the Bishop of Carcassonne.

In the account of these events within the pages of *The Holy Blood and the Holy Grail*, it is alleged that Saunière was promptly sent to Paris, at the bishop's expense, to show the documents to senior ecclesiastical scholars.[33] The book recounts that one of these scholars was Abbé Bieil, the director-general of the seminary of St Sulpice, a church long associated with esoteric spirituality. It is also claimed that the documents were shown to Bieil's nephew, Emil Hoffet, [34] who had established an impressive reputation as a scholar. Hoffet had considerable expertise in linguistics, palaeography and, most importantly, cryptology. In spite of the fact that he had a clerical role, he was deeply immersed in esoteric thought and was in regular contact with many of the groups and individuals involved in the occult revival in Paris.[35] This elite group involved literary giants such as Stèphane Mallarmé, Maurice Maeterlinck, the composer Claude Debussy and the renowned operatic diva Emma Calvé.[36] It is impossible to establish the outcome of Saunière's various meetings with his church superiors during his stay in Paris. It is alleged, however, that this simple country priest was welcomed into the illustrious circle of esotericists that revolved around Emil Hoffet, and some sources even propose that Saunière and Emma Calvé were lovers. It is also claimed that Saunière visited the Louvre and purchased copies of three paintings; one of a medieval pope, another a work of some esoteric significance by Teniers, and the third, the well-known painting Les Bergers d'Arcadie by Poussin.[37]

The Restoration of the Church Continues

When he returned to Rennes-le-Château, Saunière continued with the restoration of the church and its grounds. In the churchyard stands the tomb of Marie, Marquise d'Hautpoul, the last of the feudal lords of this area. Abbè Antoine Bigou designed the head and flagstone marking Marie's grave,[38] and he is credited with the writing of two of the mysterious documents found inside the hollow Visigoth column. As well as being the parish priest, he was also the personal chaplain to the d'Hautpoul family. It is impossible to explain why Saunière obliterated the inscriptions on the tomb, as his recorded actions at this point are somewhat odd to say the least.[39]

During this time, Saunière began spending considerable sums of money on the renovation. By 1884, records show that he was spending more on postage than his annual stipend could possibly support, and yet between 1896 and his death in early 1917 he spent more than 200,000 gold francs, which at that time would have been valued at £500,000 sterling, the equivalent of several million pounds today.[40]

The church not only benefited from the priest's generosity; Saunière paid for the construction of a modern road leading up to the village and he financed the substantial cost of providing water for his parishioners. He commissioned the building of a considerable house, the Villa Bethania,[41] and, for his own use, he built a strange edifice, the Tour de Magdala, which overlooks the valley on the steepest side of the mountaintop. The parish church was not simply restored but it was embellished with decorations that can only be described as eccentric. Emblazoned on the wall over the door entrance he placed the warning-TERRIBILIS EST LOCUS ISTE, which is usu-

Tour de Magdala
Photo Tim Wallace-Murphy

ally mis-translated by most works on Rennes-le-Château as 'this place is terrible'[42] instead of the more accurate rendition—this place is awesome. Upon entering the church, the holy water stoop is supported by a frightening statue of a demon known as Asmodeus, a prominent figure renowned in legend as the custodian of secrets, the guardian of hidden treasure and the guardian of Solomon's Temple.

As you would find in most Catholic churches there are panels here depicting the Stations of the Cross, which are painted in bright colours and the details differ considerably from those that one would expect to see in a village church of this nature. The Fourteenth Station is particular noticeable as it depicts the body of Jesus being carried out of the tomb, for here the scene is set against the background of a dark sky lit by a full moon. It is reasonable to assume that Saunière was attempting to signify that either Jesus was buried after dark, many hours later than the Bible states, or that the body of the Saviour is being carried out of the tomb under the cover of darkness.[43] It is conceivable that this is a clever symbolic reference to the age-old esoteric tradition that Jesus survived the crucifixion. That being the case, this may well be a pictorial representation of the statement made in *The Lost Gospel According to St Peter* which recounts how the soldiers guarding the tomb reported: 'And as they declared what things they had seen, again they see three men come forth from the tomb, and two of them supporting one...'[44] This would certainly lend credence to the esoteric legend that Jesus did not die on the cross but that after the crucifixion he was taken down and nursed back to health by members of the Essene sect.

The East End of the Chapel
Photo Tim Wallace-Murphy

As the decoration of the newly restored church continued, this provincial parish priest did not abandon his own comfort. He created an orangery in the grounds of the Villa Bethania, [45] and a zoological garden. He installed an impressive library in the Tour de Magdala, which is not surprising for a man of his intellectual abilities. [46] He continued to spend large sums of money to satisfy a taste he had developed in rare china, precious fabrics and antique marbles, which he collected fervently. He was not a self-centred man and continued to look after the needs of his parishioners. In addition to financing the building, the road and the water tower, he also provided them with banquets. [47] His lifestyle took on the characteristics of an oriental potentate instead of a modest parish priest in one of smallest and most impoverished parishes in France. According to *The Holy Blood and the Holy Grail*, his generosity extended well beyond his parish; he delighted in inviting a great number of important guests from the capital and from abroad, including Emma Calvé. Curiously was alleged to have included on his guest list the French Secretary of State for Culture and strangest of all, he reputedly welcomed Archduke Johann von Hapsburg, a cousin of Emperor Franz-Joseph of Austria, who was said to be travelling in disguise under the name of 'Monsieur Guillaume.' [48]

The Bishop of Carcassonne, who had sent Saunière to Paris, appeared to overlook his decadent spending and his flamboyant lifestyle. After the bishop died, however, Saunière was called before his successor, Paul-Felix Beurain de Beausejour, to account for his actions. [49] Unwilling to explain the source of his wealth and refusing to accept the bishop's order transferring him to another parish, he was accused of simony, that is selling masses and pardons. On 5 November 1910, a local tribunal called to hear his case suspended the uncooperative priest. [50] A new priest, whose ministrations were boycotted by the villagers, was appointed in his place. The Mayor of Rennes-le Château sided with Saunière and informed the bishop by letter that the church remained empty and all religious ceremonies had been replaced by civil rites. The devout villagers continued to attend masses celebrated by Saunière in the Villa Bethania while the new priest preached to an empty church. Saunière appealed directly to the Vatican seeking to be re-established as the priest of Rennes le Château and against his sentence. He was determined to sue the bishop for defamation of character and notified his lawyers of this intent. The sanctions that were imposed on him by the Bishop of Carcassonne were annulled in 1915. With his head held high and with an ironic and mysterious smile upon his face Bérenger Saunière re-entered his presbytery.

Saunière's Mysterious Death

The circumstances surrounding Saunière's illness and sudden death are peculiar. On the 17th of January 1917, the same date as inscribed on the tombstone of Marquise d'Hautpoul,[51] he suffered a major stroke. His parishioners declared that just five days before his death that he seemed to be in an enviable state of health for a man of his age. Death is a great leveller. The ceremonies for attending the rich and poor alike in 20th century France were the same. While Saunière lay on his dying bed, a priest was called in haste to hear his last confession and to administer the last rites. Upon his arrival the priest hurried to the dying man's bedside. It is claimed in *The Holy Blood and the Holy Grail* that according to eyewitness testimony, he emerged shortly in a state of considerable agitation and he refused to administer extreme unction, presumably on the basis of Saunière's deathbed confession.[52]

Saunière died on 22 January 1917 without being absolved. The ritual following his death was perplexing by any ecclesiastical standards. Dressed in a robe adorned with numerous scarlet tassels, he was seated upright in an armchair and placed on the terrace beside the Tour de Magdala. Many unidentified mourners filed past the corpse, one by one. For reasons unexplained, many of them plucked a tassel from his robe, perhaps as some ritual token of remembrance. To this day this strange rite mystifies the residents of Rennes-Le-Château as it does everyone else.[53]

Marie Dernarnaud

Marie Dernarnaud lived at the Villa Bethania in considerable comfort until 1946 when her fortunes underwent a drastic change. After the war the French Government issued new currency, and all who wanted to exchange any considerable amount of old francs for new were subjected to severe questioning in order to establish the source of their wealth. This standard was set in place to expose tax evasion, war profiteers and various other illegal operations. Marie was not going to be answerable to anyone, and she was seen in the Villa Bethania garden burning sheaves of old franc notes.[54] She was able to sustain herself for another seven years by living on the proceeds from the sale of the Villa Bethania. The property had been bought by a certain Monsieur Noel Corbu who, along with his family, looked after her until she died. Marie had repeatedly told him that he was walking on valuable treasures, which would one day make him extremely wealthy and that before her death she would reveal the secret to him. Unfortunately for M. Corbu, this did not happen as Marie suffered a sudden stroke on 29 January 1953, which left her without the ability to speak. Her secret followed her to the grave.

The comments made by Marie motivated a wave of destructive treasure hunting in the guise of archaeological excavation. If you found any buried treasure, by French Law, it was yours to keep. Ready available explosives, which were used extensively in wine growing regions to clear deep-rooted vines, exacerbated the situation. An ornate tomb in the nearby vicinity reputedly to be the one depicted by Poussin in Les Bergers d'Arcadie suffered damage from one of the dynamiting expeditions. The small hilltop village of Rennes-le-Château stands virtually on a honeycomb of tunnels, some natural, some man-made, some ancient and others very recent. When entering the village a large and rusting notice could be seen that, until very recently, declared that 'unauthorised archaeological excavations' are forbidden under a local law dating from 1966. A typewritten notice to the same effect hangs outside the Marie warning that this law still applies. Like many French laws it is honoured more by its breach than by its observance. As Tim wandered the near deserted streets on a hot summer's day in 1999, all that could be heard was the faint tapping of hammers in the tunnels underground.

CHAPTER 2
THE STORY SURFACES

Travelling through France in 1969, Henry Lincoln picked up a paperback copy of *Le Trésor Maudit* by Gérard de Sède. In it he read that the Abbé Bèrenger Saunière, parish priest of Rennes-le-Chateau had apparently deciphered certain coded documents found in his parish church. There was one strange omission in the story that intrigued Lincoln. Although the texts of two of these documents were reproduced in the book, the message alluding to the treasure was not. This was not mentioned at all by de Sède, and Lincoln was intrigued by the discovery of a concealed message within one of the published documents.[1] If he was able to decipher the message, as he was, it seems certain that de Sède would have been able to do so as well. How could such an oversight as this have happened? After all, mention of a coded message of this nature would have given a huge boost to book sales.

Lincoln was fascinated with story and presented it to the executive producer of the 'Chronicle' series of programmes for BBC as a possible theme for a television documentary and, with the producers approval, he travelled to France to meet Gérard de Sède. Lincoln questioned de Sède as to his reasons for not publishing the message hidden in the parchments. Gérard de Sède taunted him by replying 'What message?' When Lincoln pursued the point, de Sède gave an enigmatic answer: 'Because we thought it might interest someone like you to find it for yourself.'[2] Subsequently de Sède began teasing Lincoln with bits and pieces of information. The initial revelation was the text of a coded message, which spoke of the painters Poussin and Teniers. Lincoln would learn from de Sède that the key to the code was incredibly complex and had only been broken by the computer experts of the cipher department of the French army. After checking the story with experts, Lincoln's suspicions were confirmed by people within British Intelligence who stated bluntly that that this complex code was unbreakable by computer. Therefore either Sède or someone else must hold the key.

It turns out that the two parchments whose authorship was ascribed to Abbé Antoine Bigou, Saunière's predecessor, were actually excerpts from the New Testament written in Latin. Yet, neither of these documents is altogether what it first appears to be. In the first coded document, the words run together with no spaces between them and, in a number of places, some extremely unnecessary letters appear to have been inserted. The second document is completely different, lines of text are strangely abridged, sometimes in the middle of a word, and certain letters are obviously raised above the others. These two texts include a sequence of creative and highly complex codes. Both texts have since been deciphered and the following transcriptions were published in French books devoted to Rennes-le-Château and in two of the TV documentaries made for the BBC.

BERGERE PAS DE TENTATION QUE POUSSIN TE-
NIERS GARDENT

LA CLEF PAX DCLXXXI PAR LA CROIX ET CE CHE-
VAL DE DIEU

J'ACHEVE CE DAEMON DE GARDIEN A MIDI POM-
MES BLEUES

(SHEPHERDESSS, NO TEMPTATION. THAT POUS-
SIN, TENIERS, HOLD THE KEY; PEACE 681. BY THE
CROSS AND THIS HORSE OF GOD, I COMPLETE-
[OR DESTROY]—THIS DAEMON OF THE GUARD-
IAN AT NOON. BLUE APPLES)[3]

While one of the ciphers is so complex that it might have stumped Einstein, the other is quite simple and childish. In the second parchment the raised letters merely spell out the message:

A DAGOBERT II ROI ET A SION EST CE TRESOR ET
IL EST LA MORT.

(TO DAGOBERT II, KING, AND TO SION BELONGS
THIS TREASURE AND HE IS THERE DEAD.)[4]

On reflection, Lincoln thought that Saunière must have spotted the second message, but voiced his doubts that the parish priest, intelligent though he was, would have had any chance whatsoever of deciphering the more complex code.

Les Bergers d'Arcadie was Nicholas Poussin's most famous painting. De Sède told Lincoln that there was a tomb that had been discovered not far from Rennes-le-Château, which, resembled the one in Poussin's painting and forwarded him several photographs of it.[5] This additional information allowed Lincoln to make a full-length documentary that was broadcast early in 1972 under the title *The Lost Treasure of Jerusalem?* As a result of the wide public interest and controversy created by the programme, Lincoln immediately began working on another documentary entitled *The Priest, the Painter and the Devil*, which was broadcast in 1974.

The growing perplexity and mystification of the story began to exceed any one man's capacity to investigate it and, in 1975, Lincoln began collaborating with Richard Leigh and Michael Baigent and together they wrote a third documentary entitled *The Shadow of the Templars*, which was broadcast in 1979.[6] An interesting letter from a retired Anglican priest provoked the au-

Les Bergers d'Arcadie (*Shepherds of Arcadia*) by **Nicholas Poussin**

thors' curiosity, as it made startling and bizarre allegations with apparent i as to whether the authors believed them or not. The writer's bold proclamation stated that the treasure did not consist of bullion, jewellery or articles of value, but of a secret that irrefutably claimed the Jesus did not die on the cross and that he was alive and well as late as 45 CE.[7]

The Holy Blood and the Holy Grail began by undertaking the story of the priest Bèrenger Saunière and the coded documents he found, and continued with the authors' investigations into the possible source of Saunière's sudden accumulation of wealth, power and influence. How could a poor parish priest acquire such a fortune in a small, deprived village? They began by investigating the history of the area to see if it could provide any rational explanation of this and then they proposed three plausible sources: the Visigoths, the Cathars and the Knights Templar. During their research into the origins and actions of the Templars, they began to suspect that there was much more to this mystery than a mere search for buried treasure.

The Knights Templar

During their study of the accepted historical account of the founding of the Knights Templar, or the Order of the Poor Knights of the Temple of Solomon, Baigent, Leigh and Lincoln found that these raised far more questions than they answered. Guillaume de Tyre, writing between 1175 and 1185 claimed that the order was founded in 1118[8] and describes how a nobleman, Hughes de Payens, sometimes known as Huge de Payne, a vassal of the Count of Champagne, presented himself with eight companions to Baudouin (Baldwin) II, the King of Jerusalem. These nine knights avowed their purpose to 'as far as their strength permitted, to keep the roads and highways safe… with a special regard for the protection of the pilgrims'. They were granted quarters on the site believed to be that of the ancient Temple of Solomon, from which the new order derived its name[9] and, according to Guillaume, no further candidates were admitted to the ranks for the first nine years of the order's existence. The knights were warmly welcomed by the Patriarch of Jerusalem, who granted them permission to use the double-barred Cross of Lorraine as their heraldic device.

Baigent, Leigh and Lincoln noted that it was odd that the official royal historian employed by King Baudoin II, Fulk de Chartres, made no mention whatsoever of Hugh de Payens or the Knights Templar or, to use their popular name, La Milice du Christ (the Militia of Christ). There are also no contemporary records of the knights exerting themselves in the protection of pilgrims to the holy places. However, in less than ten years the Templars had acquired a certain degree of renown. The Abbot of Clairvaux, St Bernard, wrote a highly complimentary document in 1128, *In praise of the New Knighthood*, in which he declared the Templars to be the epitome of Christian values.

The Council of Troyes, which was dominated by the thinking of the Abbot of Clairvaux, [10] gave the order their rule in 1128. The first grand master of the Order was Hughes de Payens and the Knights Templar themselves were to be warrior monks, combining the discipline of the cloister with a courage that bordered on fanaticism. A papal Bull was issued in 1139 by Pope Innocent II, a protégé of St Bernard, declaring that the Templars owed no allegiance to any secular or ecclesiastical power other than himself. Strictly speaking, they could act independently and, if necessary, in defiance of the rule of kings, emperors, princes or prelates. [11] Baigent, Leigh, and Lincoln also claim to have discovered that the order had actually been founded nine years earlier, as the 'front men' for a mysterious and secretive group known as the Priory of Sion. [12] They also suggest that the true motive for its foundation was to travel to Jerusalem to locate the hidden treasure of the Temple of Solomon. [13] Apparent confirmation of this third Order to use the authors' words, 'soon thrust itself upon them. [14] It seemed as though there had been another organization working behind the scenes manipulating both the Templars and the Cistercians.

The Secret Dossiers

The wealth and variety of documentation that in appeared in France from 1956 onwards relating to Bérenger Saunière and the mystery of Rennes-le-Château implied that the subject was of great, if unexplained, importance to someone. The information emerged consistently as if to stimulate further investigations, and was presented as if it had originated from some highly privileged source. Within this information were references directly or indirectly relating Rennes-le-Château, the Cathars, the Templars, the Merovingian kings, the Rose-Croix and books on both Saunière and Rennes-le-Château.

These books and articles tell only a small part the story. Documents that were deposited in the *Bibliothèque Nationale* (National Library) in Paris, which did not seem destined for general circulation, held most interesting and perhaps more important information. The authors' identity of many of these works is often disguised by pseudonyms.[15] A work entitled, *Les Descendants Merovingians Et l'Enigme du Razès Wisigoths* (The Descendants of the Merovingians and the Enigma of the Visigoth Razès), claims on the title page to have been published by the Supreme Masonic Lodge Switzerland, the Grand Loge Alpina, which is equivalent to the Grand Orient Lodge in France and Grand Lodge in Britain; yet officials there denied all knowledge to the work.

Deposited in *Bibliothèque Nationale* are other documents relating to the mystery of Rennes-le-Château, *The Secret Dossiers,*[16] a loose collection of rather odd items-newspaper clippings, cheap pamphlets, occasional printed pages, that might well have come from some other work, letters pasted to backing sheets and numerous genealogical lists—kept within a stiff-covered document holder. Periodically some pages were removed while others were freshly inserted. Inclusions and revisions were occasionally made in small copperplate handwriting and at a later date, printed ones that incorporated all the handwritten altercations replaced these corrected pages.

Henri Lobineau had supposedly written the bulk of the section devoted to genealogical research. Further information in the Dossier indicates that Henri Lobineau is a fictitious name, possibly derived from a street, which passes St Sulpice in Paris, known as the Rue Lobineau and that someone called Leo Schidlof may have written the work. The daughter of Leo Schidlof, whom Baigent, Leigh, and Lincoln contacted for further information, protested that her father had no interest in genealogy none whatsoever in the Merovingian dynasty, and had not even heard of the mystery of Rennes-Le-Château. Soon information confirming that Miss Schidlof's story may have been true claimed, in its turn, that Henri Lobineau was not Leo Schidlof at all, but a distinguished French aristocrat, the Comte Henri de Lenoncourt.[17]

At the turn of the century events at Rennes-le-Château began to resemble a puzzle swathed in in layers of mystery, protected by a minefield of misattribution and misrepresentation. The information that had been gradually coming in since 1956, purportedly the work of people with perfectly credible names, has almost all been confirmed to be of untraceable authorship. Places that appear to have significance such as the address quoted for publishing houses and organizations proved to be non-existent. Books have been cited that cannot be traced and, to the best of our knowledge, have never been seen. Within the confines of the *Bibliothèque Nationale* certain documents have been altered, some have disappeared, others have been miscataloged, and one document, which the authors sought with persistence, seemed undetectable.

One of the privately published books, *Le Serpent Rouge*, deposited in the *Bibliothèque Nationale* mentioned the Merovingian Dynasty. The date on this volume is a seeming 'coincidence;' it is 17 January, the date of the death of the Marquise d'Hautpoul and that of the stroke suffered by Saunière. Inside this curious book is a Merovingian genealogy, two maps of France in Merovingian times with a brief commentary, a ground plan of St Sulpice in Paris outlining the various side chapels, and thirteen short prose poems, of considerably literary quality.[18] Among them are references to the decoration of the church at Rennes-le-Château, to its priest Bérenger Saunière, to the Blanchfort family, Poussin's *Les Bergers D'Arcadie* and the motto *Et In Arcadie Ego* which is found in this painting. There is peculiar and dramatic mention of a red snake described as uncoiling its length across the centuries, as an allegorical illusion to hereditary descent, a bloodline, or a dynastic lineage.

The Role of the Priory of Sion

With this abundance of material Baigent, Leigh and Lincoln summarized the key points as follows: there was a secret order known as the Priory of Sion which created the Knights Templar; the Priory of Sion was led by a series of grand masters whose names figure prominently in the development of Western European culture; after the suppression of the Knights Templar in 1314, the Priory of Sion apparently not only survived but orchestrated certain critical events in European history. It was also alleged that the Priory of Sion continued to play an influential role in both international affairs and the domestic politics of some European countries; to a large extent it is the organization responsible for the flood of information on the Rennes-le-Château mystery and the declared objective of the Priory of Sion was the restoration of the Merovingian dynasty to the thrones of Europe.[19]

Referring to the Priory documents as their source, specifically the Secret Dossiers, Baigent, Leigh and Lincoln wrote that the Order of Sion was founded by Godfroi de Bouillon in 1090, some nine years before the conquest of Jerusalem. Yet, within these documents, there are other papers that claim that the true founding date for the Order was 1099 when, shortly after the capture of Jerusalem, it is claimed that a group of anonymous but powerful people held a secret meeting to elect a King of Jerusalem. At the time there were more than one claimant for the title with Raymond Count of Toulouse being among them; however the meeting offered the throne to Godfroi de Bouillon. Godfroi declined the royal title but accepted the responsibilities. He was king in all but name, and only ruled for a little over a year. His brother who succeeded him, Baudoin I, had no hesitation in accepting the title of King of Jerusalem.

The Secret Dossiers allege that Baudoin II of Jerusalem, 'who owed his throne to Sion', was 'obliged' to accept the constitution of the Order of the Knights Templar in March 1117, the founders of which were listed in the Secret Dossiers as follows: Hughes de Payens, Bisol de St Omer, and Hughes I, Count of Champagne, along with certain members of Order of Sion who were named as André de Montbard, Archambaud Saint-Aignan, Nivard de Montdidier, Gondemar and Rossal.[20] Until 1188, the Order of Sion and the Order of the Temple, according to the Secret Dossiers, shared the same grand masters. The situation changed in 1188 as the two deviated dramatically. According to Priory documents, Jean de Gisors,[21] was the first grand master to rule exclusively over the Order of Sion.

That same year the Order of Sion changed its name to the Priory of Sion and, as a kind of subtitle, adopted the name Ormus. This peculiar name is found in early Zoroastrian and Gnostic texts, where it is associated with the principle of light. French Masonic ritual denotes that Ormus was a Gnostic adept of Alexandria who, after conversion to Christianity by St Mark, founded a new initiatory Order with the identifying symbol of a red or 'Rose Cross.' According to the Secret Dossiers, confirmed by the Priory documents, one should discern in Ormus the origins of the Order of the Rose-Croix or Rosicrucian's. To make this perfectly clear, the documents further claim that in 1188 the Priory of Sion adopted a second subtitle- *l'Ordre de la Rose-Croix Veritas* (the Order of the True Red Cross). By quoting Frances Yates, who had established no known evidence of an Order of Rosicrucians in existence earlier than the final years of the 16th century, Baigent, Leigh and Lincoln tried to achieve some semblance of balance in their narrative.[22] They also put forward, however, that if the Priory documents were authentic—which these three authors apparently accepted they were—then Yates opinion would have to be revised to accommodate the uncomfortable fact that this secretive Order had been in existence for nearly 400 years before its name became public.

Three Lists of Names

There were three lists of names contained within the Secret Dossiers. The first Baigent, Leigh and Lincoln did not consider worthy of detailed investigation, as it was simply a list of abbots who, it was claimed, presided over the Order of Sion's possessions in the Holy Land between 1152 and 1281. The second list was more interesting to them as it contained the grand masters of the Knights Templars from 1118 until 1090, from the time of the Order's official foundation until the date it supposedly separated from its parent Order, The Priory of Sion. While comparing the list with those cited by the Templar historians, they became aware of certain important discrepancies. According to academic historians' lists, the Knights Templar was led by ten grand masters between 1118 and 1190. The name André de Montbard is included in most not merely as a co-founder of the Order but also as the Templar grand master from 1153 to 1156. However, André Montbard is indicated as having never led the Order in the Secret Dossier.[23]

According to most Templar historians, Bertrand de Blanchfort became the sixth grand master of the Templar Order after the death of André de Montbard in 1156. The Secret Dossiers gives a substantially different account. Their list states that Bertrand de Blanchfort, whom Baigent, Leigh and Lincoln believed resided near Rennes-le-Château, was the fourth grand master, attaining the rank in 1153. They then raised the question, "Because it disagreed with the lists compiled by established historians, should we regard the list in the Secret Dossiers as wrong?' They justifiably assert that no absolutely definitive list of the grand master of the Knights Templar exists; the earliest one we have dates from 1342, 30 years after the dissolution of the Order and more than two centuries after its foundation. The problem was straightforward. Either the list of the Templar grand masters in the Secret Dossiers is authentic, based on information inaccessible to academic historians, or it was a forgery. With their preference for the list in the Secret Dossiers over the authentic historical record, the authors of *The Holy Blood and The Holy Grail* made their preference plain, despite their many warnings and disclaimers to the contrary. Furthermore, they went on say:

> Whether our conclusion was warranted or not, we were confronted by one indisputable fact that some had obtained ac-

cess, somehow, to a list that was more accurate than any other. And since that list-despite its divergence from others more accepted-proved so frequently to be correct, it lent considerable credibility to the Priory documents as a whole.[24]

They would further claim that if the Secret Dossiers were reliable in this critical respect then there was less reason to doubt their authenticity in others.

In view of these conclusions, they continued their examination of the third list in the Secret Dossiers. This being that of the alleged grand masters of the Priory of Sion that, in any other circumstances, they would have dismissed as a ridiculous absurdity. Within the Secret Dossiers the grand masters of the Priory of Sion, who were also known by the name Nautonnier (an old French word meaning navigator or helmsmen), included, among others:

- Jean de Gisors: 1188–1220
- Edouard de Bar: 1307–36
- Nicolas Flamel, 1398–1418
- René d'Anjou: 1418–80
- Sandro Philpeppi (otherwise known as Boticelli): 1483–1510
- Leonardo da Vinci: 1510–19
- Johann Valentin Andrea: 1637–54
- Isaac Newton: 1691–1727
- Charles Nodier, 1801–44
- Claude Debussy, 1885–1918
- Jean Cocteau, 1918–1963.[25]

The Sacred Bloodline and René D'Anjou

The alleged grand master of the Priory of Sion between 1418 and 1480, René Anjou, had a profound influence on the development of Europe's cultural heritage. He was one of the major figures, along with his distant relative, Earl William St Clair[26] of Roslin, whose work helped to fuel the explosion of cultural and intellectual development that we call the Renaissance. René was fascinated by the idea of knightly chivalry, was enamoured with Arthurian legend, and had an obsession with the search for the Holy Grail. On occasion he staged a *pas d'armes*—highly coloured events that were a strange mix of chivalric tourney and masque—in which knights not only participated in the joust but also acted in a form of courtly drama or play. One of René's most noted *pas d'armes* was called by the evocative title of '*pas d'armes* of the *shepherdess*', a pastoral assortment of Arcadian romantic themes, chivalric Arthurian pageantry and the mysteries of the Grail quest. The theme of an underground spiritual stream rich in symbolic and allegorical references was a motif René believed encompassed the entire esoteric tradition of Pythagorean, Gnostic, Hermetic and Cabalistic thought. The Dossiers Secrets proposes a different and deeper connotation, one that has a hidden meaning; the underground stream, in this context, did not simply represent the transmission of a general body of esoteric teaching but, principally, specific factual information, such as a secret of some description, which was transmitted in a hidden manner from one generation to the next. In addition to this secret are implications that this underground stream might refer to an identifiable, subterranean bloodline descending through the centuries.[27]

Following beliefs such as this, reinforced by evidence gathered from the Secret Dossiers and the dubious Priory documents, the authors of *The Holy Blood and the Holy Grail* justified what was to become the most controversial theme in the book. It was described by the devout as impious, and by non-Christians as plausible, but was fundamentally incapable of conclusive and irrefutable proof. The assertion was that, despite the accounts in the Scriptures and the teachings of the Christian churches, Jesus was married with a family and, he had left a dynasty, which was identifiable in the 20th century. The term Sangreal, a phonetic variant term for the Grail that occurs in some of the earlier Grail romances, was used as one of their supporting arguments in conjunction with all the other evidence. In a later version the writer Malory subscribes a subtle variation from Sangraal to Sangreal, which the authors then split into two words 'Sang Real',[28] the French for royal blood. Wolfram von Eschenbach, author of one of the Grail Romance, had repeatedly referred to 'a Grail family' and Baigent, Leigh and Lincoln reinforced their argument by citing this work. Developing this theory and bringing it up to date they identified who, in their opinion was not only a principal personality involved in the Modern Priory of Sion, but a probable descendant of Jesus himself. This person was Pierre Plantard,[29] or as he himself preferred to be known, Pierre Plantard de St Clair.

CHAPTER 3
ACTION AND REACTION

The notion of direct hereditary descendants from Jesus provoked an outcry from Christian authorities of all denominations; among the general public, however, it stimulated massive curiosity and interest. Even though the authors had sprayed their text with caveats, repudiations and cautionary warnings about the validity of the Secret Dossiers and the Priory of Sion documents as reliable sources, a huge swathe of the readership came to believe that the medieval Priory of Sion had as much legitimacy as the police or fire brigade, for they reacted to *The Holy Blood and the Holy Grail* as a form of modern day 'biblical text.'

Many works on subjects relating to the mystery surrounding Rennes-le-Château had been published in France long before *The Holy Blood and the Holy Grail* hit the shelves. The series of essays, books, articles, and documentaries in the English language have turned this considerable literary stream into an international deluge of banality. The works range from the near intellectual to the blatantly absurd, and all are based to some degree on the total acknowledgment and acceptance that the research and findings done for *The Holy Blood and Holy Grail* were based upon factual evidence. All was not what it seemed, and with the wide publicity generated by the publication of *The Tomb of God*,[1] the balloon went up big time.

Richard Andrews and Paul Schellenberger's book *The Tomb of God* created a public sensation with the claim that the body of Jesus had not been 'taken up' into heaven as Church teachings has contended for more than 2,000 years, but had been unearthed from a grave in Jerusalem and reburied on a mountainside near Rennes-le-Château. Not long after publication, the broadcast of another BBC documentary in the 'Timewatch' series entitled *The History of a Mystery*, amplified the dispute over this contentious idea immensely.

The documentary repudiated the claims upon which *The Tomb of God* was based upon and was exceedingly reproachful of earlier research. Bill Cram, the producer, made allegations that are pertinent to the mystery of Rennes-le-Château that are summarized as follows:

1. That the coded documents that were published as the work of Antoine Bigou, later discovered by Saunière during the restoration of the church, were modern forgeries.

2. That these documents were forged by a French aristocrat, the Marquis Philippe de Cherisey, a known associate of Pierre Plantard de St Clair. Knowledge of their true origin had been widespread in France since 1971, when Gérard de Sède had quarreled with Plantard and de Cherisey over financial matters and de Cherisey had admitted being the author of the so-called coded documents.

3. That Pierre Plantard de St Clair was not the doyen of the Resistance he claims to be, but a man with extreme right-wing views whose so-called Resistance newspaper was published not *against* the wishes of the German Government of Occupation of France, but *with* their tacit approval.

4. That Pierre Plantard, which is his true name, received no special letter of commendation from General de Gaulle for his supposed role in returning de Gaulle to power in 1958, but only a nationally distributed letter received by a large number of French citizens at that time.

5. That Pierre Plantard had a conviction recorded against him for crimes of deception.

6. That the Secret Dossiers and the so-called Priory documents were highly scholarly and intellectually astute modern fabrications that blend a profound knowledge of history with outright fantasy. The authors of these scholarly frauds were Pierre Plantard and Philippe de Cherisey.

7. The programme checked the records at the Louvre and showed beyond any doubt that the priest Saunière did *not* purchase copies of the paintings by Teniers and Poussin from there, as claimed in *The Holy Blood and the Holy Grail*.

The 'Timewatch' programme specific disclosures make it obvious that de Séde knew that the documents were fictitious, either prior to his initial interviews with Lincoln or very shortly thereafter. Lincoln began his investigations in 1970 and pursued his research for another ten years, seemingly oblivious of the coded documents' precise provenance or of the deceptive nature of the Secret Dossiers.

Bérengere Saunière

Late 1800s Paris was immersed in esoteric speculation, quasi-masonic and chivalric societies, from which sprang countless numbers of new esoteric Orders. It was into this maelstrom of speculation and intrigue that the bishop at Carcassonne dispatched Bérenger Saunière after his discovery of the mysterious secret in the church at Rennes-le-Château. It was written that Saunière procured copies of three paintings at the Louvre in Paris during his first visit there. It was discovered by producers of 'Timewatch' that there was no record of this; the closest recorded sale of a copy of Poussin's Les Bergers d'Arcadie is nearly ten years too late. It is also maintained that there are no records of his visits to St Sulpice. Would such a visit under the circumstance be recorded seeing the potentially precarious and secretive nature of his business?

Taking into consideration the serious allegations made about the forgery of coded documents and the fabrications of the Secret Dossiers by de Cherisey and Plantard, it is necessary at this juncture to review the story of Saunière. Records do disclose that at the time of his installation as the parish priest of Rennes-le-Château he was extremely poor and lived an incredibly simple life. After making some mysterious discovery in his parish church, it is alleged that he was sent to Paris by the Bishop of Carcassonne and spent some unspecified time there. On his return to Rennes-les-Chateau he began spending vast sums of money reportedly over 200,000 gold francs the source of which has never been reasonably explained. It was also claimed that for many years thereafter he lived a life of relative luxury and received several important visitors such as Emma Calvé. The Abbé was suspended by the Vatican for not revealing the source of his wealth, and reinstated in 1915. Marie Dernarnaud, his house-keeper, survived him by many years and lived a very comfortable life in circumstances of considerable affluence until the post-war issue of a new currency in France in 1946. For another seven years she lived on the funds she received from the sale of the Villa Bethania, and disclosed to Noel Corbu, the new owner, that there was a secret that would make him both powerful and rich.

It is reasonable, on this basis, to come to some tentative conclusions. Primarily, it is plausible to accept that Saunière did make a discovery in his church that either directly or indirectly brought him great wealth and a reasonable degree of protection from authority. Considering Saunière's lifestyle and that of his housekeeper, and her comments to Corbu, we can speculate that the discovery had two separate but related aspects. First, it was of a nature that could be easily exchanged into legal currency without attracting any attention; and second, it related to some form of information of truly immense importance that could endow its possessor with immunity and power as well as riches. There has been considerable speculation that suggests that it may have been some documentary source proving that Jesus and the Magdalene had children or, conceivably, an ancient Cathar copy of *The Gospel of Love*—the original initiatory and heretical gospel of St John.

The vast majority of authors who have written works about this mystery have followed the well-trodden track laid down by Baigent, Leigh and Lincoln. Many English language works on this subject appear to be simply variations of the themes established by *The Holy Blood and the Holy Grail*. Most of them accept without question the validity of the Priory of Sion, the authenticity of the Priory documents and Secret Dossiers and treat Saunières stated contacts with Emma Calvé and members of the Hapsburg family as absolute fact. We now know, and have done for over forty years, that the coded documents of the Priory of Sion and the Secret Dossiers are clever forgeries. While we acknowledge that Saunière may have met with Emma Calvè in both Paris and at Rennes-le-Château, there is no significant proof of that. It is possible, if difficult to accept that he entertained the French Minister of Culture in his remote hilltop village, and again there is no proof. Yet, when we examine the alleged contacts between this rural priest and the senior ruling family in Europe, namely the Habsburgs, we are entering the realms of pure fantasy and conjecture.

Saunière's claimed association with Parisian esoteric circles may well be an allegation based upon some form of truth and the key to this could be his known royalist and right-wing political views. Guy Patton, a respected colleague, who has earned a well-justified reputation for meticulous research, has been investigating Saunière's movements in esoteric and masonic circles for some time. He is the author of the book entitled *The Web of Gold.* Another puzzling matter that might well be explained is the markedly odd nature of Saunière's 'pre-funerary ritual.' The Abbè could have seen something similar in some of the many lodges he visited wherein some ritual a man was seated, clothed in a robe decorated with golden tassels which were plucked one-by-one by the other participants.

There was an additional facet to this intricate tale that provoked investigation. A line of inquiry that provoked Tim to re-examine the verifiable record of the activities of the Cathars and The Knights Templar in the vicinity of Rennes-le-Château. This specific line of research began after Tim had lectured on the mystical carvings of Rosslyn Chapel to a meeting of the Saunière Society in London 1994. Following the lecture, he heard an incredible story that, if it proved to have any degree of validity, would tend to not merely support but to strengthen and expand the contentious idea of a bloodline founded by Jesus and other important figures of his time.

SECTION II

Rex Deus Emerges Shyly from the Shadows

CHAPTER 4
TIM'S INTRODUCTION TO REX DEUS

In 1994 Derek Burton, the secretary of the original English Sauniére Society, invited Tim to address one of their meetings in Golders Green in London. The other speaker asked to contribute was a co-author of *The Holy Blood and the Holy Grail*, Richard Leigh, who was not the most reliable of people, and did not turn up. As a consequence, after Tim had given his talk on Rosslyn Chapel, the rest of the day was spent on a general 'barn storming' discussion about heresy, the Knights Templar and the wider field of esoteric spirituality in general. In the course of the discussion Tim's colleague, Stephen Prior, mentioned that they soon hoped to go to Jerusalem and were seeking permission to enter the tunnels under Temple Mount that had been explored by Lieutenant Warren of the Royal Engineers at the end of the 19th and the beginning of the 20th century. At the conclusion of the day's events, Tim was approached by a man who introduced himself as Michael Monkton who then began to sketch a series of symbols on a piece of paper and told Tim to keep his eyes out for these in the tunnels under the Temple Mount. When asked where he had obtained this knowledge, Michael replied that the symbols were from 'A secret tradition in my family which had been preserved for over 2,000 years.' Intrigued by this statement, Tim was even more amazed when he was told that Michael was a direct descendant of Hughes de Payens, not merely one of the co-founders, but also the first Grandmaster of the Knights Templar. Some three weeks later, Tim invited Michael to dine at

Stephen Prior's house in Croydon where, from 6 PM until 2 AM both Stephen and Tim questioned Michael almost non-stop. With Michael's permission, the whole session was tape-recorded. After it was over, Tim drove Michael back to Buckingham and was able to prolong their earlier conversation by about an hour and a half. A month or so later, Tim invited Michael to come to Totnes in Devon and spend a weekend at his home. The conversations that took place there were also tape-recorded and the following story began to take on a more comprehensible and coherent shape.

When Michael first read *The Holy Blood and the Holy Grail*, he had experienced a profound sense of relief and freedom as he felt that the revelations in the book released him from a frightening and solemn, binding oath of secrecy he had made as a young man. He stated that he was born a group of families who claimed descent from twenty-four hereditary high priestly families of the Biblical Temple in Jerusalem and that included both the Davidic and Hasmonean royal families. The families' secret traditions were passed down from father to selected children of both sexes, from generation to generation under conditions of extreme secrecy. The instructions given to each child were imparted under an oath that stated that they should never be disclosed to an outsider 'lest my heart be torn out or my throat be cut.' After the very public revelations about the descendants of Jesus as recounted in *The Holy Blood and the Holy Grail*, Michael now felt free to talk openly about these matters.

According to Michael, this group of families called themselves *Rex Deus* or, more simply, the families. Following the destruction of the Temple in Jerusalem in 70 CE they scattered and fled to a variety of destinations but swore to keep their traditions alive. Sensing that a period of persecution would follow the Jewish uprising against Rome, they all swore to outwardly follow whatever was the prevailing religion of their time and place, but secretly practice their own beliefs and pass them down through the generations. They were strictly instructed to keep accurate genealogies and only to marry within the Rex Deus group, in the same manner as the Cohenite priesthood of biblical Israel. At first sight this story seemed somewhat bizarre but as Michael was well balanced, sane and sincere, Tim decided to spend some time investigating this intriguing tale it in depth. For, if the story, or any substantial aspect of it could be proven, it might well tend to explain some of the more puzzling enigmas of European history and perhaps increase our understanding of outbreaks of heresy in Europe during the medieval era. Here is a précis of the main points of the Rex Deus story as Michael told it.

Jerusalem in the Era of Jesus

Prior to the time of Jesus there were two boarding schools at the Temple in Jerusalem, one for boys and one for girls. All pupils at these schools were drawn from the hereditary high-priestly families, the royal families and the Levites. The boys were destined for the priesthood, the rabbinate or as future leaders within Israel. The teaching staff were chosen from among the twenty-four *ma'-madot*, the hereditary high priestly families who were the only men permitted to enter into the Holy of Holies and who, on ceremonial occasions stood in ascending order of rank on the Temple steps and were ritually named, for example, as 'The Melchizedek', 'The Michael' and 'The Gabriel.' The high priests not only taught in and ran the schools but also were also responsible for impregnating each of the girls when they reached puberty. When the girls became pregnant they were found suitable husbands among the leading families of Israel and their children in turn, became pupils in the schools at the age of seven. Thus educated elite was created that, according to the Rex Deus tradition, kept the hereditary priesthood bloodlines pure and unsullied. One such female pupil at the Temple school was called Miriam or Mary, the daughter of a previous pupil named Anne. She was impregnated by the Gabriel high priest and was found a husband of Davidic descent called Joseph. Her child was the one we know as Jesus who spent his early years in Egypt before returning to Jerusalem and attending the Temple school in his turn.

The Gospels recount that Jesus was baptized by John the Baptist. Now, according to the Biblical scholar John Dominic Crossan, this baptism was a physical and external cleansing, one symbolizing that a spiritual and purification had already taken place in the baptized person.[1] This is outright heresy to those Christians who believe that Jesus was 'born without sin' and who, being Divine, was absolutely incapable of sin. According to the Rex Deus tradition as told by another informant, John the Baptist was indeed the spiritual teacher of Jesus, a role that the Christian churches have always vigorously denied. Yet, despite prevailing church teaching, one modern historian wrote that:

> People placed themselves in the position of disciples of John (the Baptist) in order to learn how to be purified effectively both inwardly and outwardly. Once they felt fairly confident of their righteousness, by John's definition, they came for immer-

sion. …Not all the people became his disciples. Once people were immersed, however, they would have already have accepted John's teaching and therefore have become his disciples before this.[2]

Thus modern scholarship completely supports the Rex Deus, Templar, and other secret traditions that all claim that John the Baptist was the spiritual teacher of Jesus. We shall reveal more about the Baptist later, but now we revert to Michael Monkton's original story.

Michael had always admitted that he only had an incomplete story and his version of events jumped dramatically from his account of the birth and education of Jesus mentioned above, to sometime in the 4th century CE. Then, he said, it was deemed safe for members of the Rex Deus families to return to Jerusalem to re-bury the body of the Messiah. The place they chose was the one that no one would ever dream of looking in, on Temple Mount itself, which, according to Judaic custom and teaching, was deemed inviolable. A place so holy that it was strictly forbidden ever to be used as a place of burial. We can understand this choice in terms of secrecy, but it is nonetheless puzzling as to why families that spring from the very peak of orthodox Jewish tradition should choose it.

After the 4th century, the Rex Deus families continued to spread their influence throughout Europe, not merely in the Roman West but also in the Byzantine Empire in the East. Once again at this point Michael mentioned his descent from Hughes de Payens. In consequence, Tim began to construct a Rex Deus hypothesis that could be tested against the historical record of the medieval era. Checking marriage records in the archives of France; examining the historical record of the Rex Deus activities in a Europe dominated by a repressive church and revisiting certain historical events which had always puzzled him, such as the family connections between the founders of the Knights Templar; the history of the Shroud of Turin and why, how, and when did the various guilds of craft-masons transform themselves into the modern worldwide craft of Freemasonry? In this book we will recount the sum total of our discoveries and the understanding we have now reached by amalgamating the contents of Tim's two previous works on the subject and incorporating other material that has come to light and then reviewing our conclusions dispassionately.

The Origins of Initiatory Spirituality

The origins of Rex Deus teaching seem to lie in Ancient Egypt, which is where we can find the earliest reliable traces of an initiatory tradition maintained by an hereditary priesthood. This revered practice was later passed on to each of the world's three major monotheistic faiths, Judaism, Christianity and Islam. To reach any reasonable and accurate understanding of early Egyptian initiatory practice and religious beliefs we need to consult translations of the oldest corpus of esoteric teaching that is still extant the so-called 'Pyramid Texts.' The odd thing about these inscriptions is that they were apparently discovered by accident and not by design; by a layman and not by an archaeologist and furthermore a layman motivated by greed rather than intellectual curiosity.

The Discovery of the Pyramid Texts

In 1879 an Arab workman standing near the Pyramid of Unas at Saqqara spied a desert fox silhouetted against the dawn light. The animal moved, then stopped and looked about as if inviting the Arab to follow him and then disappeared into a large crevice in the north face of the pyramid. Inspired by thoughts of buried treasure perhaps, the workman followed this earthly incarnation of the ancient God Upuaut—the opener of the ways—into the heart of the pyramid.[3] When the workman ignited his torch he could see that the walls of the chamber he stood in were decorated with hundreds of hieroglyphics inlaid with gold and turquoise.[4] Later, similar inscriptions were found in other pyramids, over 4,000 lines of Hymns and formulae in total. Collectively they are known, as the Pyramid texts.[5] Professor Gaston Masparo was the first European to see the Pyramid Texts in situ. Even he would have been amazed at the deep understanding of ancient beliefs and practices that would flow from an accurate translation of the texts. Unfortunately Masparo's own interpretation was inaccurate and masked their true importance for many decades, a mistake compounded by another mis-translation by the Egyptologist James Henry Breasted who mistakenly described the Pyramid Texts as the expression of a solar cult.[6] Masparo was right in one important matter when, however, he stated that the Pyramid Texts were the expression of a far older tradition that pre-dated the construction of the Pyramids at Saqqara by many centuries, one that dated back to Egypt's pre-historic era[7] that predates the Exodus by two millennia and the writing of the Christian New Testament by over 3,400 years.[8] A view that Professor Edwards confirmed when he wrote that the Pyramid Texts ' .had originated in extreme antiquity; it is hardly surprising therefore that they sometimes contain allusions to conditions that no longer prevailed at the time of Unas.'[9] The Pyramid Texts are, in the opinion of these two leading and respected Egyptologists, the oldest compilation of religious texts ever found anywhere. Despite their antiquity and importance, we had to wait until 1969 for their definitive translation. This was made by the gifted Professor of Ancient Egyptian Language, Raymond Faulkner who claimed also that 'The Pyramid Texts constitute the oldest corpus of Egyptian religious and funerary literature now extant.'[10] They are, in fact, the oldest body of esoteric writings in the known world.

Zep Tepi

Within the Pyramid Texts there are a considerable number of references to the *Time of Osiris*, that legendary time when Egypt was allegedly ruled directly by the gods who had taken human form. This mysterious era is also referred to as *Zep Tepi*, or 'The First Time' although, sadly, there is no indication of exactly when or where this was supposed to have taken place. According to the texts it was the gods who had given Egyptians the wondrous gift of 'Sacred Knowledge' and they had certainly attained an intensely profound, sophisticated and uncannily accurate knowledge of astronomy at a very early stage in history. The question now arises 'how did this level of knowledge and understanding arise in Ancient times when there is no evidence whatsoever of any developmental period preceding it?

An English author, John Anthony West, gives one indication of how this may have occurred.

> Every aspect of Egyptian knowledge seems to have been complete at the very beginning. The sciences, artistic and architectural techniques and the hieroglyphic system show virtually no signs of 'development:' indeed many of the achievements of the earlier dynasties were never surpassed or even equalled later on. ... The answer to the mystery is, of course, obvious, but because it is repellent to the prevailing case of modern thinking,

it is seldom seriously considered. Egyptian civilization was not a development, it was a legacy.[11]

Nothing arises in a vacuum, so if this knowledge was a legacy, from whom and in what culture did it originate? As there is no evidence in the Egyptian records of any developmental period therefore, this level of knowledge and understanding must have arisen in another culture and location —unless it developed in Egypt at some period for which there is, as yet, no evidence. Several explanations have been advanced to explain this phenomenon and the most plausible is that of the 'Dynastic Race Theory' first proposed by William Matthew Flinders Petrie, the so-called 'Father of Modern Egyptology.' This theory suggests that the knowledge was an import from a vastly superior culture. While this idea may seem offensive to proponents of the 'politically correct' school of thought, the fact is that history is littered with examples of one race dominating another intellectually, by force of arms or by economic means.

Archaeological Indications

Flinders Petrie and James Quibell excavated over 2,000 graves of the pre-dynastic era at Nakada between 1893 an 1894. The finds came from two distinctly different eras that Petrie named Nakada I and Nakada II. The artefacts recovered from the Nakada II sites showed distinct Mesopotamian characteristics[12] while those from the earlier period showed no foreign influence whatsoever. Petrie found Lapis Lazuli in the Nakada II graves, the only find of this precious stone in the pre-dynastic period. It was, however, a highly prized stone in Mesopotamia prior to the Nakada II era. There are several other signs of the probable Mesopotamian origins of the dynastic race including a 'pear shaped mace,' cylinder seals, the use of remarkable brick architecture and hieroglyphic writing that are all 'proof' of the foreign origins of this transformative period.[13] Douglas Derry, one of Petrie's pupils wrote in 1956:

> It is very suggestive of the presence of a dominant race, perhaps relatively few in numbers but greatly exceeding the original inhabitants in intelligence; a race which brought into Egypt the knowledge of building in stone, of sculpture, painting, reliefs and above all writing; hence the enormous jump from the primitive pre-dynastic Egyptian to the advanced civilisation of the Old Empire (the Old Kingdom).[14]

A Dutch archaeologist, another of Petrie's pupils, Henry Frankfort, claimed that the appearance of the cylinder seal in pre-dynastic Egypt was 'The strongest evidence of contact between Mesopotamia and Egypt.'[15] The sudden appearance of evidence such as this does nothing to explain how it was carried from its original source to the Nile valley. However, discoveries first made by Arthur Weighall and later explored by others including David Rohl in 1997, make a plausible case for the most probable route.

In 1908, Weighall, who was Inspector of Antiquities for the Egyptian Government between 1905 and 1914, explored the Wadi Abbad that leads from Edfu towards the Red Sea and found graffiti on the rock walls depicting high-prowed boats. Then, later, in 1936, Hans Winkler who was exploring another Wadi nearby, the Wadi Hammamat discovered similar drawings to those discovered by Weighall. Winkler suggested that these drawings recorded seafarers who had landed on the west coast of the Red Sea and then crossed the desert to the Nile valley. In his view, these inscriptions recorded a 'military expedition.'[16] In more recent times, in 1997, the brilliant young English Egyptologist, David Rohl, revisited both the Wadi Abbad and the Wadi Hammamat before extending his search into the Wadi Barramiya where he found similar inscriptions on the rock walls. Rohl claims that there is a direct connection between the people recorded by these drawings of high-prowed boats and the artefacts of Mesopotamian origin found in the Nakada II graves by Petrie.[17] Rohl was seeking evidence for the origins of people referred to in the Pyramid Texts as *The Shemsa Hor*, the followers of Horus whom he believed were the immediate predecessors and ancestors of the first pharaohs.[18] The Pyramid Texts record the earliest reference to the Shemsa Hor who are described as a succession of priestly initiates whose sacred duty was to transmit a body of sacred knowledge down though the generations. The origins of this knowledge lay in the time of the Neteru, when Egypt was, according to sacred tradition, ruled by the gods in the pre-historic era long before the first pharaohs. While not necessarily kings, these revered initiates were extremely powerful and highly enlightened priests who had been carefully selected by an elite group who had established themselves at Heliopolis in the Egyptian pre-historic era. The Egyptologist Georges Goyon claims that Heliopolis was chosen by this group of priestly astronomers, because of 'certain (unspecified) religious and scientific factors.'[19]

Ancient Egyptian Astronomers

The revered scholars of the classical world who had first hand knowledge of the ancient Egyptians were awestruck by the range and depth of sacred knowledge and wisdom displayed by the Helipolitan and Memphite priesthood. The Greek philosopher, Aristotle, speaking of the highly advanced levels of knowledge shown by the Egyptians wrote that they were people 'whose observations have been kept for many years past and from whom much of our evidence of particular stars is derived.[20] Proclus Diodachus wrote in the 5th century BCE, 'Let those who believe in observations, cause the stars to move around the pole of the zodiac by one degree on one hundred years towards the east, as Ptolemy and Hipparchus did before him know ...that the Egyptians had already taught Plato about the movements of the fixed stars...'[21] Professor I. E. S. Edwards of the British Museum came to similar conclusions.[22] The insight of one of the world's greatest scholars of Egyptian Gnosis, Schwaller de Lubicz was summed up by John Anthony West when he stated that Egyptian science, medicine, mathematics and astronomy were all of an exceptionally far higher order of sophistication and refinement than most modern scholars will acknowledge. Indeed the whole of Egyptian civilisation was founded on a total and precise understanding of universal laws.[23]

Sacred Knowledge or 'Gnosis'

The incredible depth and range of sacred knowledge attained through spiritual initiation were not preserved for the personal gain of the initiates of the Egyptian Temple Mysteries. Rank and high birth undoubtedly brought wealth and privilege in their train, but the sacred knowledge of art, architecture, medicine, science, astronomy, mathematics, metallurgy and navigation were used for the benefit of the whole population. Gnosis was always to be employed in service to others. Imbued with sacred knowledge and protected by the seemingly boundless desert that separated it from other cultures, the Egyptian nation and way of life developed a degree of stability, sophistication and complexity that has never been exceeded. Egyptian Gnosis has come down to us in the 21st century recorded in part within the Pyramid Texts, the Edfu Texts and the Egyptian books of the dead. Other references can be found inscribed on the walls of the many temples and tombs that have survived. The authors,

Robert Bauval and Graham Hancock wrote that 'The language of all these texts is exotic, lade with the dualistic thinking that lay at the heart of Egyptian society and that may have been the engine of its greatest achievements.'[24] This knowledge was revered, indeed the Edfu texts repeatedly refer to 'the wisdom of the sages' and stress the fact that the gift that the Egyptians valued most, was knowledge.[25]

That incredibly insightful French scholar, Schwaller de Lubicz discerned that the ancient Egyptians had their own unique way of understanding the universe and man's place within it and that this was comprised of an understanding and knowledge system that was totally different from the one understood and revered by modern man today.[26] The ancient Egyptian 'Way of knowing' could not be transmitted by the use of language, but only through mythology and symbolism.[27] Schwaller de Lubicz begins his explanation of Egyptian symbolism by stating that there are always two ways of interpreting their religious texts, the exoteric and the esoteric. The exoteric is the basis for the standard, or more usual, interpretation found in textbooks on religion and history. This outward form also serves as a vehicle for the esoteric of hidden interpretation that de Lubicz called the symbolique meaning.[28] He claimed that this form of the transmission of esoteric knowledge has largely been forgotten but that symbolic remnants of it have been passed on, in one form or another, to all the great monotheistic faiths that spring from Egyptian origins, namely Judaism, Christianity and Islam.[29]

La Symbolique

The immense power of symbols and hieroglyphics to provoke complex and profound responses far exceeds that of mere words no matter how beautifully written. All who have studied the work of the medieval craft masons or have immersed themselves in Egyptology or who are followers of the 20th century initiate Rudolf Steiner; know this from their own personal experience. In the mid-20th century the insightful authors, Pauwels and Berger described this aspect of ancient symbolism and the initiates who employed it in the following terms:

> They... wrote in stone their hermetic message, Signs, incomprehensible to men whose consciousness had not undergone transmutations... These men were not secretive because they

loved secrecy, but simply because their discoveries about the Laws of Energy, of matter and of the mind had been made in another state of consciousness and could not be communicated directly.[30]

The sages and initiates of every religion and culture that is known to mankind have traditionally, used symbols for this form of communication. The ancient Egyptians did not restrict this form of transmission to religious matters, they also used it to record and reinforce the divine origin and lineal descent of the pharaohs.

For millennia, depictions of the Pharaohs showed them wearing the double crown of both upper and lower Egypt. On the front of this ceremonial headdress are twin symbols depicting a falcon's head and a cobra. The falcon's head indicates symbolically, the pharaoh as the living embodiment of Horus, while the cobra carries a double symbolic meaning, each important in its own right. Firstly, as an indication of Divine Wisdom, or Gnosis, and, secondly, as an indication of the divine ancestry of the royal family. While Egyptian Temples varied in design, to a certain extent, they were almost invariably adorned with symbols celebrating the power, wisdom and earthly conquests of the pharaoh. The pharaohs erected a pair of obelisks on the approach road to the major temples, each surmounted by a pyramidal shaped 'ben-ben' stone the symbolic resting place of the phoenix. The bird that, according to legend, underwent spontaneous combustion and then recreated itself from its own ashes, a symbolic representation of spiritual death and rebirth.

The Pharaoh Tuthmosis III (1476–1422 BCE) changed this form of symbolism into one that still persists to this day. Instead of erecting the two traditional obelisks on the approach to the Temple at Karnak, he had two pillars placed there. Neither holds anything up, indeed they fulfil no architectural purpose whatsoever. The Egyptologist David Rohl claims that they are symbolic of the two kingdoms of Egypt and describes the carving on them in the following words:

> The pillar on the south side has three tall stems ending in an elaborately stylised flower with partly pendent petioles. If one were to trace its outline and transfer the design to the coat of arms of the French monarchy, you would immediately recognise 'the Fleur de Lys.'[31]

The lily is not a plant that was native to Egypt and could only be cultivated there at that time with considerable difficulty. They were grown for the pharaoh's use alone as they had 'mood altering' qualities when their bulbs were ingested. Thus, they became symbolic of the gnosis gained during these times of change in consciousness. In this manner, the lily became a symbol of royal descent and innate wisdom while the two pillars came to represent strength and wisdom.

CHAPTER 5

THE BIRTHPLACE OF JUDAISM— ANCIENT EGYPT

Strange to relate that the modern science of Egyptology was born on a military expedition that was, thanks to the perception of the General in charge, accompanied by scores of scholars of repute. The General was Napoleon, the expedition was his invasion of Egypt and the time was 1798. Napoleon arrived with 400 ships carrying 54,000 troops. However, this Egyptian invasion was to be very different from his previous military adventures, for Napoleon had brought along 150 savants—scientists, engineers and scholars—whose responsibility was to study ancient Egyptian culture and history. And while the military invasion was an ultimate failure, the scholarly one was successful beyond anyone's expectations and, in fact, laid the foundations for the systematic study of Egyptology. At first this scholastic endeavor was dominated by French academics, but the English soon joined them in ever increasing numbers. Scholars of both nationalities were inspired by the understandable desire of trying to discover an historical basis for events described in the Old Testament. Despite the increasing secularization of advanced studies, this is still the clearly stated objective of the 'Egypt Exploration Society' in England.

That, of course, is where the real problems start. Viewing the Bible as an historical document is fraught with danger and even if one adopts the view that it is simply a superb piece of religious mythology based loosely on some form of real events, trying to accurately date anything described within it is damnably difficult, if not impossible. This unpalatable fact remains a stumbling block to any real understanding as the Egyptian records, full and detailed as they are, do not match up in any comprehensible way with the slipshod and vague nature of the scriptural accounts and their implied but grossly misleading chronologies. How can we expect any scholar, however gifted, to find corroborative evidence for any biblical event when the Old Testament cites no dates, names no identifiable pharaohs or dynasties and does not cite any specific and identifiable event recorded in Egypt's voluminous and detailed historical records. It is truly a nightmare world. And, right at the beginning, the search is masked by the need of the people who write the biblical account, to mask, disguise or deny any reference to Egypt for political reasons highly pertinent at the time of their writing—i.e. when they were exiled in Babylon after a war that they had fought as allies of Egypt.

The Patriarch Abraham

According to the Bible, the Patriarch Abraham arrived in Egypt somewhere about the time of 1500–1460 BCE. The scriptural account continues by telling us that this man, a wandering shepherd, was warmly welcomed by the pharaoh, allegedly because of the beauty of his wife Sarah.[1] Hardly the most plausible passage in the scriptures. The Bible claims that Abraham came from the city of Ur, which we suspect was a simple, but effective, way of disguising Abraham's true origins. Despite this attempt to hide Abraham's origins, enough evidence remains within the scriptures to enable us to discern the truth. The accounts in Genesis disclose several facts about Abraham and his family that prove that they were indeed Egyptian. It is written that Abraham says of his wife '… and yet indeed she is my sister; she is the daughter of my father but not the daughter of my mother and she became my wife.'[2] This really gives the game away and discloses that Abraham was, indeed, not merely Egyptian but very high born at that, for this type of incestuous marriage was only permitted in the pharaonic royal family. This makes Abraham's warm welcome by the pharaoh far more credible and also explains the comments of the medieval biblical scholar, Rabbi Raschi, who wrote that 'You should know that the family of Abraham was of a very high line.'[3] This not only confirms our own conclusions but also, and more importantly, denies the description of Abraham as a nomadic shepherd and indicates his true social status.

If any further indication of the truth concerning our assertion about the origin and status of Abraham were needed, it can be found in the translation of the patriarch's original name of Abram—'exalted father'[4]—a ritual name given to the kings of Egypt. There is no credible explanation given for his strange change of name or that of his wife Sarai. The new names, Abraham and Sarah are usually held to indicate 'father of many nations' in the Judeo/Christian tradition and Sarah is the Egyptian name for Princess. The scriptures also record that Hagar, Sarah's handmaiden, was the daughter of a pharaoh by one of his concubines[5] and that Abraham's son, Ishmael, took an Egyptian wife.[6]

The weird liaison between Abraham's wife, Sarah, and the un-named pharaoh has given many scholars grave pause for thought. Both the Babylonian Talmud[7] and the Holy Koran[8] imply that there are serious doubts about the paternity of Abraham's first-born son Isaac. Both texts suggest that Abraham was not the boy's real father, but that he was the child of the pharaoh. So, the sacred scriptures are written in such a way as to raise serious doubts about Abraham's place of birth, his social status and, perhaps more importantly in his role as 'founder of the people of Israel.' Are so-called 'people of Israel' descended from the pharaoh or from Abraham? Whatever the truth may be of this contentious matter, the meeting between Abraham and the pharaoh certainly signaled the beginning of a highly productive cross-fertilization of spiritual and religious ideas between the Egyptians and the emerging people of Israel that ultimately led to the foundation of the Jewish religion.

Scholars of international fame and repute such as Ernst Sellin[9] and Sigmund Freud[10] have both written persuasively about the profound influence of Egyptian religious thought on early Judaism. The term used by both Abraham and Melchizedek, 'the most high god' is one used in Egypt to describe the supreme god of the pantheon. It is also noteworthy that Abraham adopted for himself and all his descendants the practice of Circumcision. This had been common practice among the Egyptian royal family, hereditary priesthood and nobility since 4,000 BCE. Furthermore, the story of Moses being hidden in the bulrushes, the first step in the story of the Exodus, rests on the extremely dubious assumption that the people of Israel were a distinct and identifiable people, race or tribe in Egypt at that time. It also begs the question of a *berît* or covenant with the God of Abraham—the foundation not only of Judaism, but also of Christianity and Islam. In order to discern some basis of truth that may lie behind this magical mythology, we need to examine and study the religious practices of that time and then, with an open mind, explore the historical reality behind the scriptural account of the Exodus. We can gain a reasonable and acceptable time frame from the works of two recent authors, namely Robert Feather and Ahmed Osman. It was the Muslim scholar Osman who claimed that the pharaoh who welcomed Abraham was Tuthmosis III (1476—1422 BCE) while Feather opts for Amenhotep I (1517- 1496 BCE).

Joseph of the Coat of Many Colors

It was the Muslim lawyer and scholar Ahmed Osman who made the crucial breakthrough by identifying the patriarch Joseph with a real, historically verifiable character in the Egyptian historical records.[11] The key scriptural phrase that identified Joseph was:

> …it was not you that sent me hither, but God and he hath made me a father to Pharaoh and lord of all his house, and a ruler throughout the land of Egypt.[12]

This precise phrasing enabled Osman to identify the Patriarch Joseph with an important Egyptian personage whose tomb was discovered in the Valley of the Kings by Quibell and Weighall in 1905. That person was Yuya who, in Weighall's own words:

> …was a person of commanding presence, whose powerful character showed in his face. One must picture him now as a tall man, with a fine shock of white hair; a great hooked nose like that of a Syrian; full strong lips and a prominent, determined jaw. He has the face of an ecclesiastic, and there is something about his mouth which reminds one of the late Pope Leo XIII. One feels on looking at his well-preserved features that there may be found the originator of the great religious movement, which his daughter and grandson carried into execution.[13]

The distinctive and telling phrase 'a father to the pharaoh' recorded in the Old Testament[14] is repeated exactly in Yuya's book of the dead.[15] The identification of Joseph as Yuya is an essential foundation any realistic attempt to find a historical basis for the Exodus. Yuya was appointed to ministerial rank by the Pharaoh Tuthmosis IV and a later pharaoh, Amenhotep III married Yuya's daughter Tiye. Again we see another linkage between the founders of the people of Israel, Abraham and his great-grandson Joseph on the one hand and the Egyptian royal family on the other.

Who was Moses?

One Jewish scholar working in the early years of the 20th century seemed to succeed in identifying the biblical character Moses with someone credible from the Egyptian historical records. Dr Karl Abraham published an article that suggested that the monotheistic Pharaoh Akenhaten may have been the real person on whom the biblical Moses was based. This idea received a degree of confirmation when, just before the outbreak of World War II, Sigmund Freud published his final work *Moses and Monotheism*, for in this book Freud demonstrated that the story of Moses birth as recounted in the scriptures was clearly based on a mixture of the mythology surrounding Sargon (2,800 BCE) and that of the birth of Horus. Both of whom, according to myth and legend, had been hidden in a bed of reeds. According to Freud, the biblical account was to hide the fact that far from being of humble origin, Moses was a member of the Egyptian Royal family. He also recorded that the name Moses was a variation on the Egyptian word *mos* or child.

Neither Abraham nor Freud were alone on claiming that Moses was in fact an Egyptian. This had been mentioned much earlier by historians such as Mantheo—an Egyptian high priest of the 3rd century BCE—the Jewish historian Philo Judaeus of Alexandria in the 1st century BCE or Flavius Josephus the Jewish historian of the 1st century of the Christian era. An early father of the Christian church Justin Martyr also made a similar claim, in the 2nd century CE. The modern English scholar, Robert Feather wrote that:

> Detailed analysis of the Torah, the Talmud and the Midrash led me to the conclusion that Moses was not only born and raised as an Egyptian, but was, in fact, a Prince of Egypt—a son of the Royal House of Pharaoh.[16]

The Exodus

The claim that the people of Israel lived in Egypt is highly dubious and, as a result, estimates for the period of time they allegedly spent there are specious in the extreme. Estimates vary wildly from four hundred years to one century. Attempting to construct a reasonable time-scale for the Exodus tends to depend upon identifying 'the pharaoh who knew not Joseph ⁷ whom Osman names as Horumheb.[18] Therefore Osman concludes that the pharaoh at the time of the Exodus was Ramses I. By this time, Egyptian culture had achieved a sophistication, complexity and stability that was never to be exceeded. Religion had evolved and developed into a mainly solar cult whose panoply of gods was headed by Amun and temples dedicated to him, such as the one at Karnak, derived enormous benefit from royal patronage and national prosperity. However this stability was more apparent than real and, when the monotheistic Pharaoh Akenhaten, the grandson of Yuya, tried to abolish the entire pantheon of gods and replace them with one, The Aten, this brought both economic and religious chaos to the land. Akenhaten was deposed and seems to have completely disappeared from the record. To use modern parlance he had become a 'non-person' and his name was erased from inscriptions and his statues defaced.

Several modern authors such as Karl Abraham and Maurice Cotterell have concluded that the Exodus took place at the time of Akenhaten.[19] Sigmund Freud claimed that Moses was an official in Akenhaten's entourage named Tuthmosis who some scholars claim was the brother of the pharaoh.[20] The skilled lawyer and scholar, Ahmed Osman, managed to prove beyond all reasonable doubt that the figure we know as Moses was not Tuthmosis, but Abraham's original choice, Akenhaten himself.

Atenism

Freud described in some detail many of the similarities that link emergent Judaism and the worship of the Aten. He claimed, quite clearly and simply, that Akenhaten simply changed the worship of Aten to the new Jewish faith. Freud stated that the prayer that is so central to Jewish worship, *Shema Yisrael Adonai Elohenu Adonai Echod* (Hear O Israel the Lord Thy God is One God), was neither unique nor a new post Exodus creation but was an almost exact copy of a prayer to the Aten. He proposed that in translation, 'd' in Hebrew has been transliterated from the Egyptian 't' and the Egyptian 'e' has now become 'o'. Thus the Egyptian version of the prayer reads *'Hear O Israel, our God Aten is the only God.'* Over two thousand years before Freud published *Moses and Monotheism*, the priest and historian Mantheo wrote that Moses had discharged priestly duties in Egypt.[21] Akenhaten was not merely the Pharaoh, but also the high priest of Atenism and often officiated at the temple at Amarna.

In accounts of Judaism as it was practiced during the Exodus, we find more direct links with Egyptian religious custom and ritual. Egyptian priests were, as we mentioned earlier, a hereditary caste that preserved sacred knowledge. In emergent Judaism, there was again a hereditary priestly elite created by extending the rights, duties and obligations of the Atenist priesthood as the Levites. These heirs to traditional practice were also expected to preserve sacred knowledge among their number as before.

The Ten Commandments

The holy law of the Jews, The Torah, rests on the firm foundation of the Ten Commandments. But, where did they come from? Given to Moses on Mount Sinai? Or do they have another origin? Also, in Atenism, according to Professor Flinders Petrie, Aten was deemed to be the only God. Petrie also stressed the fact that 'The Aten was the only instance of a jealous God in Egypt, and his worship was exclusive of all others and claims universality.'[22] Compare that statement with this extract from the Ten Commandments found in the book of Deuteronomy '…Thou shalt have no other gods before me… for I, the Lord Thy God, am a jealous God,…'[23] The Israeli historians of the Exodus, Messod and Roger Sabbah also stress the fact that Atenism abolished all the images and idols of all the other gods and instituted the worship of one God—abstract, invisible, transcendental and all knowing. This unique and novel concept was of a God who was the sole creator of the Universe in a manner that fitted perfectly within the context of ancient Egyptian sacred wisdom.[24] Thus the edict forbidding graven images listed in Deuteronomy's version of the Ten Commandments also replicates the same injunctions in the Atenist code. If we consult the Ten Commandments listed in Exodus we find, to our surprise, that they mirror passages in the Egyptian Book of the Dead that list the principles by which a soul is tried after death, in the Court of Osiris.[25] The Jewish people have always claimed that while the Ten Commandments were a unique, Divine, revelation made to directly to the 'chosen people', they were, nonetheless, of a universal application. No one doubts the universality of their application but we can now see that the hypothesis that Judaism sprang directly from the religion of Akenhaten is almost certainly true.

Further indications of the probable truth of this provocative and controversial statement can be found when we compare Psalm 104 in the Old Testament with Akenhaten's *Hymn to the Aten*. Verse 24 of the Psalm reads as follows:

O Lord how manifold are Thy works
In wisdom hast thou made them all:
The earth is full of thy riches.

In *The Hymn to the Aten* we find:

How manifold are all your works,
They are hidden from before us,
A sole God whose powers no other possesses
You did create the earth
According to your desire.

Now, the word for ark or casket is identical in both Hebrew and Egyptian, indeed in Hebrew *ark* is described as a 'loan word' of Egyptian origin. Indeed, a 19th century specialist in Semitic languages, Antoine Fabre d'Olivier stated categorically that 'I regard the idiom of Hebrew sensed in the *Sepher* (the Scriptural rolls of the Torah) as a transplanted branch of the Egyptian language.[26] The veneration and ritual usage of the Ark in both the Egyptian and Jewish religious systems repays detailed comparison. In the temple at Amarna in Egypt, the Ark was used as a symbolic form of transport for the God Aten: the biblical account in Exodus recounts how the Ark was used to transport items of Divine revelation, such as the tablets of stone inscribed with the Ten Commandments. After the people of Israel arrived in the Promised Land, the Ark was housed at Shiloh in a sanctuary built for it and staffed by priests of the House of Eli who traced their ancestry back to Egypt. It was only after Solomon built his Temple in Jerusalem that Ark was moved there.

Other religious practices that are common to both cultures include: the ten *sephirot*, or attributes of God described within Judaism's mystical tradition, the Kabbala. These include the following terms: *crown, wisdom, intelligence, mercy, power, beauty, victory, foundation and royalty*. All of which, according to the Israeli historians Messod and Roger Sabbah, were terms used as attributes of the Egyptian Pharaohs.[27] Akenhaten's new city of Armana was described as 'the Holy City.' The animals he sacrificed there to the God Aten were the same as those Moses sacrificed. The land surrounding Armana was called 'the Holy Land' a term that evokes considerable meaning for both Jews and Christians today. Another habit that seems to have migrated painlessly from Egyptian to Jewish culture was one found in Armana. The worshippers of the Aten ritually inscribed sacred texts above the entrances to his temples, in most orthodox Jewish homes today, we find a startlingly similar practice, above the entrance to these homes are fixed small boxes, or mezzuzot, containing holy texts within them.

Ahmed Osman's identification of Akenhaten as Moses, convincing as it is, was not the end of the matter. David Rohl suggests that the Exodus took place during the reign of the Pharaoh Dudimose, yet, despite this divergence, most modern Egyptologists and serious scholars of this era are convinced that Judaism emerged and evolved from Egyptian religious practice. Also it should be noted that, Osman, Feather, Abraham and Freud all agree upon the other issue central to any real understanding of the Exodus—that the followers of Akenhaten made up the vast majority of the so-called 'people of Israel' *who* followed Moses into the wilderness.

> The strange desertion of Amarna and the sudden disappearance of all who lived in it, imparts a high degree of plausibility to this new version of the Exodus. Not only did the nobility and priesthood vanish, but also so did all the artisans, craftsmen, workers and servants. Akenhaten's Egyptian priests, scribes and notables—the national elite—were the first true monotheists in humanity and believed in one god, Aten. Capable of unity like so many persecuted people, they were chased from their town and country of origin, bringing with them not only material riches but also the greater part of their culture, spirituality, and oral and written traditions.[28]

These dis-possessed people were joined by other dissidents, as well as by foreign residents. The medieval Jewish scholar Raschi described them as a mixture of nations newly converted to monotheism. Arriving in the Egyptian colony of Canaan, they brought with them their own religious and ancestral traditions and, adapting Phoenician writing created a new written language—Hebraic-Hieroglyphic.

The True Origins of the 'People of Israel'

One major fact that has confused many of these issues is that it has proved to be impossible to find any identifiable trace whatsoever of 'the people of Israel' in the vast and detailed Egyptian records. Various attempts have been made to identify them with the Hyksos or the Hebiru, none with any degree of either plausibility or success. The fact that confuses all scholars studying Egyptian history is that there is no trace of any credible mention of pre-Exodus Jews living in Egypt anywhere in the voluminous Egyptian records. Indeed many scholars and historians, both Israeli and Gentile, have voiced profound doubts about the historicity of the Exodus and have claimed that the whole Biblical account is simply a matter of myth and legend. Freud himself, wrote that he had found no trace of the term 'Hebrew' prior to the Babylonian Exile [29] when the scriptures, as we now know them, were first transcribed from oral tradition into written form. The Israeli scholars, Messod and Roger Sabbah state that there is no proof whatsoever of the existence of the Hebrew People as a nation or tribe at the time of Moses as described in the Bible.[30] In fact they go further when they write:

> How could a people so impregnated with such a major part of the wisdom of Egypt disappear from the (Egyptian) historical record so mysteriously? More than 200 years of research in the deserts, tombs and temples have shown nothing.[31]

The Post Exodus Period

Official records in any country or culture always record the deeds; power and victories of the rulers, the vast range of the detailed Egyptian records do exactly the same. The power and victories of the Two Kingdoms of Egypt are recorded in great detail; the defeats and failures are completely ignored. In respect of Akenhaten, his heresy and the financial ruin he brought on the country, they went further. In modern Soviet double-speak, he became a 'non-person:' his name was deleted from inscriptions on temple walls and monuments. Therefore, any mention of 'the fallen one of Akenhaten' would not merely go unrecorded but be completely expunged. The Biblical accounts of the recently liberated slaves, the people of Israel, carrying vast quantities of valuables with them as they fled, including 'jewels of silver and jewels of gold' is hard to believe.[32] According to Robert Feather, this treasure was made up of the personal wealth of Akenhaten and the treasure of the temple at Armana.[33] It is also possible that the new pharaoh contributed to pay off the dissidents and speed them on their way. The Israeli Sabbah brothers state that the pharaoh also granted the emigrés the right to settle in Canaan along with permission to export the treasures of Armana.[34]

The facts that we have recounted above have all been widely recognised by Egyptologists and a large number of Biblical scholars. It is somewhat sad, especially in these troubled times that they have been completely ignored by the public at large and the blinkered and prejudiced thinkers of the worlds of Judaism, Christianity and Islam. Also, as we shall demonstrate, the Jewish religion continued to evolve and develop from the Exodus until after the time of Jesus, and owes far more to the influences of polytheism, paganism and the wisdom tradition than most modern religious preachers would be prepared to admit from any pulpit.

CHAPTER 6
DEVELOPING JUDAISM

While the 'Old Testament' of the Bible is undoubtedly the one of the most powerful, spiritually inspiring documents in the world, as an historical record it leaves a very great deal indeed, to be desired. What it is most certainly is *not* is the inerrant word of God as many fundamentalist Christians loudly and wrongfully claim. The Book of Exodus, for example, was not an account of contemporary events, but a highly imaginative and colorful description of a long gone period of history, shrouded in myth and legend that took place some seven centuries before the scriptures began to take written form. This fanciful account was also deliberately distorted for pressing political reasons that were current at the time of its composition. Therefore historians and biblical scholars tend to view its accounts with considerable caution and a deep and abiding skepticism and rightly so. For example, the Jewish historian Sigmund Freud described the era of the settlement of the people of Israel in the promised land as one 'that was particularly impenetrable to investigation.'[1'] The Dead Sea Scrolls scholar, John Allegro wrote:

> We are in a shadowy half-world, where the hard facts of history fade off into mythology, and where the clear dividing line we like to draw between fact and fiction has no place. ...[2]

Indeed several Israeli scholars of repute deny the historicity of the Exodus and have declared that this story is simply a myth. The American and Jewish scholar Norman Cantor was particularly astute, when he wrote:

> ...perhaps the whole Egyptian sojourn was fabricated in later centuries for some ideologically conditioned or socially advantageous purpose...[3]

There are Orthodox Jews who would be outraged at that statement and many fundamentalist Christians would also be horrified by it. The whole idea that 'the inerrant word of God' could be factually inaccurate would completely destroy the very foundations of their faith. What would they make of another of Cantor's observations about the sojourn in Egypt and the Exodus?

> Such is the Biblical story whose verification defies the course of historical and archaeological science. **It is a romantic fantasy.** (Our emphasis) [4]

Even the staunchly Catholic historian Paul Johnson who normally accepts scriptural accounts without question expressed doubts about this era when he wrote:

> Some other sites mentioned in Exodus have been tentatively identified. But plotting these wanderings on a map, though often attempted, and undoubtedly entertaining, can produce nothing more than conjecture.[5]

However, while the Biblical account of the Exodus is undoubtedly highly questionable as history, even its critics recognize the essential and vibrant 'spiritual' truth that shines from its pages. John Allegro wrote:

> During the desert wanderings under Moses, following their providential escape from Egypt, the Israelites were welded into a nation, allowed to know the secret name of God, and given the inestimable gift of the *Torah*, or Law.[6]

Embedded in the accounts of the post Exodus settlement of the Promised Land we can find clear and unequivocal indications of the importance of the Egyptian mystical, or Gnostic, roots of Judaism even though these are set against an almost legendary background that cannot be verified by either history or archaeology to any substantive degree.

Pillars of Faith?

Everything we know and see in this world is in a constant state of evolutionary change and development. Religious thought is no exception to this and the very idea that Judaism has not changed from the time of Moses to the present day does not bear close examination. In the immediate post-Exodus period this monotheistic belief system changed in ways that would have horrified Moses and many present-day monotheists.

From the era of the Exodus onwards as recorded in the scriptures we come across symbolism of plainly Egyptian origin that has exerted a profound influence on mystical Judaism down to this day. The Pillar symbolism that arose with the erection of the two pillars on the entrance road to the Temple at Karnak were vibrantly transformed to stress the divinely inspired and sacred purpose of the account of the Exodus. As Moses led his people through the wilderness we read that:

> The Lord went before them by day in a pillar of cloud to lead the along the way, and by night in a pillar of fire to give them light, that they might travel by day and night; the pillar of fire by night and the pillar of cloud by day did not depart from the people.[7]

This symbolism was used again to reinforce the presence of Almighty God in the tabernacle:

> When Moses entered the tent, the pillar of cloud would descend and stand at the door of the tent, and the Lord would speak with Moses. And when all the people saw the pillar of cloud standing at the door of the tent, all the people would rise up and worship, every man at his tent door. Thus the Lord would speak to Moses face to face, as a man speaks to his friend.[8]

Later on in the scriptures, the Psalmists tell us that God spoke to them in a pillar of cloud [9] that was later interpreted to be the seat of Wisdom herself. Many passages that refer to the wisdom tradition do so in a manner that implies that Wisdom was a separate Divine entity from the Lord God of Israel. 'Sacred Wisdom', or 'Gnosis', was just as important and central to the belief system of the new hereditary priesthood as it had been to their Egyptian predecessors. In

Proverbs 9:1 we read that Wisdom was God's helper in the act of creation and was described in this context as 'the consort of God' a term to give us all pause for thought. How, in any truly monotheistic system, can God have a consort? As the centuries passed and Judaism became more sophisticated the understanding of the term 'Wisdom' changed and evolved and was described as 'a creation of God.' Later, according to the author Karen Armstrong, it developed further and was called an attribute of God.[10]

The so-called Conquest of Canaan

In archaeological terms, probably the two most heavily excavated countries in the world are Israel and Egypt, and in most cases, the motivation was to investigate the historical accuracy of events described in the Old Testament. A series of excavations by Albright at Jericho between 1935 and 1965 were at first trumpeted as proof of the truth of the biblical story, substantiating the phrase in the Negro spiritual 'and the walls came tumbling down.' When Albright discovered evidence for collapsed city walls, this was loudly proclaimed as proof of the historicity of the Bible, news that was greeted with unbridled delight by Jews, Christians and Muslims alike. This euphoria did not last long, however, for later excavations by Kathleen Kenyon demonstrated clearly that the ruined walls found by Albright dated from a far earlier period than the alleged conquest of the city by Joshua and the Israelites.[11] Excavations over many decades in Israel have found absolutely nothing that can be plausibly claimed as evidence of conquest in the era of implantation of the people of Israel in the promised land. The biblical historian Robin Lane Fox states unequivocally that 'There is no sign of foreign invasion in the highlands which would become the Israelite heartland.'[12] The modern scholarly view is that, far from being founded by force of arms, the nation or tribe that became known as the people of Israel emerged peacefully and gradually from elements that arose from within Canaanite society.[13] The English historian Paul Johnson described this process in the following terms:

> Much of the settlement was a process on infiltration, or reinforcement of affiliated tribes who, as we have already seen, held towns such as Sechem.[14]

However, be that as it may, by 1207 BCE, Israel was established as either a nation or a major tribe and this is commemorated by a stele erected by the Egyptian Pharaoh Mernephtah on which is inscribed the words: 'Israel is laid waste, its seed is not...'

The modern scholarly consensus strongly suggests that there appear to have been three main waves of Hebrew settlement in the land of Canaan: the first under Abraham that is recorded in Genesis; the second led by Jacob, or Israel, who settled in Sechem—and these became the founders of the twelve tribes of Israel. The third and final wave was the Akenhaten/Moses 'mixed multitude' whose numbers and wealth allowed them to dominate the other Semitic tribes that were already established in Canaan. In the words of Karen Armstrong:

> The Bible makes it clear that the people we call the ancient Israelites were a confederation of various ethnic groups, bound principally together by their loyalty to Yaweh, the God of Moses.[15]

Thus echoing the words of the medieval Jewish scribe, Raschi cited above.

The Era of the Book of Judges

The apparent coherence in historical terms of the Book of Judges is particularly deceptive. Those listed did not rule in sequence, each ruled one of or another of the twelve tribes and therefore many of them were in power at the same time. From the scriptures it is virtually impossible to clarify this complex and chaotic situation. There are other complications also, to the extent that even Paul Johnson was moved to write:

> The Book of Judges, though undoubted history and full of fascinating information about Canaan in the late Bronze Age, is flavored with mythical material and fantasy and presented in a confused fashion, so that it is difficult to work out a consecutive history of the period.[16]

That is putting it mildly. Constructing a plausible chronology based on the Book of Judges is to enter into a nightmare world of educated guesswork founded on flimsy or highly questionable evidence. However, when we study the religious beliefs of the people of this time we are on far more solid ground wherein Biblical statements can be confirmed from outside, independent sources and archaeology. The Scriptures record in some detail, the backsliding and lapses from true monotheism that were recurrent among the people of Israel from the time of their implantation in the Promised Land until the Babylonian Exile some seven hundred years later. This scathing scriptural self-criticism that could easily have been either omitted or glossed over by the scribes who wrote the scriptures, is undeniably true and is confirmed by the archaeological evidence regarding Canaanite beliefs that have come to light since the dawn of the 20th century.

From the scriptural accounts we can soon discern that for some centuries, at least those covered by the Books of Judges and Kings, the emerging people of Israel were far from monotheistic as we now understand the term. While the majority of the Israelites described Yahweh as 'the one True God' and believed that they should worship him and no other, large numbers continued to worship the many gods of the Egyptian pantheon or local deities in Canaan. This pluralistic time of worship lasted up to the time of the Babylonian Exile when the Scriptures first began to take on their present written form. The composition of the Old Testament signaled that moment in history when the people of Israel as a whole decided that Yahweh was the sole God and there were no others.[17] Prior to that time, the people of Israel were far from being entirely and enthusiastically monotheistic. They participated in the fertility rites of Ba'al; worshipped many Syrian deities and also venerated the goddess Asherah, indeed one King of Israel, Manasseh, erected an altar to her in the Temple.[18]

The Lord God of Israel

Concepts of God evolve as do the belief systems built upon them. As first Yahweh was regarded as the one True God who has chosen a people to follow him. Following the building of Solomon's Temple and with Yaweh mystically enthroned in the Holy of Holies, while he was still believed to have chosen his people, he was now also recognized as the creator of all things. When King David moved the Ark of the Covenant from Shiloh to Jerusalem to symbolize Divine blessing on his conquest and to make the city the religious capital of the nation, he made Zadok, a Jebusite, as one of the high priests. Zadok, a priest in the tradition of Melchizedek had previously served the god El Elyon. Zadok held a collaborative appointment, the other high priest was Abiathar who had served Yaweh by looking after the Ark at Shiloh.[19] This dual appointment must have served some political purpose but it created problems later when the high priests at the Temple in Jerusalem had to prove their descent from Zadook and not Abiathar.[20] In order to 'legitimize' this weird idea, a genealogy had to be fabricated for Zadok that considerably exceeds in length any other credible, parallel lineage.[21]

The Myth of Solomon's Temple?

Even the biblical descriptions of Solomon's Temple in Jerusalem carry distinct overtones of polytheistic symbolism. The design described is similar to that of earlier Egyptian, Syrian of Canaanite temples.[22] The building comprised three, square edifices, each within the other with the central and smallest being known as the Most Holy Place, or the Holy of Holies. This small, innermost cube shaped building housed the Ark of the Covenant.[23] Despite the commandment forbidding graven images, the Temple is said to have contained ten carved Cherubim each of which was ten cubits high[24] in addition to carved depictions of flowers and palm trees. In conformity to ancient Egyptian temple tradition, there were two free-standing pillars of thirty five cubits height named Boaz and Joachim.[25] A large bronze altar, a huge bronze basin supported by bronze bulls that symbolized Yam, the primal sea of Canaanite mythology.[26] Lastly in this list of apparent anomalies, there were two forty feet high free-standing pillars representing the fertility of Asherah. Solomon himself is reported to have worshiped pagan deities and is described as building high places to Shemosh the Moabite god and Moelch the Ammonite deity.[27] Therefore, despite the fact that Solomon was reputed to have built the first Temple to Yaweh in the city of Jerusalem, he can hardly be described as a true monotheist—according to the biblical accounts at least.

The scriptural accounts disclose further anomalies in respect of Solomon's Temple. The account in Kings is strange in that it makes no mention of priests[28] while the very different story recounted in Chronicles gives detailed and inordinately lengthy descriptions of the duties of the priests at the Temple.[29] One perceptive biblical scholar Sanmell explained this confusing issue when he wrote:

> The ordinary view of modern scholars is that in Chronicles
> the ecclesiastical organization which arose in the later part of

the post-exilic period was anachronistically read back into the time of David and Solomon, thereby giving the sanction of antiquity to the ecclesiastical system of the post exilic period. This ecclesiastical organization provided for twenty-four *ma'madot*, priestly teams who took turns in serving at the Temple in Jerusalem.[30]

Again we are beset with the same problems mentioned above when we read scriptural accounts of the reigns of both David and Solomon for the biblical passages in question were written more than four centuries after the events they purport to describe and, furthermore as we shall see later, were inflated for political and religious purposes. The scriptures started to take written form during the Babylonian Exile and, by that time, Judaism had changed considerably from the religion practiced by either King David or King Solomon and had evolved into a truly monotheistic system, served at its core by an hereditary priestly caste who presided over a highly legalistic religion based firmly on the 613 strictures of The Law. The scribe responsible for creating the Old Testament continually stressed the importance of Sacred Wisdom—and nowhere was this more obvious than in their description of King Solomon. One early father of the Christian church, Eusabius, quoted Aristobulus, to stress the importance of Wisdom at the time of Solomon:

> One of our ancestors, Solomon (the reputed author of the biblical book of Proverbs) said more clearly and better that Wisdom existed before heaven and earth, which agrees with what has been said (by the Greek Philosophers).[31]

In the Old Testament we read:

> God gave Solomon Wisdom and very great insight and a breadth of understanding as measureless as the sand on the seashore. Solomon's wisdom was greater that the wisdom of the men of the East and greater than the wisdom of Egypt.[32]

Thus the scriptures themselves relate the Wisdom of Solomon to that of Egypt and it also tells us that the King prayed for wisdom.[33] The wondrous gift of wisdom is extolled still further in the apocryphal book The Wisdom of Solomon and, we are told in the Bible, was the principal reason for the visit of the Queen of Sheba to the King of Israel.[34]

The Queen of Sheba and King Solomon

Modern archaeology suggest that, in the time of King Solomon, Sheba was a land of considerable wealth and culture that lay in the area of modern day Yemen and Ethiopia. Its principal exports were myrrh and frankincense so; the motivation behind the visit of the Queen of Sheba to King Solomon almost immediately after he had completed the Temple could have been commercial among other reasons. One widely respected document, the *Kebra Nagast* records the most significant result of the Queen's visit to the King of Israel, a son called Menelik. The Kebra Nagast is as important and sacred to the Ethiopian people as the Torah is to the Jews. Furthermore, according to the Egyptologist Wallis Budge, Judaism was introduced into Ethiopia at about 950 BCE as not only Menelik became Jewish but also the Queen of Sheba herself.[35] It was in this fashion that the Royal House of David gained an Ethiopian branch and, over the centuries, Judaism began to spread far beyond the borders of either Israel or Egypt.

While the story of King Solomon in the Bible is fascinating in the extreme and has given rise to teaching, rites and rituals in the world wide brotherhood of Freemasonry there is considerable doubt about the truth of the Biblical story. Despite the descriptions of Solomon's alleged wealth, wisdom and power, the size and influence of his empire and the overwhelming importance of the Temple he is reported to have built in Jerusalem, no indisputable archaeological proof of his palace, temple or empire has ever been found. Furthermore, in the voluminous and detailed records of surrounding countries, there is no mention of this allegedly powerful empire. The English author Graham Philips writes:

> There is not a single contemporary reference to Solomon in the many neighboring countries that were keeping records in the 10th century BCE. At the time when the Bible tells us that Solomon created a major empire in the Middle East, none of his contemporaries seem to have noticed it, not even the Phoenicians with whom he apparently traded, worked closely and forged an alliance. The Egyptian pharaoh was supposedly his father-in-law, yet no Egyptian records of the period, of which many survive, make any reference to him. …Without the Biblical accounts we would be unaware of Solomon's existence.[36]

Despite the scant or non-existent evidence regarding his empire, the lack of any archaeological proof that his temple was ever built, Solomon was undoubtedly of supreme importance to the scribes who wrote the scriptures. From those accounts it is obvious that at this time Yaweh was not regarded as the only deity but as the national god, which left room for a variety of cults as well as the veneration of a number of local gods, as political expediency, the need for marital alliances or trade may have dictated. This lack of religious unity was reflected in the factionalism among the people of Israel and after Solomon's death, the nation paid a high price for this.

CHAPTER 7

THE WRITING OF THE OLD TESTAMENT

Shortly after the death of King Solomon, the Kingdom split into two. In the north was the Kingdom of Ephraim, later called Israel that eventually became Samaria. To the south was the Kingdom of Judea with Jerusalem as its capital. Samaria ceased to exist after its conquest and capture by the Assyrians in 722 BCE. This conquest and the deportation of the Samarian people is one of the very few events described in the Old Testament during the first Temple period that can be verified from external sources. Documents recording the reign of King Sargon of Assyria state that:

> In the beginning of my royal rule, I have besieged and conquered the city of the Samarians ...I have led away 27,290 of its inhabitants as captives.[1]

Ever since that momentous event, Jewish consciousness has been haunted by the ghostly spectre of 'the lost ten tribes of Israel.' In 702 BCE the Assyrians struck again and besieged Jerusalem, but the holy city did not fall. Its respite was relatively short for in 598 BCE a new invader, Nebuchadnezzar the King of Babylon, entered Judea and in 597 BCE Jerusalem fell. Ten thousand captives, including the city notables and the heir to the throne were led away into captivity.[2] The Exile in Babylon had begun. This was simply one terrible event in a long catalogue of disasters for there were six enforced deportations between 734 BCE and 581 BCE and, at the same time, many thousands of Jews fled for safety into Egypt and other nearby countries.[3]

These tragic events heralded the beginning of the Diaspora, a situation that has lasted from that day to this, wherein more Jews live outside the Holy Land than within its borders. The great fear was, that without the Temple, their national centre of worship and without a land of their own, the people of Israel faced absorption by the heathen peoples who had either enslaved or scattered them. However they had one significant trump card, they had the Lord God of Israel and the Torah. Using the religious concept of a chosen people their leaders resolved to centre all things Jewish around God and the Torah and create a new form of Judaism, stripped of all geographical and political limitations and founded firmly and exclusively on piety, learning, religion and study.[4] The Jewish people used the enforced exile in Babylon to totally transform their lives, their culture and their religion and, in the process, welded their people into a nation, an entity that was to survive conquest, dispersion, persecution, genocide and repression for all time. They turned adversity to advantage in a truly magnificent and lasting manner. How did they do this?

The leaders of the exiled people of Israel, its priests and its scribes needed to provide a logical and credible explanation of why this series of disasters had befallen their people. They also had to create a viable form of Judaism that could survive and prosper without access to the Temple in Jerusalem and give the Jews a communal way of life that they could use to unite the people and that was also practical, accessible and devout. They had the sacred Law, the Torah, the Book of Deuteronomy that had been fortuitously rediscovered just before the fall of Jerusalem, a few scanty records of the past, their oral traditions and the sayings of the prophets, above all they had a passionate sense of purpose, a divinely inspired plan that allowed them to plan for the future and also project their current ideas back into the past. From this heady cocktail they distilled the literary, spiritual and religious masterpiece that they call the Tanakh that most gentiles call the Old Testament. A collection of books that has transformed not only the people of Israel, but the entire monotheistic world.

Today, among biblical scholars, there is broad agreement as to how and when the Old Testament as we now know it, took written form. Various contributions for the sources named above can be identified either from the manner in which they describe God of from the bias and emphasis that discloses their priestly origins. Starting in Babylon a process began which blended them all into a coherent, if sometimes contradictory manuscript in which the original scribes utilised their understanding of Israelite history, tradition and mythology to impart a compelling and persuasive narrative style. According to the modern scholarly consensus, at least four major different sources can be detected. The J authors who described God as Yaweh or Jehovah; the E authors who refer to God as the Elohim; D the scribe who wrote Deuteronomy and, finally P the priestly source.[5] Today the majority of students of the Bible accept this hypothesis in one variation or another, be they Christian or Jewish. The traditional concept that the first five books of the Bible, the Pentateuch, were written by Moses has now been discarded. The Bible began to take written form during the Babylonian Exile and continued its evolution with the addition of new work, until the 2nd century of the Christian era. The Hebrew Bible, the Tanakh, consists of three major component parts: The Torah or Pentateuch, The Nevim or Prophets, and lastly the Ketuvim or sayings. The language of parts of Daniel, Ezra and Jeremiah is Aramaic but the rest are written in Hebrew.[6]

In archives throughout the world there is no such thing as an unbiased record of anything, the authors always had their own motivation and a personal interest to promote and the Bible is no exception to this rule. The spiritually inspired scribes, scholars and priests who composed the Old Testament stressed the role and importance of the hereditary priestly caste with particular emphasis being laid upon the twenty-four *ma'madot* or priestly teams who served in the Temple in Jerusalem. They laid distinct and specific emphasis on descent from Zadok the priest as an absolute and essential qualification for the high priesthood.

The Biblical authors 'invented' a credible and acceptable explanation for the trials and tribulations suffered by the people of Israel in their exile in Babylon. The constant and recurring lapses from faith, the repeated national apostasy that they listed in such detail in their Biblical accounts was given as the reason for God's anger with his chosen people. The Israelites had suffered conquest, diaspora, enslavement and exile as a direct result of their individual and collective deliberate failure to keep the covenant, or *berit*, with the Lord God of Israel. They had, in fact, brought ruin on themselves. The Exile and all it represented was a direct consequence of their backsliding, paganism and sinful past from the time of the fall of Jericho to the Babylonian conquest of Jerusalem.

This simple and understandable explanation gave all Jews at that time, a chance to understand their intolerable predicament and regain their self-respect and God's blessing by a life of repentance and righteousness.[7] Now they could once more come closer to Jaweh by 'doing Torah.' In Deuteronomy there were lists of obligatory laws, including the Ten Commandments, which the scribes elaborated into the complex and demanding list of 613 Command-ments or *mitzvoth* of the Pentateuch. Judaism had been transformed into a complex, highly legalistic and demanding code of living that impinged on every aspect of a member's life. Exiled in Babylon, the Jews were physically separated from the central shrine of the Temple in Jerusalem. There was a pressing need to establish new centres of worship for religious observance and the preaching of the new scriptures, thus the creation of synagogues can be traced back to this time. Denied access to the Temple and the opportunity to make ritual sac-rifice there, these new religious meeting places not only acted as centres of sa-cred teaching but also as places where exiled Jewish people could maintain and sustain a sense of national identity. So regular meetings, prayer and religious teaching, began to become codified in a recognisable and effective manner.

It was while the people of Israel were exiled in Babylon that they began to speak Aramaic, a local Semitic language that closely resembled Hebrew but was, nonetheless, distinct and different from it.[8] When the Israelites returned to Jerusalem and Judea, it became the commonly spoken language of all the Jewish people there too, and was still very much the common language at the time of Jesus. Even today, in Orthodox Judaism, *Kaddish*, the ritual prayers for the dead are said in Aramaic. The holy language of Hebrew was reserved for the scriptures and religious worship. This remained the case until a little while before the establishment of the state of Israel when Hebrew was estab-lished as the official language of the new state. According to Sigmund Freud, the term 'Hebrew' as a description of the people is not found prior to the Babylonian Exile.

Biblical Israelite Initiatory Tradition

The Jewish historian Norman Cantor reports that other scholars, including John Allegra and Professor Morton Smith, believe that it was during the Exile in Babylon that the Jewish people refined their monotheism. As a defeated nation who had been allies of Babylon's traditional enemy Egypt, the scribes played down, omitted or minimised the true Egyptian roots of the people of Israel. Thus Abraham was not described as being of the Egyptian royal family but as a wandering shepherd from Ur. Both Allegro and Smith argue that post exilic Judaism was strongly influenced by a volatile variety of esoteric spirituality from other sources to compliment and enhance the seemingly sedate and legalistic religion that is seen on the surface today.[9] What is certainly unarguable from the scriptures, as they were written, is that the Jews held their own initiatory mystical traditions in high esteem. The inspired writings in the Tanakh constantly stress their importance and centrality to the faith. The mystical vision of the Prophets, of King David and of Solomon was constantly extolled and the esoteric, spiritual concept of ascending degrees of holiness pervaded every aspect of Jewish life and extended into the precincts of the Temple itself. Indeed, the prophet Ezekiel, after a mystical vision that he experienced while in Exile in Babylon, made this explicit in his description of the ideal Temple that he had see in his vision.

Ezekiel spoke of a very special area of holiness surrounding both Jerusalem and the Temple that was to be occupied solely and exclusively by the religious elites: the King, the High Priests and the servants of the Temple, the Levites. This area was holier that the rest of the Promised Land occupied by the twelve tribes of Israel. Outside, far beyond this sacred land, was the profane, wider world, occupied by the Goyim. Just as the Lord God of Israel was separate from his people, his people, in their turn, needed to be separated from the profane world and peoples beyond their borders. Thus, in the name of sacred separation there was to be no fraternizing with the Goyim nor flirting with false gods. If the people of Israel made themselves sufficiently holy and righteous, God would dwell among them and they would know that they were holier than their pagan neighbours.[10]

The Early Scriptures

The newly required righteous lifestyle described in the Priestly writings is made particularly obvious in the books of Leviticus and Numbers. The scribes referred to as P rewrote the history of their people, using oral tradition and mythology, as seen from the priestly perspective to describe their 'forty years' of wandering in the wilderness. When they codified the Sacred Law that God allegedly gave to Moses on Mount Sinai, they also described a series of ascending graded areas of holiness that had at its heart the Tabernacle housing the Ark, symbolising the 'glory' of Yaweh. The only person permitted to enter this sacred space was Aaron the high priest. The encampment of the Israelites was sanctified and holy because of the presence of God within it, outside its boundaries was the profane, Godless sweep of the desert sands. These priestly scribes described Yaweh as a God of 'no fixed abode' who moved his abode with his people.

For the priestly scribes, P, the Israelites only truly became a people when Yaweh decided to dwell among them. They 'knew' that the on-going presence of God among his people was just as important as The Law. They wrote that the Lord God of Israel had revealed the divine plan for the Tabernacle at the same time as he gave The Law, or Torah, to Moses. In this manner they informed the people that Yaweh went with his people wherever they were and was still with them in Exile in Babylon just as he had moved with them in their wanderings in the Wilderness centuries before.

The new scriptures succeeded beyond the scribe's wildest dreams, Israel became exclusively and completely monotheistic and united as a people around the 613 structures of The Law, the dietary laws, the new synagogues and the new religious vision of the scribes. Karen Armstrong described this process as follows:

> Yaweh had finally absorbed his rivals in the religious imagination of Israel; in exile the lure of paganism lost its attraction and the religion of Judaism was born.[11]

The heart of this form of Judaism was the amalgamation of several existing strands of thought, uniting the prophetic, mystical and initiatory tradition with the new legalistic approach to the Law thus creating a religion of command and high moral purpose. This showed itself symbolically in the new form of worship. In the First Temple era, worship had been noisy, joyful and tumultuous; by contrast, post-exilic Judaism became quiet, solemn and sober. After the exile, Jews had become aware that their sins, individually and collectively had brought about the destruction of Jerusalem and now their new forms of worship reflected this. A new festival was instituted to mark this change, Yom Kippur, the feast of Atonement, when the high priest entered the Devir, the Holy of Holies and, on behalf of his people, begged God, on his knees, for Divine forgiveness for the sins of the entire nation.[12]

The Torah

As a direct result of the writing of the scriptures, the Torah was no longer the exclusive property of the priestly class and became accessible to all who wished to know it and 'doing Torah' became the central issue in life for the vast majority of devout Jews. Over the next few decades or so, it became the ultimate source of every Jewish practice, rule and custom. This influence spread far beyond people's personal lives and extended into all religious matters, into morality into political life and every social domestic and economic aspect of life among the people of Israel. The establishment of the Torah as the central issue of life transformed Judaism from a just another priestly religion into one that embraced every aspect of living. Henceforth, according to Isadore Epstein, the people of Israel became in effect a theocratic state where every religious announcement was, at the same time a political one and each political statement was also religious.[13] This seminal change in religious thinking was not restricted to Jerusalem and Judea but extended God's Law and rule to every Jew in the wider Diaspora.

God's message to his chosen people was inscribed in the ever-evolving scriptures that vast in bulk and sometimes almost impenetrable in their obscurity gave birth to an ever-increasing army of scribes, priests and exegesists whose commentaries and explanations filled libraries and gave rise to endless debates and arguments. In consequence, Judaism became luxuriant with internal conflicts that, over time, gave rise to a wide variety of sects and divisions that co-existed under the religion's broad spiritual umbrella. As each male Jew was under a sacred obligation to 'do Torah' they first had to be able to understand it and the result of this form of Talmudic scholarship was the saying 'where you have two Jews you have three arguments'. Under Persian rule this tendency grew, as the Persians were tolerant of their subject people's religion. Then in 333 BCE when Alexander the Great's army conquered Judea, the Jews were again granted considerable autonomy. In both cases the high priests remained the religious and political leaders of the Israelites and the only burden laid upon the people was an extra level of taxation. Later, when under the rule of the Selucid King Antiochus IV, this taxation doubled and he deposed the Zadokite high priest and appointed his own. The son of the deposed high priest moved to Egypt and built his own Jewish Temple at Lentopolis. The more devout members of the ma'madot deserted the Temple that they believed to have been profaned and formed their own sect centred at Qumran. This group, who later became known as the Essenes, based their new form of worship on strict ritual purity, and devoted adherence to the Torah under the guidance of their spiritual leader whom they called 'the Teacher of Righteousness.'

Thus the inherent tendency towards religious division was becoming ever more apparent. Things became far worse when Antiochus IV decided to eliminate Judaism in its entirety: all forms of religious service and ritual, circumcision. Fasting and the observation of all Jewish festivals were made capital offences. The Temple was dedicated to the Greek god Zeus, swine flesh was sacrificed at the altar and prostitutes were imported into the sacred precincts of the Temple.

The people of Israel rose in revolt and, under the leadership of the Maccabeans the fight to preserve Judaism began. At first the rebels attacked the apostates who had obeyed the Greek edicts, then they went for the Greek occupiers. The Maccabean family led the Israelites to victory and the Temple was cleansed and rededicated to Yaweh at a new festival called Hannukkah. Simon Maccabeus was named as both high priest and ethnarch and so, for the first time in many centuries, the people of Israel had their own Priest-King. However, the twenty-four hereditary high priestly families stood aside and remained at Qumran as Simon Maccabeus was not a direct descendant of Zadok and, in their eyes, the Temple was still defiled.

At first the people of Israel prospered and, following a series of wars, the country expanded to the point that, under the rule of Alexander Jananeus it was compared to the realm of the legendary King Solomon. This did not last long and the country was riven by civil war during which one side invoked the help of Rome. Under Roman rule a king was appointed who was described as 'a friend of Rome'—a complex, skilled political manipulator and cruel man known as Herod the Great.

CHAPTER 8
JERUSALEM AT THE TIME OF JESUS

Right across the developed world most Christians feel they have a reasonable understanding of life and conditions in biblical Israel in that era. This fantasy originates in 2,000 years of blind and uncritical belief based on documents of great spiritual import with virtually no historical validity. The New Testament imparts little or no understanding of either the social customs or religious obligations of the Jews, at that time. The Gospels imply that there were only two major factions within Judaism at that time—the Sadducees and the Pharisees—with a passing mention of the Samaritans. Aside from that, the inference is that Judaism was a moderately united religion. Contemporary historical documents give us an extremely different and detailed account.

There were four main sects within Judaism in the 1st century of the Common Era described by the Jewish Historian Flavius Josephus: the Essens, the Sadducees, the Pharisees, and the "fourth philosophy."[1] The Essens, now commonly referred to as the Essenes, were of the spiritual lineal descendants of those Zadokite priests of the ma'madot who withdrew to the wilderness as protest against the defilement of the temple by Antiochus and the appointment of non-Zadokite high priests by the Maccabeans.[2] They held all their goods in common, maintained ritual purity, lived austere lives, believed that soul was immortal, and held as major aspect of their belief, an almost obsessive insistence on "doing Torah"- that is, living life in strict accordance with God's

Law. The contemporary Jewish historian Josephus described the Essenes in these words: "They exceed all other men that addict themselves to virtue and this in righteousness."[3]

The Sects of the Sadducees and Pharisees

The Sadducees did not believe in an afterlife or the immortality of the soul, however, they believed that the law of the Torah or written law had to be followed without the slightest deviation.[4] They were so profoundly influenced by the Hellenistic culture that they incorporated certain Greek ideas into their lives, and being mainly of the property-owning class, they preached cooperation with Rome. The major differences between the Sadducees and the Pharisees was summarized by Isadore Epstein:

> The Pharisees desired all the affairs of the State should be governed on strict Torah lines, with no concern for any other consideration. The Sadducees, on the other hand, maintained that whilst it was well to recognize the Torah as the basic constitution of the State, it was impossible to carry on a Government, which, under changed conditions, necessarily demanded close relations with heathen powers without making political expediency and economic interest the final arbiter of things.[5]

Epstein maintained that the Pharisees were the only party suitable for dealing with the needs of the times. The foundation of their beliefs was the oral law that had been revealed in spiritual teaching to Moses when he received the Ten Commandments on Mount Sinai. They were open-minded in their effort to understand this body of oral law and tradition, attempting to adapt its meaning and observance in order to make it applicable to the lives of the people, an attitude that gained them considerable support. The Sadducees vehemently opposed all these beliefs, especially those deriving from the oral law. Therefore, in many respects, the rise of the Pharisees can be seen as an inspired response to the demanding, anachronistic legalism of the Sadducees; in others, it can be viewed as a reaction to the more profound Hellenization this ultra-conservative, powerful priestly, and propertied class represented.[6]

The God of the Pharisees was not exclusive to the people of Israel alone; he was the God of every individual, Gentile and Jew alike. In their view, he was the God of the entire world, of all mankind.[7] Furthermore, scholars researching the Dead Sea Scrolls have recently found another, less flattering, description of the Pharisees—one that portrays them as "seekers after smooth things" who were only too willing to make accommodation with foreigners, which made them look like collaborators to their more extremist "Zealot" opponents.[8] Since the time of the Maccabeans, the Sadducees and the Pharisees became active rivals and competitors for the control of the state.[9] There is a fourth sect among the Jews, mentioned by Josephus, the Zealots, described as having an "inviolable attachment to liberty which causes the nation to go mad with distemper and makes them revolt against the Romans.[10]"

Various Jewish Sects

During the last centuries of the Second Temple period there were other groups who contributed to the varied tapestry of religious belief in biblical Israel. There was a distinctive trend of charismatic Judaism that had a Galilean origin,[11] as well as a many-facet mystical trend of truly Egyptian/Hebraic roots. For instance, from the 2nd century BCE, the Devir, or Holy of Holies, that had once held the Ark of the Covenant, God's throne on Earth, became the focus for visionaries who imagined ascending directly to God's heavenly palace and approaching his celestial throne. We read of Jewish mystics getting ready for this mystical ascension by special disciplines.[12] Further mystical beliefs found in the Talmud focus on the *maaseh bereshith* (the work of creation) depicted in the first chapter of Genesis, and the *maaseh merkabah*, (the divine chariot) in the narrative of Ezekiel's vision. Throughout Talmudic times, these mystical doctrines were prudently protected and it was forbidden to communicate them except to a few chosen disciples in the traditional Egyptian manner.

In addition there are "the Psalms of ascent" in the Bible and the Ascents tradition that took written form many centuries later in the Kabbala—that is, the ascent through the various degrees of Neoplatonic enlightenment or gnosis, or—ascent to the higher heavens, another variation of the Merkabah tradition that was also known as Hekaloth.[13] The tradition that was received from Aaron over twelve centuries later took written form as the Kabbala, the major Jewish mystical tradition. One of its highly recognized tenets is the idea of the Zaddik, or the Righteous Ones.[14] The Righteous Man, as Ezekiel proclaims, will not suffer for someone else's sins; he will not die. "The man who has sinned is the one that must die. A son is not to suffer the sins of his father, nor the father the sins of his son."[15] It is written in the Sephar-al Zohar that Noah was a righteous one who was called the Foundation of the World, "and the earth is established thereon, for this is the Pillar that upholds the world. Thus, Noah was called 'Righteousness…and the embodiment of the world's Covenant of peace.[16]'"

Apocalyptic Creeds

Within the Essene tradition, although not necessarily relating to the sect, was a group of visionaries whose ideas are preserved in the body of literature known as the Apocalypse.[17] In obvious contrast to the Essenes and the Apocalyptists, who embodied an ostensibly negative reaction against the misery and oppression of the times, were Zealots, who were out to fight against the Roman oppressor—the Kittim—and make an end to tyranny. They were extremely fervent patriots who combined a devotion to the Torah with a passionate love of their country and were ready to fight and die for both.[18] In reality, despite what is written or implied in the New Testament sources, Judaism at the time was comprised of at least twenty-four parties and sects that were not regarded as heretical, but as an essential part of mainstream Judaism.[19] Moreover, a devout Jew could sit at the feet of a teacher in one or several of these groups at various times in pursuit of spiritual knowledge and righteousness, without apparent contradiction.

Herod The Great

The Jewish state of Judea in 63 BCE became a puppet state of Rome as a result of Pompey's interference in the civil war between the Pharisees and the Jewish rulers Hyrcanus and Aristobulus.[20] Initially, Rome was not sure how to manage these difficult people, but soon placed Judea under the control of the Roman Governor of Syria. In 43 BCE, Herod the Great seized the throne of Judea, and four years later, was confirmed as King of the Jews by Rome. Herod was "so supreme to his predecessors, according to Strabo, particularly in intercourse with Romans and in his administrations of the affairs of state, that he received the title of King."[21]

In contrast to general belief, Herod was, at first a brave and resourceful king—a builder, an administrator, and a supremely able politician who brought order and stability to Judea. He completely restored the temple in Jerusalem, which became a source of wonder for both the Jew and Gentile, established the port of Caesarea, and constructed a fortress as far south as Jordan and another in Damascus to the north. Herod was an Iduminean who did not take his Judaism seriously, not only did he rebuild the Jerusalem Temple, but he also built temples to pagan gods: three were built to Roma and Augustus—one at Caesarea, another in Sebaste, and the third in Panias.[22] Likewise, he constructed a temple to Ba'al at Sia and assisted in the temple building at Berytus and Tyre.[23] Herod also aided in the restoration of the temple of Pythian Apollo in Rhodes.[24] As a friend of both Pompey and Julius Caesar, he built the Antonia for Marc Antony that later became the permanent residence of the Roman proconsuls and was eventually occupied by Pontius Pilate.

Herod is one the most familiar characters in the New Testament and one of the most-documented characters in that period of history and it is well recorded that he behaved atrociously and murderously toward members of his own family whom he perceived as a threat to his power.[25] The Roman Emperor Augustus is noted as having said, "I would rather be Herod's pig than his son,"[26] which sums up the views of a powerful ruler on the actions of one his most trusted subordinates. Shortly before the end of his life, Herod developed an even more cruel and violent streak that destroyed his reputation for all time, culminating in the execution of Rabbi Mathias and his students for pulling down the sacrilegious Roman eagle from the temple.[27] The accepted biblical narrative that vilifies him unjustly, however, is the New Testament account of his "slaughter of the innocents"[28] Josephus's signal failure to mention this event in his thorough list of Herod's cruelties, gives us grave cause to question it. Moreover, as there is no mention whatsoever of it in the Talmudic literature of the period, we are inevitably led to believe that it simply did not happen.

During the early decades of Herod's reign, Rome's relationship with the Jews, both in Palestine and the Diaspora, was fruitful.[29] The Romans, who intervened as little as possible with internal affairs of defeated provinces, allowed the Jews a large measure of autonomy and the people were permitted full freedom of religious worship. Along with Herod's skilful political administration, this managed to keep the lid on the seething source of nationalist discontent fuelled by the activities of the Zealots and Hassidim. This discontent had been the constant backdrop to the affairs of the state since the time of Antiochus IV (169 B.C.E), long before the arrival of the Romans.

As before the occupation, the Sanhedrin continued to exercise its jurisdiction in all cases, whether civil or religious involving an infraction of Jewish law. Also there was the political Sanhedrin staffed by men chosen by the high priest, other Sadducees, who acted as arbitrators between the Roman administration and the people. They were accountable for policing cases of sedition and insurrection and handing over the accused to the Roman procurators. Regrettably, however, the procurators who governed Judea abused their power and did everything to render the lot of their Jewish subjects miserable and bitter.[30]

The Roman Occupation

Following Herod's death, his kingdom was divided between his sons, and there was also intermittent rule by the Romans procurators, Jewish nationalistic and religious fervour rose to the surface repeatedly in violent confirmations with the hated Roman occupiers, the *Kittim*. The Talmud records the first major rebellion called Varus' War. The Roman governor of Syria, Varus, reported a major revolt at the feast of the Pentecost that spread from Jerusalem into Judea, Galilee, Perea, and Idumea. With typical Roman efficiency, Varus put his legions into the field, burned Emmaus and Sephoris, and enslaved the survivors of those cities.[31] After that, he exercised the standard Roman punishment for sedition and ruthlessly crucified 2,000 Jews for rebellion.[32] This war was just one of many in a series of violent episodes arising from Jewish discontent with the Roman occupation. This potent blend of religious fervour and political agitation gathered momentum as the Herodian Kings and their Roman masters continually increased taxation. Overall, biblical Israel was a theocracy, in that the Torah was the law of the land and Roman law an additional imposition. Under these conditions, it was impossible to make a religious statement without it being a political statement, and it was just as difficult for the Romans to impose any political constraints upon the people without them having overtones of religious infringements. This was the reality that created the tumultuous environment for the life and ministry of Jesus—not the gentle, rural atmosphere of peace implied by the Gospels.

Robert Eisenman, biblical scholar and the director of the Centre for the Study of Judeo-Christians Origins at California State University, proposes that the apparently peaceful, Hellenized country where the Galilean fishermen cast their nets, the New Testament scenes depicting Roman officials and soldiers as "near saints," and the vindictiveness of the Jewish mob described in the Gospels have to be understood in the light of the fact that these allegedly "divinely inspired" accounts were written in complete subservience to the ever-present realities of Roman power.[33] Josephus made a similar observation more than 2,000 years ago, when he wrote that all historical accounts of that period suffered from two major effects—"Flattery of the Romans and vilification of the Jews, adulation and abuse being substituted for real historical record.[34]"

Moreover, by the time the gospels were written, in the decades following the destruction of Jerusalem by the Romans in 70 CE, Christian doctrine and mythology were already well developed. Consequently, the Jesus described in the Gospels must be distinguished from the very different Jesus of history.[35] It is, however, possible to construct a picture of Jesus, John the Baptist and James, and, more important, some realistic indications of the nature of their true teaching by utilising a combination of non-canonical sources—contemporary histories, apocryphal materials, the Dead Sea Scrolls, non-canonical acts such as the Pseudo-Clementine Recognitions, the Nag Hammadi Scrolls, early church literature, and modern scholarship.

Josephus makes specific reference of the frequent acts of rebellion against Roman occupation inspired by leaders or prophets of the apocalyptic tradition of Judaism, a visionary train of thought that spoke of God's intervention in the ultimate battle of the righteous against the forces of evil. This was an important aspect of messianic teaching within Judaism. The Zadokite/Essene and the Pharisaic traditions both expected two messiahs, not one: a priestly messiah and a kingly messiah. Both schools also believed that, until the elect of Israel adhered strictly to the covenant of God, the final redemption and the triumph of good over evil could not take place.[36] The role of the priestly messiah was to purify the elect and the kingly messiah was to lead them to victory in a war against evildoers. The Old Testament announced the coming of the messenger of the covenant who would "purify the sons of Levi."[37] It also foretold the return of Elijah as reconciler.[38]

The Essene "John the Baptist"

The historian Paul Johnson describes how at this time, the example of the Essenes led to the creation of a number of Baptist movements in the Jordan valley, where the entire countryside between the Lake of Genasseret and the

Dead Sea was alive with Holy eccentrics, many of whom had been to Qumran where they had absorbed Essene teaching. Johnson and most scholars specializing in that era are convinced that John the Baptist was an Essene who saw as his mission the creation of an elite within an elite to hasten the purification that was the necessary prelude to the coming apocalypse.[39]

Within the prophetic tradition, John's position is indicated by the fact that his own people believed him to be Elijah come again [40] and Josephus gives us an insight into John's mission and execution in the following terms:

> Herod had put him [John surnamed the Baptist] to death, though he was good man and had exhorted to the Jews to lead righteous lives, to practice justice towards their fellows and piety towards God, and so doing to join in baptism. In his view this was a necessary preliminary if baptism was to be acceptable to God. They must not employ it to gain pardon for whatever sins they had committed, but as a consecration of the body implying that the soul was already cleansed by right behaviour. While others too joined the crowds about him, because they were aroused to the highest degree by his sermons, Herod became alarmed. Eloquence that had so great effect on mankind might lead to some sort of sedition…John, because of Herod's suspicions, was brought in chains to Machareus… and there put to death.[41]

In the historical context of the times already described, Josephus' logic for John's execution is entirely credible. Nevertheless, the version given in the New Testament is also likely to have occurred because of his connections with the Essenes, who railed against what they called "fornication." The two versions are different, but not mutually exclusive and both may accurately reflect different aspects of Herod's motivation.

The Biblical scholar John Dominic Crossan, states that Josephus' view means that John's baptism was not a ritual act that removed sin, but rather a physical and external cleansing symbolizing that spiritual and internal purification had **already** taken place among the followers.[42] A modern historian, utilising exactly the matters raised above, wrote:

> People placed themselves in positions of disciples of John [the Baptist] in order to learn how to be purified effectively both

inwardly and outwardly. Once they felt fairly confident of their righteousness, by John's definition, then they came for immersion... Not all the people became his disciples. Once people were immersed, however, they would already have accepted John's teaching and therefore become his disciples before this.[43]

Church doctrine has continuously denied any teaching role of John the Baptist in his relationship with Jesus, yet modern scholarship tends to support the "heretical" view that Jesus was his pupil, a tradition that has been kept alive for 2,000 years among the hidden stream of spirituality preserved by the descendants of the ma'madot, chiefly the Rex Deus families and their spiritual heirs, the Templars and the Freemasons.

Jesus the Nazorean

The relationship between John and Jesus as teacher-pupil presented an array of problems for the Church. The Church minimised the truth in their explanations of the relationship between these two inspired figures for Jesus, as a disciple of John must have been a sinner who was restored to righteousness in order to qualify for baptism—an unimaginable idea for those who believe Jesus was divine and born without sin. It is impossible to accept that Jesus ever considered himself divine for this would have been the ultimate blasphemy for Jesus and all other Jews. He was, above all else, a devout Jew so committed to "doing Torah" that he became a pupil of John the Baptist and underwent purification from sin before his baptism. The modern author A.N Wilson came to the same conclusion and wrote that Jesus was a Galilean *hasid*, or a holy man, a healer in the prophetic tradition. Wilson asserts emphatically:

> I had to admit that I found it impossible to believe that a 1st century Galilean holy man had at any time of his life believed himself to be the Second Person of the Trinity. It was such an inherently improbable thing for a monotheistic Jew to believe.[44]

There is only one archaeological artefact that makes any reference to Jesus, which was discovered in 2001, except for a plethora of so-called medieval relics of highly dubious provenance. This artefact was an ossuary found inscribed in Aramaic with words that translate as "James son of Joseph and the brother of Jesus." Of course, this discovery was regarded with extreme scepticism when it first came to light. Unhappily, it proved later to be a clever modern fake, created and sold for mere profit. Falsehoods such as this are nothing new; the manufacture of "holy relics" was a big business during the medieval days. Regrettably, artefacts such as these, be they ancient or modern, do nothing to corroborate or bear witness to the historical reality of Jesus. Certainly, attempting to achieve any sensible comprehension of the full extent and nature of his teachings is exceedingly difficult, for outside the canonical Gospels he made little impact. Thus, we have to reconstruct a context of his true teachings from the Apocryphal Gospels and Acts, expanded and supported by pertinent documentation found among more recent discoveries at Qumran and Nag-Hammadi.

The Teaching of Jesus

The New Testament tells us more about the authors' viewpoint than they do about Jesus the man, with one or two notable exceptions. Nevertheless, these few exceptions are, interesting, especially when they contradict church teaching. For instance, Karen Armstrong emphasizes one episode when she remarks: "Certainly Jesus' disciples did not think they had founded a new religion: they continued to live as fully observant Jews and went every day in a body to worship at the Temple,"[45] her comment is based upon a passage from the Act of the Apostles.[46] One of the earliest apologists for Christianity, Aristides, declares that the worship of the first Jerusalem "Christians" was essentially more monotheistic than even that of the Jews. His disciples and apostles, therefore, did not regard the teaching of Jesus, as either the foundation of a new form of religion or as a condemnation of Judaism. The solitary difference between them and their Jewish neighbours was their fanatical adherence to Jesus' interpretation of the Torah, reinforced and supported by their faith in the messianic nature of his role.

The name Jesus of Nazareth is inaccurate, as Nazareth simply did not exist at that time. Jesus the Nazorean is a more accurate description, as the Nazorean sect was an offshoot of the Essenes. The initiatory, gnostic nature of Jesus' teaching is made profusely clear in a segment from The Gospel of Thomas uncovered among the Nag Hammadi Scrolls in 1945 in Egypt, that notes him saying: "He who will drink from my mouth will become like me. I myself shall become he, and things that are hidden will be revealed to him."[47] In his role of supreme teacher of righteousness, Jesus initiated the elite among his followers into the Nazoreans by a form of baptism. Professor Morton Smith discovered proof of this in his studies into the *Secret Gospel of Mark*, to which he found reference in the monastery of Mar Saba in Israel.[48] It is highly probably that this document was the one originally known as the *Gospel of Hebrews*.

For reasons such as this, we can only safely accept the recounted sayings of Jesus in the canonical Gospels when they are authenticated in apocryphal works, or can be validated by the material covering the beliefs of Jesus' brother, James the Just. Others are reasonable when they are obviously uncontaminated by pro-Roman bias or are consistent with mainstream Jewish belief, practice and phraseology. For instance, Jesus is quoted as saying, "Go not into the way of Gentiles and into any city of the Samaritans enter ye not; but go rather to the lost sheep of Israel,"[49] which is entirely in the line with Essene teaching and can be taken to be an authentic reflection of what he actually might have said.

By contrast, Jesus is attributed as saying, " Go ye therefore and make disciples of all nations, baptizing them in the name of the Father and of the Son and of the Holy Spirit," should be rejected as an impossible concept to be held by anyone of the Essene tradition, [50] not only because of its instruction to preach to the gentiles but, more importantly, because of the use of the phrase, "In the name of the Father and of the Son and of the Holy Spirit," would be an abomination to any Jew. The Jews, whether they were Nazoreans, Essenes, Zealots, or any of the other sects, believed in monotheism, observing one God, the God of Israel. The expression, "Father, Son, and Holy Spirit," does not arise in any authentic Jewish document and did not come into general use among the Christians until long after the destruction of Jerusalem.

A vital event to understand is the one that begins with Jesus' triumphal entry into Jerusalem and his crucifixion occurring less than a week later. This calculated staging of his entry into the Holy city a week prior to Passover, as described in the Gospels, [51] gave advance warning to the Romans that serious trouble was brewing. Furthermore, one Gospels notes that he was hailed with words "Blessed is the King of Israel, [52]" which would be interpreted by the Romans as an open call to rebellion. Two centuries before this there were similar reverberations of an entry into Jerusalem of the triumphant Simon Maccabees, who purified the temple after he was greeted with popular approval, "with praise and palm branches:"[53] a warning to the Romans that was amplified when Jesus upset the tables of the money-changers in the temple soon after he entered the city.[54]

All this, happening shortly before Judaism's most important feast when the city was saturated with Sadducees, Pharisees, Zealots, Hassidim, and various apocalyptic fundamentalists excited by nationalistic and religious fervour, constituted a religious and political powder keg, with Jesus' entry acting as the fuse.

The Governor of Judea, Pontius Pilate

The Roman in charge at the time was by no means the ideal choice to deal with these delicate and explosive circumstances. Pontius Pilate had a reputation for corruption, violence, robbery, and executions without a trial.[55] By now, Pilate had already weakened the power and influence of the Sanhedrin by depriving them of their jurisdiction in religious matters and burdened the Sanhedrin with responsibility of arresting anyone suspected of plotting against Rome and handing them over to the Romans for judgement.

Acting under the instructions of the political Sanhedrin, the temple guards arrested Jesus and handed him over to Pilate.[56] There was never a night-time trial of Jesus by the Sanhedrin as recorded in the Gospels, for this would have been illegal according to Jewish Law. There was no appearance before Herod and absolutely no prevarication on Pilate's part, for why should he concern himself with the life of one man when his predecessor, Varus, had crucified 2,000 Jews for sedition? The inevitable fact is that Jesus was crucified by the Romans for sedition and not arraigned in accord with Judaic tradition. He was judged and executed by Pontius Pilate, Roman procurator,[57] a man renowned for his cruelty, in order to circumvent any potential insurrection. The Romans' standard punishment for sedition, rebellion, and mutiny was crucifixion; and death by stoning was the Jewish penalty for blasphemy, as we shall see later.

Discovering who led the Nazoreans after the death of Jesus, how Jerusalem came to be destroyed by the Romans, and, most important, how, after the traumatic event, Judaism and the teachings of Jesus came to transformed into two markedly different religions, we must study the life and teachings of the brother of Jesus, James the Just, high priest of the temple and the so-called "first bishop of Jerusalem."

CHAPTER 9

JAMES THE JUST, ST. PAUL, AND THE DESTRUCTION OF THE TEMPLE

The accepted tradition that Jesus appointed Peter to be the leader of the disciples after the crucifixion was an invention by the Church, some considerable time later, to proclaim the supremacy of Rome over all other centres of Christianity. Within the New Testament, the works of early fathers of the Church, and in a passage of the Apocryphal Gospels we can discover the truth about leadership of the original disciples. The Gospel of Thomas, suppressed by the Church, vanished from sight more than 1,500 years ago, until a copy was rediscovered among other long-lost documents at Nag Hammadi in 1945. Within it is found the following passage:

> The disciples said to Jesus:
> We know that you will depart from us,
> Who is to be our leader?
> Jesus said to them:
> Wherever you are, you are to go to
> James the righteous,
> For whose sake heaven and earth came into being.[1]

The expression, "For whose sake heaven and earth came into being," has distinct and deliberate connotations of the traditional Kabbalistic description of Noah, of whom it was said, "The Righteous One is the Foundation of the

World." Occurring within the Pseudo-Clementine Recognitions is another reference to Jesus' direct appointment of James as his successor,[2] and, according to another early Church father and historian of Christianity, Epiphanius, James was described as "The first to whom the Lord entrusted his Throne upon the earth.[3]" Clementine of Alexandria, though, tells of the election of James by the Apostles and not of a direct appointment by Jesus. Thus, whether by appointment or election, it is established that it was James and not Peter, who was the true successor of Jesus. The New Testament also acknowledges this when it defines James as "the first bishop of Jerusalem,"[4] Robert Eisenman takes this to its logical conclusion when he declares that:

> James was the true heir and successor of his more famous brother Jesus and the leader at that time of whatever the movement was we now call "Christianity," not the more Hellenized character we know through his Greek cognomen Peter, the 'Rock' of, in any event the Roman Church.[5]

The creation of the Petrine foundation myth forced the Church to marginalize the role of James. The Gospels make it clear that Jesus was from a large family that included brothers James, Joses, Simon, and Judas Thomas, as well as several unnamed sisters,[6] which tends to explain Jesus' choice of successor. Certainly his brother, who knew his beliefs, would have been deemed sufficiently trustworthy to carry on his teachings unaltered; James had already acquired a reputation for righteousness. A further cause for an embarrassed reaction to James on the part of the Christian theologians began in the 2nd century when, in its divinely guided wisdom, the Church decided that Mary, the mother of Jesus, was a virgin, that Jesus was her only child, and that he was celibate.

The Gospels record Jesus as being a member of a large family and this was not the only awkward problem that the Church theologians had to overcome. Another problem needed answering and that was the question surrounding Jesus' marital status. According to Jewish custom in that era, it demanded that all males, especially rabbis, marry and produce a family. There are only a few exceptions to this rule which are clearly delineated in sacred literature, one being his brother James, for example, who was described by early Church fathers and theologians as a Nazorite who was "dedicated to Holiness from his mother's womb[7]" and, as such, would have been celibate. Jesus, as a rabbi, was subject to the 613 strictures of the Law and was obligated to marry. Furthermore, as he was of the direct line of David, it was incumbent upon him to produce an heir.

The Marriage of Jesus

Professor of New Testament Theology at the Ecole Biblique in Jerusalem, Father Jerome Murphy-O'Connor, stated, in a BBC radio broadcast, that:

> Paul was certainly married... Marriage is not a matter of choice for Jews, that's why you have so few in the early centuries who weren't married and that's why... Paul... must have [been married].[8]

The Church has clearly failed to apply the same reasoning used by Fr. Murphy O'Connor in respect of Paul to the case of Jesus, in spite of the fact that there is no mention in the New Testament that Jesus was unmarried, a situation that would have caused considerable comment at the time. Nonetheless, undertones of Jesus' marital status and clues to the identity of his wife can be found in the Gospels. A. N. Wilson, an English scholar, proposes that, "The story of the wedding feast at Cana contains a hazy memory of Jesus' own wedding,"[9] and the Muslim scholar Professor Fida Hassnain says of it:

> The question arises who is the guest and who is the bride? I would suggest Mary is the host for she orders the procuring of the wine or the guests, which Jesus deals with. One wonders whether it is *his* own marriage with Mary Magdalene, and whether the whole episode has been kept under camouflage... I believe that Mary Magdalene behaved as the chief consort of Jesus, and he also took her as his spouse.[10]

The account of the wedding feast is found in the Gospel of John:

> And the third day there was a marriage in Cana of Galilee; and The mother of Jesus was there: And both Jesus was called, and his disciples, to the marriage. And when they wanted wine, the mother of Jesus sayeth unto him, they have no wine, Jesus sayeth unto her, Woman, what have I to do with thee? Mine hour is not yet come. His mother sayeth unto the servants, whatsoever he sayeth unto you, do it.[11]

As the narrative continues, Jesus changes the water into wine and orders the servants to distribute it. A research of Jewish custom of time reveals that only the bridegroom or the groom's mother would have the necessary authority to give orders to the servants at a wedding,[12] which indicates that this was actually Jesus' own wedding being described.

Further on in the Gospel, we read of circumstance that, again interpreted according to the strict legalistic customs of the time, reveal the true nature of the relationship between Jesus the Nazorean and Mary Magdalene.

> Then Martha, as soon as she heard that Jesus was coming, went and met him: but Mary sat still in the house... And when she had said so, she went her way, and called her sister secretly, saying the Master is come and calleth for thee. As soon as she heard that, she arose quickly, and came unto him.[13]

The Mary being discussed is Mary of Bethany, better known as Mary Magdalene, who is clearly playing the role of a dutiful wife, the only woman permitted to sit at a man's feet. The Gospel of Luke gives the following account: "And she had a sister called Mary, which also sat at Jesus' feet and heard his word,"[14] thus indicating, according to Jewish custom, that Jesus and Mary Magdalene were husband and wife.

Margaret Starbird, an American Roman Catholic theologian, was so incensed at the apparent heresy of Jesus' marriage as described in *The Holy Blood and the Holy Grail* that she set out to refute it. It is a reflection to her spiritual and intellectual integrity that the book she published after several years of detailed research, *The Woman with the Alabaster Jar*,[15] is a superbly argued and detailed exposition of the conclusive evidence proving the marriage of Jesus and Mary Magdalene and their foundation of a dynasty. The alabaster jar being referred to held an expensive perfume that Mary poured on Jesus' head:

> While Jesus was in Bethany in the home of a man known as Simon the Leper, a woman came to him with an alabaster jar of very expensive perfume, which she poured on his head as he was reclining at table.[16]

In keeping with Jewish custom, in that era, and to other Near Eastern traditions from Sumer, Babylon, and Canaan, the king's head was ritually anointed with oil, usually by the royal priestess or royal bride in her ancient role of goddess. The Greeks referred to this ritual as *hieros gamos*, or the sacred marriage. This ritual union with the priestess was essential if the king was to be recognized in his divinely blessed and royal role, as the true "anointed one," or the messiah.[17] For that reason, Western art and Church iconography nearly always portray Mary Magdalene as the Lady with the alabaster jar.

The First Church in Jerusalem

The vast amount of material describing the belief of James the Just and the Essenes helps us clarify the basis for the true teachings of Jesus. It is also an important aid in stripping away the veneer of theological obfuscation that resulted from the mythologizing of this gifted spiritual teacher. In spite of its later marked divergence from the initiatory teachings of Jesus, the social structure of the early Christian Church was chiefly shaped by Essene teaching, tradition, and practice.[18]

The early Church is acknowledged as having used a handbook known as the *Didache*, or "the teaching of the Lord." The semblance between the *Didache* and the *Community Rule* found among the Dead Sea Scrolls is quite startling—especially in view of the Church's determined attempt to date the latter to an earlier era. They both begin with information describing "the two ways"—the way of light and the way of the darkness—and continue in a manner that leaves no doubt as to which is the parent document.

The first "Christian Church" in Jerusalem was governed by a triumvirate of elders, based clearly on the model of the Essene community. The three leaders of the followers of Jesus was recognized as "the Pillars," and they are listed in the New Testament as James, the brother of Jesus and the so-called "first bishop of Jerusalem," Simon Peter, and John.[19] This shows that the well-established use of pillar symbolism had evolved even further from its original Egyptian use as a sign of divinely inspired wisdom or gnosis, through its significance of the divine presence during the forty years in the wilderness, to a symbolic representation of an individual who had attained enlightenment or righteousness. Robert Eisenman, the Dead Sea Scrolls scholar equates James the Just with the Teacher of Righteousness of the Essenes.[20]

James the Just, the Brother of Jesus

Epiphanius, described James' function as high priest in the following terms:

> I find that he also exercised the Priesthood according to the Ancient Priesthood, [the Rechabite or Nazorite one—possibly even the one Hebrews are calling the "Priesthood after the Order of Melchizedek"]. For this reason he was permitted to enter the Holy of Holies once a year, as the Bible lays

down in the Law commanding the high Priests. He was also allowed to wear the High Priestly diadem on his head as afore-men-tioned trustworthy—men Eusabius, Clement and others haverelated—in their accounts.[21]

One other early Church father, Hegesippus, describes James being brought to the temple by Scribes and Pharisees to quiet the Passover crowd hungering after the messiah. These establishment figures were, definitely, intent on pacifying the crowd in order to coexist peacefully with the Roman occupiers.

However, James was of a different persuasion, for he was the centre of agitation at the temple in the years leading up to the war against Rome.[22] Instead of alleviating the agitation of the crowd, he did the opposite and fanned the flames of revolt.[23] Found within *The Antiquities of the Jews* cited above, Josephus describes the beliefs and activities of the "fourth philosophy," those zealous for freedom and liberty, merging part of his earlier descriptions of the Essenes in *War of the Jews* with that of this nationalistic group. He implies, by that comment, that the Essenes and the Zealots were either following the same religious and political direction or, more likely, had become almost indistinguishable from one another. It is also suggestive of this trend that Josephus uses the term *Zealots*, when referring to the people opposed to the high-priest Ananias who eventually murdered James.

James, the leader of a group of strict, extremely religious, nationalistic Jews, was the man to whom Jesus appointed the leadership of his own disciples. Consequently, could there have been any significant difference between the true teachings of Jesus and those of his brother James? Absolutely not! There are no major or compelling deviations conceivable. This raises a question, however: How and why is the version of Jesus' teaching recorded in the canonical Gospels so different from the sectarian, Torah-based, ultra-orthodox practices revered by James the Righteous and the Essenes? In order to truly understand that, we must look at the character of a man whose changes of direction were confusing in their complexity—one who started by persecuting the followers of Jesus, was "miraculous converted," joined James and others, and later, betrayed them.

Saul of Tarsus (St. Paul)

The man who, centuries later, became known as the Father of Christianity was the strange and complex Saulus, or Saul, of Tarsus, better known as

St. Paul in Christianity. In his own writings, St. Paul establishes that he was both a Roman citizen and a Pharisee who spent some time relentlessly persecuting the followers of Jesus after the crucifixion.[24] Following his so-called miraculous conversion on the road to Damascus, he did a complete about face and not only changed his religion but his name as well. After spending a mysterious three years in Arabia,[25] he joined James in Jerusalem, learning the "True Way" as taught by Jesus,[26] before setting out on a series of prolonged evangelical journeys.

Paul's missionary travels took him to many important cities of the eastern Mediterranean, so neither his perseverance nor his stamina can be attacked. Nevertheless, within a surprising short time, he was subject to scathing criticism by James and the original disciples in Jerusalem. It is evident, from both the New Testament accounts and other sources, that there was a major fundamental difference between the Way as interpreted by James and his Essene companions and the version preached by Paul. Thus, conflict was inevitable and is mentioned, albeit, in an evasive manner, in the account of the Council of Jerusalem in the Acts of the Apostles. This somewhat diplomatic version of events indicates that, after some discussion, Paul's version of the message was deemed acceptable and valid.[27] Conversely, knowing that James the Just and his disciples who walked with Jesus had a righteous and absolute dedication to the Torah, the strict prohibition against mixing with Gentiles, keeping strictly to the dietary laws of Judaism, and trying to create a purified "elite within the elite of Israel" in the readiness for the eventual victory of the power of light over darkness in the Last Days, we must recognize this as an unimaginable scenario—particular when we read Paul's personal beliefs, which are expressed so clearly in his epistles.

Paul associated with the Gentiles, claiming that the covenant and its laws no longer applied. According to him, circumcision was not necessary for converts, and faith alone was all that was needed for the salvation in the run up to the Parousia, or End of Times, when Jesus would come again. In his studies of the Dead Sea Scrolls and related documents, Robert Eisenman has found records of this dispute that have enabled him to construct a more accurate version of these events. Within this, it becomes apparent that the dispute hinges on Paul's preaching to the Gentiles and his denial of the validity of the Torah. This gave rise to a dramatic confrontation between a man called the Liar and those of his persuasion on one side, and the righteous on the other.

The importance of this harsh dispute is emphasized by the reference to treachery in the underlying text, which refers to factional strife within the community.[28] The Essenes insistence on ritual purity, doing Torah, refusing to eat food sacrificed to idols, and forbidding social contact with Gentiles was rigidly enforced within the group. In the Qumran Community Rule it is said that:

> Any man who enters the Council of Holiness walking in the Way of Perfection as commanded by God and, whether overtly or covertly, transgresses one word of the *Torah* of Moses on any point whatsoever… shall be expelled from the Council of the Community and return no more. No Man of Holiness shall associate with him in monetary manners or in approach *on any matter whatsoever.*[29]

Paul's teaching was clearly out of step with that of Jesus and his twelve apostles and the fate quoted above from the Community Rule is exactly what happened to the self-appointed apostle who gives three different contradictory accounts of his miraculous conversion. After his expulsion, even his closes companion, Barnabas, deserted him, as he recounts in the Epistle to the Galatians.[30] His absolute abrogation of the Law and his insistence that salvation is by faith alone and not by doing the Torah, which he holds as worthless, is made evident later in the same letter.[31] Paul Johnson, Catholic historian, declares that, from the time of this dispute, the evangelical mission of St. Paul steadily lost ground to that of the evangelists duly accredited by James the Just of Jerusalem.

Paul makes a disparaging mention of this practice of accreditation when he writes: "Or do we need, like some other people, letters of recommendation to you…"[32] Johnson makes it perfectly clear that, if it had not been for the destruction of Jerusalem by the Romans a few years later, Paul's monumental effort would have been consigned to a minor footnote of history, or, more likely, forgotten altogether.[33] From this time forth, few, if any, Jewish disciples have anything more to do with Paul. Following his expulsion, his traveling companions and collaborators are Judeo-Greeks such as Timothy, "whose mother was a believing Jewess,"[34] a remarkably similar description to the one applies to another of his companions and converts, the Herodian Princess Drusilla.[35] Like Paul, Drusilla was a Roman citizen. The majority of Paul's own letters written after this event express resentment and bitterness about his treatment and express his pain at the charge that he is a liar and not a true apostle. For instance:

> Am I not free? Am I not an apostle? Have I not seen Jesus our Lord? ...Even though I might not be an apostle to others, surely I am to you![36]

Is it more likely that the true teachings of Jesus and his disciples had drifted off course, or that Paul should lie? Paul writes in a letter verse that:

> ...and for this purpose I was appointed a herald and an apostle—I am telling the truth and I am not lying... (I Timothy 2:7)

He was clearly a controversial and an unusual character in the New Testament account, with his constant complaining and contradictory teachings to those laid down by Jesus and his disciples recorded in the canonical Gospels. When reading all of the epistles of Paul one after the other, it is impossible not to perceive this, for his constantly self-pitying tone and the sense of resentful defensiveness that emerges is readily apparent. It is not hard to see Paul in a very different light when they are read in sequence.[37]

Considering his anti-Torah teaching, for James and his followers in Jerusalem, Paul was a false prophet. The Bishop of Lyons, one early Church father, Iraneus, quotes an Ebionite document that describes Paul as "an apostate of the Law."[38] The Ebionites also called "the Poor" were the names by which the followers of Jesus became known during and after James' ministry. An early 2nd CE document by the Ebionites, the *Kerymata Petrou*, describes Paul as a "Spouter of wickedness and lies," and "the distorter of the true teachings of Jesus." This same document gives a short shrift to Paul's description of the visions leading to his so-called miraculous conversion on the road to Damascus, classifying them as "dreams and illusions inspired by the devils."

Altogether, it seems justifiable to propose that the family and disciples of Jesus held Paul in considerable contempt. Regarding Paul's letters, we can sense that this mistrust and dislike were mutual. He describes his own position versus the community in Jerusalem in these terms:

> Therefore stand fast in the freedom with which Christ has made us free and no doubt [submit] again to the yoke of slavery... Everyone who accepts circumcision is obliged to do the whole Law. Whosoever is justified by the Law are set aside from Christ.[39]

Paul's epistles were observed by James and his brethren as full of blasphemous ideas and dotted with gratuitous insults maligning circumcision, circumcisers and the Torah generally. They also accused him of being simultaneously a "Law-Keeper to those who keep the Law" and a "Law breaker to those" who do not.[40] Thus, it is not surprising that the dispute between James and Paul did not end with Paul's expulsion from the true disciples in Jerusalem. It changed from verbal antagonism to murderous violence.

Paul's Arrest

Paul physically assaulted James the Just and attempted to murder him by throwing him down the temple steps and breaking his legs leaving him for dead. This attempt on James' life is recorded in the *Pseudo-Clementine Recognitions* and is also part of the subject matter of a lost work about James from which Epiphanius quotes several passages, the *Anabathmoi Jacobou*, or *The Ascent of Jacob*. The most erudite and conclusive study of these disturbing matters can be found in Robert Eisenman's master-work, *James the Brother of Jesus*.[41]

Following the assault, Paul was arrested,[42] allegedly because he had incensed the mob at the temple by his blasphemy in preaching the Gospel. However, it seems that the real reason for his arrest was to protect him since the mob wished to kill him in revenge for his attempt on James' life. At the time he was in custody, he was warned of another plot to kill him, so he then told the Roman arresting officer who took him to Caesarea under a large military escort of two hundred spearmen[43]—a suspiciously large escort for a blasphemer whom the Romans would normally have left to the none-to-tender mercies of the Sanhedrin, who would have sentenced him to death by stoning. Still no one in the Christian world seems to question why so much importance is attached to Paul or why such an expenditure of military resources is committed to his removal at a time of potential rebellion. Could the reason be that Paul was a Herodian, a member of the ruling family and a long-term friend of Rome?

The first reference we have of this pivotal relationship with the Herodians occurs in one of Paul's own letters. In a passage whose importance has signally failed to make an impression on modern Christianity of any denomination, Paul states:

> Greet those who belong to the household of Aristobulus. Greet Herodian my relative.[44]

The Aristobolus he alluded to was the son of Agippa I's brother, Herod of Chalcis, who had a son called Herod, known as Herodian, or the Littlest Herod. These family and political connections explains how, as a comparatively young man, Paul exerted power in Jerusalem as a member of the temple guard authorized by the high priest to persecute the followers of Jesus. As a group of nationalistic, zealous Jews, the Jesus group would have been a prime target for temple authorities bent on suppressing rebellion against their Roman masters. The English author A.N. Wilsons asserts that: "It does not seem unreasonable to support that he was in the same position in the temple guard when Jesus was arrested."[45] The important political power that goes with royal connections may explain Paul's comfortable status during his two-year imprisonment at Caesarea at the behest of the Roman governor, Felix.[46] Within this same narrative, we learn that Felix was married to a lady called Drusilla, who was a Jewess, the third daughter of Agrippa I, and the sister of Agrippa II. She had divorced her first husband in order to marry Felix,[47] who was also well connected, being the brother of Nero's favourite freedman, Pallas. This is the same Drusilla referred to earlier who was among the loyal followers of Paul after his expulsion by James. Josephus writes that the original Antipater, the father of Herod the Great, was awarded hereditary Roman citizenship for services to Caesar,[48] so Paul and Drusilla, as Herodians, both relatives of King Agrippa II,[49] were born into a highly privileged position that they exploited to the full.

In his epistle to Philippians, Paul acknowledges that one of his converts, Epaphroditus, was a senior advisor to the Roman Emperor Nero[50]—an important connection he stresses later in the same letter, "Greetings, especially those in Caesar's household.[51]" Paul, or Saul as the Romans and Herodians knew him, was extremely well connected with people in high places. These political links and important relationships reveal to us how Paul, allegedly a simple tent-maker, travelled the world with incredible ease, has so many miraculous escapes from prison, and was treated as the welcome guest of people of considerable power and influence. It is not by chance, therefore, that the community at Antioch, who were the first believers to be called Christians, consisted chiefly of other Herodians; Paul was receiving considerable support from his family.

These influential, strong Herodian and pro-Roman links explain the castrating of Jesus' message that occurred when Paul stripped it of all nationalistic fervour and substituted so many calls to obey lawful authorities. Like his ancestor, Herod the Great, Paul wore his Judaism very lightly; otherwise it would be impossible to conceive how any Jew of his supposedly Pharisaic background could have indulged in the kind of anti-Semitic and anti-Torah teaching he promoted. The striking contrast between Paul's message of subservience to lawful, i.e. Roman, authority and his preaching of a New Covenant that denied most of the strictures of the Torah was the total repudiation of the teaching of James and the original disciples of Jesus in Jerusalem. James' zealous and intrinsically Jewish posture had a very political aspect. He was at the centre of the agitation at the temple, actively advocating a pro-Torah, distinctly nationalistic, anti-Herodian, anti-Roman policy that led to a collision with the authorities in Jerusalem, namely the Sadducee high priests and their principal ally, Paul's close relative, King Agrippa II.

The Murder of James the Just

The hostility came to a crisis point after King Agrippa appointed a new Sadducee high priest, Ananias. Following his orders the Sanhedrin was convened to try James for blasphemy. Procedures were already set in place for men deemed popular with the people. They are recorded in the *Mishna Sanhedrin*, which recommends that the priests gather around the condemned, jostle him and cause him to fall from the temple wall. He was then stoned and they beat out his brains with clubs.[52] This is literally what happened to James the Just. He was thrown down from the temple wall, stoned, and then given the deathblow with a fuller's club.

The early Church father, Jerome, who translated the Bible into Latin, writes that, "James was of such great Holiness and enjoyed so great a reputation among the people that the downfall of Jerusalem was believed to be on the account his death."[53] The 3rd century Christian theologian Origen, and Eusebius, the bishop of Caesarea, both claimed to have examined a copy of Josephus different from the one we presently have, probably the Slavonic version, which recorded that the fall of Jerusalem was a consequence of the death of James, not the death of Jesus—a significant admission for two of the most respected early fathers of the Church.[54] Following this traumatic event the Ebionites and the other members of the ma'madot, now under the leadership of James' "cousin," Simeon, decided to leave Jerusalem and cross the Jordan into Pella.[55] The leadership remained among the descendants of the family of Jesus known as the Desposyni for more than 150 years after their flight to Pella.[56] The opinion among the other Jews in Jerusalem and Judea remained sharply divided.

Zealots incited immediately rebellion against Rome, the Sadducees, "Hellenizers," and Herodians. Others wanted to maintain the current position and keep the peace. The die was cast by 66 CE and the move towards war was inevitable. At this point, Saul, the kinsman of Agrippa, comes back into the picture. Josephus records that, when the war broke out in 66 CE and the Jewish Zealot forces occupied Jerusalem:

> The men of power [Sadducees], perceiving that the sedition was too hard for them to subdue...endeavoured to save themselves, and sent ambassadors, some to Florus [the Roman Procurator]...and others to Agrippa, among whom the most eminent was Saul, and Antipas, and Costobarus, who were of the king's kindred.[57]

The intention of these messages was to ensure prompt military action by the Romans in order to subdue the rebellion before it got out of hand—a motivation entirely consistent with the general thrust of Paul's "obey lawful authorities" philosophy expressed so clearly in his writings. When this failed, the insurrection became unstoppable and, a deputation was sent to the Emperor Nero at Corinth—then called Achia. Once more Josephus provides the details:

> Cestius sent Saul and his friends, at their own desire, to Achia, to Nero, to inform him of the great distress they were in...[58]

After this meeting, Nero appointed Vespasian as general in command of the legions in Palestine, thereby sealing the fate of Jerusalem. Finally, after fours years of prolonged and bitter fighting, Jerusalem was besieged and fell to the Romans amid scenes of unprecedented carnage and brutality. The surviving inhabitants were put to the sword, or sold into slavery, and the city itself and the temple were razed to the ground. In this barbarous manner, the Jews were finally deprived of their centre of worship, the home of the Lord God of Israel, and the heart was brutally torn out of their culture, religion and tradition. In spite of their prophecies and the righteous behaviour of the Essenes and the bravery of the Zealots, the forces of darkness had triumphed over the sons of the light. At this moment everything changed, not only for the Jews, but also for the entire world.

CHAPTER 10

THE TRANSFORMATION OF JUDAISM, THE EVOLUTION OF THE CHRISTIAN RELIGION, AND REX DEUS

With both the Temple and the city of Jerusalem a smoking ruin, Rome's suppression of the rebellious people of Israel was complete. The Holy City was a veritable charnel house, the streets and alleyways choked with putrefying corpses, the Temple destroyed and razed to the ground and the whole stinking city ringed with crucified victims signifying the futility of rebellion against Rome. There were, nonetheless, many thousands of survivors and the vast majority of them were paraded in triumph through the streets of Rome to the delight of the cheering crowds. The victorious legions showed off their trophies of battle, the treasures of the Temple in Jerusalem. Roman imperial tradition was, of course, strictly observed with the public execution of the Jewish leaders among the captives while their unfortunate companions were despatched to the slave markets, the mines or the galleys. The failure of the Jewish revolt for which the people of Israel had paid such a high price, transformed the world. It took many years to even begin to assess the full impact of this horrendous failure but, with the passage of time, we can now state with absolute certainty that it shaped the world to come from that day to this. At the time this was far from obvious, indeed one modern commentator described the immediate results in the following terms:

> The defeat of apocalyptic hope and the physical destruction of the Judeo-Christian sect cleared the way for Pauline Christians to de-nationalize Jesus, cauterise his revolutionary message and re-package him as a 'saviour god' dispensing opiate for the masses.[1]

The Jews had to recast their lives and religious practices in order to continue to exist in the Roman world, the Temple was gone forever and mainstream Judaism had to change substantially to avoid simply being absorbed by the great ravening maw of Roman power.[2] Among the followers of Jesus, those who swallowed Paul's distorted message gradually took control and created the fundamental basis of Christianity as we now know it.

One leading Pharisee, Rabbi Yohanen ben Zakkai, who had been totally and absolutely opposed to the revolt and the extreme doctrine of the Zealots, was smuggled out of Jerusalem during the early stages of the siege. After the fall of the city and as a result of his moderation, he was one of the few Jewish leaders who retained any degree of credibility with both his own people and the Romans. He approached the Emperor Vespasian and sought permission to start a school at Jamnia where his fellow Jews could study, pray and resurrect their religion. He told the Emperor that this school would be a centre of spirituality and not a focus for revolution. There, Judaism was quietly and effectively stripped of all its messianic and nationalistic fervour.[3] With the Temple destroyed, the rabbinate now taught their congregations to experience God in their neighbours and many preached that the *mitzvah*, 'Thou shalt love thy neighbour as thyself' was the greatest principle of the Torah.[4] In order to ensure the survival of both their religion and their people, the new rabbinate simply modified the emphasis, but *not* the substance of their faith and created a new form of worship and ritual that was acceptable to the Romans. Drawing heavily on the scriptures and well established tenets of belief and using the vast store of scholarship and exegesis their predecessors had created they could continue to speak of Judaism in the present tense despite the fact that the Temple had been destroyed. The spiritual reality that the Temple had symbolized was still true—God's mystical presence on earth became the ever-beating spiritual heart of Judaism from that time onwards.[5]

The Rex Deus Diaspora

Under the leadership of Simeon, the cousin of Jesus, the Ebionites and the surviving members of the ma'madot returned from Pella and established themselves near Mount Sion in the ruins of Jerusalem.[6] However this did not and could not last as several Emperors including Vespasian, Titus, Domitian and Trajan repeatedly instructed the men of the tenth legion, Rome's principal occupation force, to seek out and execute any Jew who was, or claimed to be, a descendant of King David.[7] According to Rex Deus tradition, this type of edict had earlier been the cause of the separation of the children of Jesus to try and ensure their survival.[8] His son James was put into the care of Jesus twin brother Thomas Didymus and sent for sanctuary to King Abgar of Edessa.[9] Jesus' pregnant wife, Mary Magdalene fled first to Egypt where she gave birth to her daughter Sarah and then crossed the sea to present day France.[10]

With Imperial death sentences hanging over all their heads, it was time for the living members of the Davidic royal line to run and hide. They scattered themselves right across Europe, to England, Italy, France, Spain, to various places in Eastern Europe and the Middle East. Before they left the ruined city of Jerusalem, they swore to keep up their Cohenite marital practices in order to preserve the sacred bloodlines and began to modify and transform their outward beliefs in order to ensure the survival of their sacred teaching. They had rejected worship at the Temple as it had been, in their eyes, polluted. Now they began to discard their fervent nationalism and anti-Roman attitudes and laid far greater emphasis on 'doing Torah'—focussing on their behaviour and reverting to their old central core belief—creating an elite within the elite, sworn to sacred brotherhood founded firmly on the twin gnostic foundations of Truth and Justice. In this manner they had some semblance of hope that they might preserve the spiritual core of their teaching, and do Torah, without interference by the Romans. Their teachings would be passed down in the tried and trusted manner of old, master to pupil or, in this case, from father to selected children.

One early father of the Catholic Church, Epiphanius, recorded some of their beliefs and practices:

> Beside a daily ritual bath, they have a baptism of initiation and each year they celebrate certain mysteries . ...In these myster-ies they use unleavened bread and for the other part, pure wa-ter. They say that Jesus was begotten of human seed ...that he was not begotten by God the Father, but that he was created ...and they too receive the Gospel of Matthew and this they use ...to the exclusion of all others. But they call it the Gospel of the Hebrews.[11]

The renowned English author, Karen Armstrong gave the perfectly valid reasons why the Ebionites believed that Jesus was human and not Divine when she wrote: 'after all, some of them had known him since he was a child and could not see him as a god.[12]' Paul and his followers had no trouble bringing their beliefs into line with the new Roman requirements. Paul was a Roman citizen, a friend of Caesar and a relative of the Herodian royal family. In Paul's eyes, the Torah had been superseded by faith, and he instructed his flock to 'render unto Caesar what is Caesar's.' The nationalistic aspirations of Jesus and the original disciples were ignored and the esoteric pathway to the Lord God of Israel who had been guiding and protecting his people since the time of Abraham was now hijacked and perverted if not negated entirely.[13]

After the disastrous failure of the Jewish revolt, the followers of Jesus split into two principal groups: the original disciples now known as the Nazoreans or the Ebionites under the leadership of James the Just and then his successor, Simeon and their theological opponents, the so-called Christians who were the followers of Paul. As we have mentioned above, the Ebionites were in the process of scattering to avoid the unwelcome and lethal attentions of the Roman authorities while the Pauline flock were relatively settled in various cities around the Mediterranean and supremacy among them eventually fell to those living in Rome. It was the thinking and theology of these Pauline; Roman Christians that eventually became the central core of belief for the 'new' religion of Christianity.

The Ebionites, or the 'poor,' were completely dependent on the oral transmission of the teaching of Jesus that they had received either from him or from his brother James, directly from the people who had walked and talked with the master while he was on earth. The Pauline followers, on the other hand, received their instruction, directly or indirectly, from a man who, on his own admission, had never met Jesus in the flesh. Paul claimed that his teaching had been given to him in a vision directly from the one he called 'the risen Lord.' Contrary to what most Christians believe, the New Testament does not list its books in the order in which they were written. The earliest so-called Christian texts are the Epistles of St Paul, which were written and circulated in or about 47 CE more than three decades before the first Gospel took written form and more than fifty years before the last one.[14] Before the Gospels were written, the Epistles of Paul were the only surviving documents circulating among Paul's followers, he had the field completely to himself as he was working mainly in the Diaspora while James and the true disciples remained in Jerusalem. There was at least one other document, referred to in scholarly circles as 'Q' that gave some indication of the teachings of Jesus and his ministry. The Q document was used, according to modern scholars, as source material for the later synoptic gospels of Matthew, Mark and Luke. Robert Eisenman describes the situation in the following passage:

> In using the letters of Paul as our primary source material, we are on the firmest ground imaginable, for these are indisputably the earliest reliable documents of Christianity and can be dated with a high degree of certainty. They are patently earlier than the Gospels or the Book of Acts, which precede them in the present arrangement of the New Testament and which are in large part doctrinally dependent on Paul. Acts is to some extent dependant on Paul's letters for historical information as well.[15]

Indeed, the nearly complete doctrinal dependence of the Acts of the Apostles and the four Gospels on the works of Paul is completely unrecognised by the vast majority of today's Christians because of the ordering of these works in the New Testament,—a matter which is hardly accidental. This bizarre ordering, which was the result of decisions taken several centuries later, implies quite strongly that this is the order in which these works were written and this completely distorts any realistic, theological interpretation that is put upon them.

The activities, teaching and writings of Paul predominate so much in the New Testament stories about Jesus that it is damnably difficult, if not impossible, to filter out 'the true teachings of Jesus' from the Pauline theology. This completely dominates, masks, hides and virtually excludes any realistic appreciation of the genuine apostles and their views on 'the Way' as described by Jesus. In the New Testament, dominated as it is by the theology of Paul, we can only gain scant and often misleading glimpses of the substantial Nazorean movement that Jesus led.[16]

The Gospels Take Written Form

In the scholarly consensus that has arisen over the writing of the gospels, it is now generally accepted that *The Gospel According to Mark*, which was written between 70 and 80 CE, was the first to be completed and circulated. *The Gospel According to Matthew* appeared some ten years later, with *The Gospel According to Luke* and *The Acts of the Apostles* in the first decade of the 2nd century CE. *The Gospel According to John* came somewhat later, sometime between 100 to 120 CE.[17]

As we have mentioned above, the synoptic Gospels of Matthew, Mark and Luke are believed to have been founded on a common source document, now lost, named Q by scholars. There was such a great consensus about this document that a group of respected biblical scholars made a successful attempt to re-create it. The Professor of New Testament Studies at Claremont School of Theology in California, Burton L Mack, comments on this recreated Q document in the following words:

> The remarkable thing is that the authors of Q did not think about Jesus as the Messiah or the Christ, nor did they understand his teachings to be an indictment of Judaism. They certainly did not regard his crucifixion as a divinely inspired or saving event. Nor did they believe that he had been raised from the dead to rule over the world. They thought of him as a Jewish prophet whose teaching made it possible to live an attainable and righteous life in very troubled times. As a result they neither gathered to worship in his name, honoured him as a god—which to them as devout Jews would have been the ultimate blasphemy—nor celebrated his memory through hymns, prayers or rituals.[18]

Yet, despite this, the Gospels largely based on Q, speak of Jesus as Divine, however any unbiased examination of Jewish beliefs at that time soon shows the *a priori* improbability, if not the impossibility, of the concept of Jesus's divinity. Jesus was born a Jew, educated as a Jew and was a Jew teaching others Jews about their religion. The Roman idea of a divine human was completely alien to Jewish thought and teaching. No Jewish rabbi teaching other Jews could present himself as divine without being stoned to death for blasphemy. Therefore the deification of Jesus was a Gentile and heretical intrusion foisted on the world by someone else. The very idea of his deification was always staunchly and vehemently resisted by those who knew him personally the disciples and family who walked and talked with him here on earth. It was an entirely alien idea that Jesus himself would have been the first to refute.[19]

Chapter 11
The Council of Nicea

fter the destruction of the temple, there was constant agitation and trouble among the people. A number of divergent and often bickering sects who all claimed to hold some form of allegiance to Jesus the Nazarene took root throughout the eastern Mediterranean, Greece, and Rome. At this time, Pauline theologians began to strengthen their hold over the emerging 'Christian Church;' they used what were by then the traditional means of falsehood and personal insult to strengthen their case. The general tenor of debate in these theological disputes was so far separated from any form of spiritual or intellectual purity that it became known as *odium theologicum*, a form of harsh ecclesiastical verbal abuse that simply depended on slander and condemnation of the worst order.[1] One questionable concept in particular was used with devastating effect to bolster authority of the developing Christian power structure centred on Rome.[2]

To give substance to its claim to divinely sanctioned authority the Church used the completely unjustifiable assertion that both St Peter and St Paul had been martyred in Rome, despite credible evidence to the contrary in the case of St Peter and no evidence whatsoever of the violent death of St Paul in Rome or anywhere else. They used these claims as the basis for the doctrine of 'apostolic succession,'[3] which professed to show a continuum of power and authority that derived from the apostolic martyrs and was then passed to successive Bishops of Rome. In order to protect the developing Church's reputation as the authentic 'guardians of divinely revealed truth', the gaps in the early years of this episcopal succession were filled by the use of devout fabrication. From that time to the present, this fictitious absurdity has been used to support the claim of absolute authority for the Bishops of Rome—the Popes.

The pagan Roman Empire was usually exceedingly tolerant to the various forms of religions practiced by those it governed. As long as people made due obeisance and sacrifice to the gods of Rome on the appointed days, they were free to follow other religions.[4] The devout followers of the new 'Christian' religion often refused to make the ritual sacrifices and occasionally some emperors, such as Nero, would use the Christians as scapegoats to deflect attention away from the their own deficiencies; only rarely would systematic persecution be employed against them by the State. Whenever this happened, as in the 3rd century, it was often accompanied by confiscation of lands and property, actions that began to have a marked effect on a property-owning Church.[5] Salvation, when it came, did not arise from the faithfulness of the congregations nor from the charismatic leadership within the Church itself, but from a pagan general who sought the highly prized imperial purple.

The First 'Christian' Emperor Constantine

After the civil war ended with his victory at the battle of the Milvian bridge in 312 CE, Constantine the Great became Emperor of Rome. Soon after, he issued the Edict of Milan granting the Christian Church freedom from persecution, religious toleration and guaranteed its property rights.[6] The night before the battle that decided the religious fate of Europe for the next 1,700 years, this sun-worshipping military leader had a strange vision of the Cross of Christ and the legend *In Hoc Signo Vinces*—'In this sign you conquer.' To commemorate this victory and give thanks to the God who had inspired him, Constantine erected a triumphal arch in Rome inscribed with the cross of Christ and the words: 'By this saving sign, I have delivered your city from the tyrants and restored liberty to the senate and the people of Rome.'

The Emperor's motives were far from philanthropic. His intent was to use the Christian religion as a form of social cement to unite the divided peoples of the Empire.[7] Whenever a new emperor ascended the throne of Rome the entire system of government changed. He established the guidelines for fashion, food, social habits, intellectual adventure and religious belief and would surround himself with military, civil and financial advisers who were loyal to him personally. It was the concern of all who desired power under the new ruler to win his favour by any means possible, including flattery, imitation and corruption.[8]

In spite of his professed gratitude for the Christian sign granted to him before his pivotal battle, Constantine was no Christian. As a follower of the Mithraic sun-worshipping cult[9] of Sol Invictus, he was biased in favour of religious toleration for a complex mix of reasons, among which may have been gratitude, as well as the influence of his mother, the Empress Helena, who undoubtedly was a devout Christian. His chief reason, however, was political. His objective was to use the disciplined law-abiding traditions of the Christians and their beliefs to act as a socially cohesive force in healing the bitter divisions caused by the civil war.[10] So when Constantine began to display significant signs of favour for the new religion, many who sought friendship and influence became Christian as a mere act of political advantage. Yet strange though it might seem, Christianity did not become the officially preferred religion for a further 70 years.

Constantine's empire was divided into two parts, each with its own capital. In the west the seat of power was Rome, while in the east he founded a new capital named after him—Constantinople. He was shocked to discover that the most active source of disunity within his realm sprang from the very organization that he had chosen to act as a form of social cohesion. The empire was in grave danger of being torn apart by doctrinal argument, intolerance and venomous theological debate within the Christian Church.[11] With the interest of the state being his principal purpose, Constantine was anxious to bring about reconciliation by whatever means possible. Being a statesman and pagan he placed unity, order and stability far higher than religious dogma in his order of priority; the rule of law took precedence over divinely revealed truth. In order to impose his will on the contentious clerics he convened the first ecumenical council of the Church at Nicea in 325 CE.[12]

The Disputed Nature of Jesus

The primary theological argument that had to be settled by the Council of Nicea came from the different views as to the nature of Jesus, with the Pauline theologians on one side and the followers of Arius[13] on the other. In its later development, Pauline teaching preached that Jesus was not merely divine, the only begotten Son of God, but was co-eternal and equal with God the Father. According to his critics in the Church, Arius preached that the Father alone was the 'One True God', inaccessible and unique. Then, Christ, the Logos, was neither co-eternal nor uncreated because he had received life and being from the eternal father: 'If the Son is a true Son, then the Father must have existed before the Son; therefore there was a time when the Son did not exist; therefore he was created or made.' Arius went on to conclude that although Christ was divinely guided because the Father willed him to be so, he was not God necessarily and essentially. Arius would further affirm that it would have been possible for God the Son to sin. The Arian heresy showed the convoluted heights of absurdity attained by early theologians in attempting to define the ridiculous concept promulgated by Paul, that Jesus, the orthodox and scholarly Jew, was God. The controversy over Arianism caused chaos and, in order to clarify this, the Church was compelled to come up with a working definition that clarified exactly in what sense Jesus was a god.

The Council of Nicea

Constantine was not only a successful general but was also a superb politician and manipulator. During the Council of Nicea he used these qualities with remarkable acuity and showed clearly that he was the first man in history who had truly mastered the art of convening and corrupting an international conference.[14] The early Church father Eusebius noted that as each delegate entered the palace:

> …units of the bodyguard and other troops surrounded the palace with drawn swords, and through them the men of God proceeded without fear into the innermost rooms of the Emperor, in which some were his companions at table, while others reclined on the couches at either side.[15]

Constantine formally opened the council and during the proceedings was evidently excelling himself. He arranged elaborate and dramatic ceremonial entrances, religious processions and services with considerable talent, in stark contrast to the simplicity and purity of the first Church in Jerusalem led by the 'three Pillars' and the event portrayed in the Acts of the Apostles known as the council of Jerusalem. Paul Johnson, a Catholic historian, claims that 'Constantine, in fact, may be said to have created the decor and ritual of Christian conciliar practice.'[16]

Bishop Hosius chaired the majority of the working sessions of the council. The Pope, Sylvester I, did not attend the assembly and in his stead he sent two presbyters as his representatives. There were two hundred and twenty bishops present, mostly from the eastern sees, with only five from the west, all of whom had suffered persecutions by previous administrations in Rome, but were now under imperial protection and sponsorship.[17] At the emperor's expense, they travelled to and stayed at Nicea. When the Council finished, they were entertained at a massive banquet held to celebrate the emperor's anniversary. According to their rank, presents were distributed to each guest as they left the palace.[18]

The first ecumenical council of the Church achieved an extremely necessary political objective in what was, for the time, a novel manner—by vote. The carefully chosen episcopal delegates were assembled from diverse cultural groups within the Church. Those in attendance included a country bishop, who is noted to have driven a herd of sheep before him as he made his way to Nicea, as well as some of the most learned and sophisticated bishops from the Eastern Empire.[19] The decisions made by the council were promulgated as declarations of Church doctrine, some of which were to have devastating and long-lasting effect. The first was directly in line with the political intentions of the emperor—the Church and State were to be aligned with each other and Arius' teachings were condemned as heretical.[20] Certain Mithraic traditions and practises were also formalized into Christian doctrine by Constantine. These comprised many of the issues we mentioned earlier: the holy birth in a grotto attended by shepherds, the apocalyptic events of a judgement day, the resurrection of the body and a second coming of their god—but, this time following the teaching of St Paul, it was Jesus who was to come again and not Mithras.

Decisions at Nicea

During the council, decisions were made in regard to the marital status of the men who had taken holy orders. Priests who had been ordained were forbidden to marry, although those who were already married were allowed to continue with their family life.[21] Before the council, many of the Christian churches had celebrated Easter on different dates, the variations generally stemming from the traditions of evangelists who had first converted their local population. The council assigned a universal date for Easter and imposed it on all. As a final order of business at Nicea, a decision was taken to make Sunday the holy day of the Christian week. Consequently, the ancient Jewish Sabbath observed by Jesus and his immediate followers that ran from dusk on Friday to sundown on Saturday, was replaced by 'Sunday', the day dedicated to Sol Invictus, the god Constantine truly worshipped. Following the condemning of the Arian heresy, a creed presented by certain Arian bishops was rejected and a new one, the Creed of Nicea (which is not to be confused with the Nicene Creed), was declared binding on the Church. The Nicene Creed was proposed during the second ecumenical council in 381, and finally confirmed during the fourth council at Chalcedon in 451.[22] Both creeds are similar in intent but not identical. The Creed of Nicea determined as a basic tenant of belief the doctrine that Jesus the Nazarene was divine and equal to God the Father in every way. This set a precedent that was to have bloody repercussions for centuries to come, the council vowed to excommunicate anyone who did not accept that Jesus was completely divine.

Constantine's polished skill at manipulating the conference reached its peak of corrupt perfection in the way the votes of the delegates were recorded. Bishop Hossius was the first to announce and sign the creed, which was then taken to each bishop by a cohort of Constantine's own notaries under the leadership of Philumenus, a high-ranking imperial official. It has been suggested that many of the bishops signed under extreme pressure, for who would dare to disagree with the emperor who had so recently granted them their freedom and whose troops ringed the palace? One of his final acts at the council illustrates the 'freedom of conscience' enjoyed by delegates; Constantine imposed criminal sentences of exile on those who refused to sign. He published a letter in 326 addressed to the newly defined heretical sects declaring that their places of worship would be confiscated,[23] but his intolerance did not end there. In the year 333 CE Constantine authorised savage actions against Arian writings:

> ...if any treatise composed by Arius is discovered, let it be consigned to the flames...in order that no memorial of him whatever be left... [and] if anyone shall be caught concealing a book by Arius, and does not instantly bring it out and burn it, the

penalty shall be death; the criminal shall suffer punishment immediately after conviction.[24]

Fantasy Becomes Fact?

With the creation of the first official Church/State establishment in Christian history, based firmly on the deeply spiritual principles of corruption, fear and repression, Constantine the Great had brought about apparent unity within the Church. He did not care to any degree what grounds were used to forge this unity. The horrendous price ultimately paid for this includes the long litany of names of the unfortunate, the sincere and the devout that were to be persecuted, tortured and burnt on charges of heresy throughout the centuries to come. However, this unity was largely illusory, for this was not the last attempt to define the impossible. A vast amount of time and effort was wasted during the first 520 years of Christian history trying to define the nature and the person of Jesus the Nazarene. Since the theologians who followed the heretical doctrines and mythology created by Paul could not accept that Jesus was an extraordinary man, a great teacher and a devout Jew, they had to go to great lengths to substantiate Pauls fantasy that Jesus was divine. This led them into more complex debates attempting to define the indefinable.

It created further reasons for dispute that eventually culminated in the great schism that continues to separate the Orthodox Churches in the East from Roman Catholicism on the West. Ultimately, Jesus was defined as being the **only begotten** son of God, **born of a virgin**, who was both **completely divine** and **completely human**.[25] The specious arguments brought in to support this incredible fantasy attained new heights of absolute absurdity. The Jesus of Church doctrine and Pauline Christianity was described as having two natures and two wills yet, paradoxically, was not in any way two persons, but one. Is it likely that the disciples that followed the rabbi and devoted teacher of the Torah in Israel would have recognized this deified and rather schizophrenic distortion? The phrase 'only begotten' brought further confusion, as did the phrase 'born of a virgin'. This implied that God had sired no other son and that Mary had issued no other children into the world. This outcome would be hilarious if its repercussions had not been so tragic; the Gospels, those inerrant words of God, had got it wrong! A virgin with a large family, how could this be?

The creation of dogma rarely resulted in any degree of unanimity among the bickering theologians, for it did not emanate from any valid source of spiritual insight. Dogma was formulated in a similar way to the conclusions of the Council of Nicea, as a statement of the will of the majority in a vain attempt to paper over the many differences of belief that emerged from a collection of churches founded on differing evangelical traditions. The Church, in the name of divinely revealed truth, simply used compromise allied to repression to control its squabbling flock. Therefore, any dogma or policy that supported the fundamentally flawed theology of Paul, and that could be used as an instrument of Church governance, was built into its teaching. Any statement or fact that repudiated or debased the Church teaching was declared heretical and punished by exile, confiscation of property or death.

The phrase from the New Testament 'thou art Peter and upon this rock I will build my church' was used ruthlessly to strengthen the authority of the Church and the new Church/State establishment. The Greek word *petra*, which originally related to the 'Rock of Israel', was purposely mistranslated as if it was a play on words and was thereby related to the Greek *petros* (or stone), a metaphor for Peter. This allegation was expanded to the point where the Bishops of Rome claimed that only those who had received authority in a direct line of succession from Peter had divine blessing to be the leaders of the Church. A heretical document of the Gnostics known as *The Apocalypse of Peter* defined these self-same bishops as 'dry canals' and stated:

> They name themselves bishops and deacons as if they had received their authority directly from God…Although they do not understand the mystery they nonetheless boast the secret of Truth is theirs alone.[26]

The bishops of Rome, these dry canals, who were later to be called 'Popes', assumed to themselves a dramatic new role that was a complete reversal of previous practice. Between 90 and 95 CE, the Council of Nicea authorized a claim made by Clement, the Bishop of Rome who was supposedly the fourth in succession after Peter. Clement forcibly declared the opinion that the leaders of the Church had been sanctioned by Almighty God to rule on earth in His name and, as they held 'the keys to the Kingdom', they had divine authority to exert judgement and discipline over the congregations, which he called the 'laity'. Following the Council of Nicea, it became part of the dogma of the Church that the Bishop of Rome and the hierarchy who served under him were God's appointed representatives on earth and their pronouncements were made with divine authority. So the position held by the leader of the first Christian Church in Jerusalem, James the Just had been completely negated. As High Priest, James the Just had been the spokesman of his people seeking forgiveness and guidance from Almighty God. His apparent successors had now become the spokesmen of God who ruled their congregations with absolute and irrefutable authority. This transformation was disastrous in the extreme; James the Just had *served* his people before God, the Bishops of Rome *ruled* their people in the name of God. After St Augustine perfected the doctrine that 'outside the Church there is no salvation', the absolute political control that was the ultimate objective of the Church hierarchy became explicit. This was made manifest by one saying in particular which emerged after the Council of Nicea: 'If you want God as your Father you *must* have the Church as your Mother' [our emphasis].

Those who claimed spiritual or dynastic authority that differed with the Church/State alliance were swept aside. The writer Laurence Gardner noted this when he described how the Bishop of Rome, Pope Sylvester, notified a delegation of Desposyni, the true descendants of the Messiah, that they simply had no place in the new Christian order.[27] In spite of the claim by the Church that it was preaching the same message as Jesus, Sylvester informed the delegation that the teachings of the Messiah had been superseded by Church doctrine and dogma that had been amended to bring it more in line with imperial desires. Even though Jesus had been elevated to divine and co-equal status with Almighty God, the Pope, allegedly God's representative on earth, informed them that the power of salvation rested not in Jesus the Messiah but in the Roman Emperor, Constantine the Great.

For over two centuries doctrinal disputes continued to exert significant pressure on the Church with both Church and State continuing in their efforts to unify it and train it to be the obedient, respectful and fearful creature of the Pope in Rome. After Constantine created the effective tool of the Church/State establishment, it continued to be used with increasing effect except for the brief period when Julian the Apostate ruled the empire.

The Church's Monopoly

Fighting vicious battles with those of contrary opinions to their dogma, the Church grew in power and became the official religion of the State. It then turned its attention to the pagan religions and there all potential rivals were mercilessly pushed aside, ancient Greek mystery sects were done away with and Gnostic sects within Christianity were ruthlessly suppressed, their leaders tormented and their scriptures destroyed.

The religious establishment of Rome monopolized all access to the sacred Western Empire by the 6th century. To accomplish this it instituted dogmatism within its own structures and eliminated all the rival religions, cults and centres of worship outside them; the ancient temples were shut and the oracles of old were silence forever.[28] The Church not only exerted meticulous control over all spiritual matters, but it silenced, for centuries to come, the search for truth and knowledge in the secular world.[29] With its control and possession of all learning centres; no student was admitted who had not taken holy orders; the clergy alone was literate, the laity were to remain illiterate.[30] The individual citizen was denied personal access to the sacred except through the ministrations of the Church and was kept in the incessant slavery of total ignorance. If simple faith and obedience were all that were required for salvation, then, what use was learning? The difference between the attitudes to education and learning that were current in Classical Greece and the Roman Empire could not have been greater. This contrast was emphasised by the 20th century English philosopher Bertrand Russell who wrote:

> [Socrates] always says he knows nothing, he does not think knowledge lies beyond our reach. What matters is precisely that we should try to seek knowledge. For he holds that what makes a man sin is lack of knowledge. If only he knew, he would not sin. The one overriding cause of evil is therefore ignorance. Hence, to reach the Good we must have knowledge, and so the Good is knowledge. The link between the Good and knowledge is a mark of Greek thought throughout. Christian ethics is quite opposed to this. There, the important thing is a pure heart, and that is likely to be found more readily among the ignorant.[31]

The Church was not satisfied in dominating the peasants, the slaves and the merchants, it desired to control the leaders of nations and perpetually stated that earthly kings and emperors only existed as God's chosen rulers, therefore God's Church was of far greater authority than the State or those who ruled it. This kind of thinking would go on to form the mould for European history and the brutality and intolerance that ensued make a bitter contrast to the doctrine of 'love thy neighbour as thyself'. The theology of 'the word of God' had killed the essential, liberating the teaching of Jesus.

Christianity Spreads

Outside the frontiers guarded by the legions of Rome missionary activities had been virtually non-existent, but with the disintegration of the empire new methods had to be found both to defend the Church and extend its influence. The Church was clearly the repository of stability and the sole channel of culture, civilisation and administrative expertise; the authoritative guardian of all that could be used to bridge the gulf between the old imperial system of Rome and the semi-barbaric condition of tribal Europe.

The Church was the only institution with any clear idea of where it was going, and how and why, in the fluctuating chaos of emerging Europe. Invading hordes had occupied tribal areas and taken over lands which had lost the unifying structure and stability provided by the old empire. While the Gothic tribes settled in Italy and beyond, the Church made its first successful invasions into other areas and began to convert the Franks and Burgundians. The Bishops were not only spiritual leaders but they took on the role of military commanders of districts, thus reinforcing the Church's reputation for establishing stability and order. This led to the rise of an extensive bureaucracy in Rome that soon acquired considerable expertise in matters of civil administration.

Following hard on the heels of the missionaries, the administrators brought the benefits of civilisation along with the blessings of the Church. In the developing states, the Church became the major lawmaker, with much of the customary law of the tribes being absorbed and codified into civil law by the clergy. They recorded the oral legends, myths and stories of the newly converted people, adding their own gloss, omitting all that was offensive to accepted doctrine, keeping this, adding that, subtly changing the histories and forming the mould for new, essentially Christian cultures. With this pervasive way the Church was able to distort the histories of entire peoples, devaluing for all time any potential rivals in the field of religious beliefs, thus increasing its grip not only on the current reality of the tribes but also on their ancient cultural heritage.[32] The success of its missionary activities is ascribed to its superb administrative skills and, perhaps more important, its agricultural proficiency. The Church not only brought stability, law and administrative order to starving people and to tribes living at subsistence; it brought a more important agricultural practice that provided a stable and reliable food source.

Christian 'Love' in Action?

Following the Council at Nicea, Constantine made it completely clear that the benefits and privileges that he had granted to the Christian Church 'must benefit only adherents of the Catholic faith,'[33] which he defined as those who completely accept the doctrine enshrined in the new creed and the authority of the Bishop of Rome. As for those of differing belief he stated 'heretics and schismatics shall not only be alien from these privileges but shall be bound and subjugated to various public services.' Constantine's successors had the same disposition, with membership of a heretical sect acquiring a degree of legal notoriety and a loss of civil rights. Emperor Theodosius I prohibited all heretics from public office and conducted purges against them.[34] St Augustine of Hippo, a theologian, who created the guilt inducing doctrine of Original Sin, also formulated justification for religious coercion and the most vigorous investigation of heresy. In 383 Priscillian of Avila was the first person to be executed for heresy in the West.[35]

A period of calm and unity of religious belief seemed to pervade Europe after the effective end of the Arian faith in the 5th century. By means of the Church's monopoly on all forms of education, intellectual speculation was stifled and the superstitious populace remained dormant in a state of ignorance and fear. Following their admonition by Pope Sylvester, the Desposyni and the other families of the Rex Deus group went underground in order to ensure their survival. It was not until the later part of the 11th century that they finally began to act publicly and in concert in a manner that is discernable in the historical record.

CHAPTER 12
THE RISE TO POWER OF THE REX DEUS ARISTOCRACY

The Rex Deus families, the descendants of the ma'madot, which included the Desposyni the direct descendants of Jesus, spread throughout Europe, Asia Minor and the Middle East seeking sanctuary from Imperial persecution. Utilising their natural talents and family connections they began to gain power and importance among the trading and landowning classes. Those who were lucky enough, or clever enough, to gain positions of influence close to some of the royal families used their position to promote other members of the group to positions of power and aristocratic privilege.[1] Despite the emphasis laid upon the Merovingian dynasty as important conduits of power in *The Holy Blood and the Holy Grail*, it was their usurpers, the Carolingians who were instrumental in placing Rex Deus family members in positions of real influence throughout much of Europe. The Carolingians, were identified over seventy years ago, by Dr Walter Johannes Stein as 'the true family of the Grail.' When Charles Martel, Charles the Hammer, won his decisive victory over the Moors at Poitiers in 732 CE, he was officially the Mayor of the Palace. His second son, Pepin the Short, usurped the Merovingian throne and became King of the Franks. His son, Charles the Great better known as Charlemagne was the man who deliberately placed Rex Deus members into positions of power all over Europe. Charlemagne expanded his already considerable empire by warfare until he ruled over a huge swath of land that stretched from the River Danube in the north to the Mediterranean coast on the south. In this process he consolidated his family's hold on the so-called 'Spanish Marches', the area known as Septimania that is now the department of modern France called Languedoc/ Rousillion.

Septimania

There had ben a significant Jewish population centred near Narbonne for many centuries before the time of Charlemagne. This had been increased considerably by large numbers of Jews fleeing from Visigothic Spain before the Moorish conquest. This flourishing and prosperous community was recognised by King Pepin the Short who granted them permission to import their own prince, or *nasi*, from Baghdad after his capture of Narbonne in 759 CE.[2] However the actual installation of the Jewish prince did not take place until the reign of Charlemagne. There is one Latin Romance that is endorsed by a variety of papal and Hebrew documents that claims that the city was surrendered to Pepin in return for a promise of self-government under their own king.[3]

Charlemagne assured Jewish rights in Septimania, as he was shrewd enough to see where both the commercial and military advantages lay. Knowing that the Jews were one of the necessary keys to success in international trade, he encouraged their immigration into all of his lands and many of his charters granting protection to Jewish merchants are still extant.[4] Also he used Septimania as a military 'buffer zone' to repel any possible invasion by the Moors from across the border in El Andalus. Thus the main objective of strengthening the power of the Jewish princedom was to ensure that the Nasi would lead the Jews of Septimania and the Toulousians to repel any invasion by the Arabs of Spain or North Africa. However, apart from these politically and commercially important reasons, Charlemagne had another, much more personal and pressing motive for favouring the Jews of Septimania.

The 19th century Austrian historian of the Carolingian era, P Munz, wrote that Charlemagne claimed descent from the ancient Israelite, Royal House of David. He wrote about these matters over a century and a half before the Rex Deus tradition first became widely known in Europe. It is a matter of record that Charlemagne sent a Jewish interpreter to travel with the ambassador he despatched to Haroun al-Rashid the Caliph of Baghdad in 797 CE. This led to the installation of the first nasi or Jewish prince of Septimania, Rabbi Makhi to whom Charlemagne gave many possessions.[5] There is an age old Jewish tradition in Europe that Charlemagne also facilitated and encouraged the transfer of the main centre of Torah studies from Baghdad to Narbonne[6]—a matter that is highly credible when viewed in the light of Charlemagne's Rex Deus membership. The Austrian historian Munz, claimed that Charlemagne had yet another motive for encouraging the appointment of a Jewish prince in Narbonne, namely that he planned to unite the Carolingian dynasty with that of the nasi, thereby endowing his own reign with some sort of 'divine sanction.' While such a marriage did not in fact take place, the descendants of the nasi generally proved to be loyal and courageous subjects of the Carolingians and their eventual successors. This Jewish community grew and prospered until the time of the Crusade against the Cathars and was not finally extinguished until the expulsion of the Jews by King Philippe le Bel in 1306 CE. The renowned Jewish chronicler, Benjamin of Tudela, described the situation in Narbonne in the 12th century in the following terms:

> Narbonne is an ancient city of the Torah. From it the Torah goes out to all lands. Therein there are sages, magnates, and princes (nas'im) at the head of whom is R. Kalonymo… a descendant of the House of David as stated in his family tree. He holds hereditaments and other (landed) properties from the ruler of the country and no one may dispossess him by force.[7]

The vast extent of Jewish properties at the time of their final expulsion indicates that until the end of the 14th century they held many large estates in the countryside as well as a considerable proportion of the city of Narbonne itself. Charlemagne's astute political skills, his success as a general and his commercial acumen resulted in an ever-expanding kingdom. As the principal protector of the Papal States, he was crowned as Holy Roman Emperor in 800.

In order to rule this sprawling and ramshackle empire effectively in the days before good communications, he needed subordinates in whom he had a high degree of trust. He created a warrior aristocracy[8] and, over time he created over 600 counties throughout his empire.[9] To rule over these, he appointed the only people he knew he could trust, fellow members of the Rex Deus families. Thus by the time of Charlemagne's death on 814, much of Europe, especially France, Septimania, Provence, Northern Italy and Saxony was under the rule of an increasingly powerful Rex Deus nobility.

European Rex Deus Families

Various Rex Deus families had originally sought refuge in parts of Europe that lay far beyond the boundaries of the Holt Roman Empire ruled by Charlemagne and were, thereby, out of reach of the growing, repressive Christian church. Their Cohenite marriage patterns enable us to identify them especially after they began to marry into the Rex Deus families within mainstream, Christian Europe. Our original informant, Michael Monkton, told us that one significant branch became the Saxon royal house of England in the 11th century. After the Norman conquest of England in 1066, the daughter of the deposed Saxon king, Princess Margaret, fled to Hungary for safety. This descendant of both the Hasmonean and Davidic lines became betrothed to King Malcolm Canmore of Scotland. On her travels from Hungary to Scotland she was accompanied by two knights of the Rex Deus line, the Hungarian knight, Sir Bartholomew Ladislaus Leslyn and a Norman chevalier, Sir William 'the seemly' St Clair. Both were duly rewarded by the Scots King, Leslyn became the founder of one of the great Scottish noble lines, the Leslies[10] while Sir William St Clair, who was born near St Lo in Normandy, [11] was granted lands near Roslin.

The Lordly Line of the High St Clairs

William St Clair was a descendant of Røganvald the Mighty, Jarl of Möre, an area near the modern city of Trondheim.[12] It was Røganvald's second son Rollo who conquered Normandy and was granted the title of Count (later changed to Duke) by the Capetian King of France Charles the Simple at the treaty of St Clair-sur-Epte in 912. Charles was a member of the Rex Deus families and he gave his daughter, Gisele, as the bride for Rollo.[13] Contrary to the widely held belief among present day Sinclairs, the family do *not* take their name from the town of St Clair-sur-Epte, indeed it never belonged to them and was not even a part of Normandy. The French Genealogist L A de St. Clair wrote in 1905:

> It is therefore highly unlikely that our family used the name of St Clair-sur-Epte as its family name. **It is the town of St Clair near St Lo, near the western limit of the Bessin that is the true origin of the name of the noble house of St Clair.**[14]
> (authors' emphasis).

Furthermore it was only during the reign of the forth Duke of Normandy, Richard II, that families began to adopt the name of the area or the city they ruled as their family names.[15]

Rollo, as Duke of Normandy, lived in Caen surrounded by other members of his family and loyal supporters. Marital alliances between his family and other families of the Rex Deus group included, over time, the Saxon royal family of England, the Count of Brittany and the count of Chartres.[16] There were also marital alliances with the families of Chaumont, Gisors, d'Evereaux and Blois—the family of Champagne—and, the ducal house of Burgundy. Other important unions married them into the Capetian dynasty of France who claimed descent from the Magdelene, and the house of Flanders, thereby linking the St Clairs with Godfroi de Bouliion the first effective ruler of the later kingdom of Jerusalem.[17] There appeared to be an unseemly scramble to marry into the St Clair family which is a rather odd and otherwise inexplicable scenario to contemplate when we consider the reputation these Vikings had for pillage, rape and plunder. It is only their Rex Deus connections that can satisfactorily explain why marital union with these 'Viking raiders' was so attractive to the great and good of an extremely elitist, snobbish Rex Deus aristocracy.

William the Seemly St Clair, now Lord of Roslin, was appointed as the cup-bearer to the Queen. His son, Henri de St Clair of Roslin took part in the First Crusade along with Godfroi de Boullion and was present at the capture of Jerusalem.[18] He was accompanied by knights from eleven other leading Scottish aristocratic families who had all met regularly at Roslin prior to the crusade and continued to do so for many centuries afterwards. This important group included the Stuarts, with whom the St Clairs intermarried, the Setons, the Dalhousies, the Montgomerys, the Douglases, the Ramseys, the Leslies and the Lindsays—a group of families linked by shared loyalties and a common ancestry that reached back though biblical times to ancient Egypt. The Rex Deus families extended their influence throughout Europe and did not neglect to spread into the ranks of their sworn enemy, the church. Rollo, first Duke of Normandy, besieged the city of Chartres in 911. The city did not fall but its defence so impressed Rollo that he brought the city under his protection. He made the following declaration:

> I Rollo, Duke of Normandy, give to the brotherhood of the
> church of Notre Dame de Chartres my castle at Malmaison,
> which I took with my sword, and with my sword I shall be
> their guarantor.[19]

The Chartres Masters

Bishop Fulbertus was installed as Bishop of Chartres in 1007. A Rex Deus member who had joined the church to try and change it from the inside, he operated under the protection and patronage of local Rex Deus nobility and made the city a centre of learning as well as of pilgrimage.[20] The Chartres Theological School soon gained an international reputation for excellence and over the next two centuries attracted such luminaries as Bernardus, William of Conches, Thierry of Chartres and William of Salisbury.[21] The pupils of Fulbertus and his successors were the first in Western Christian Europe to read the works of the great classical Greek philosophers such as Plato, Aristotle and Pythagorus as well as Latin classics by Cicero, for example. Previously these works had been condemned as pagan. They had been treasured in the Islamic Empire and were translated in Moorish Spain by Jewish scholars and sent by Rex Deus members in that country to their counterparts in France. They were not translated from the original Greek and Latin, but from Arabic. Under Fulbertus, a system developed of outwardly teaching the seven liberal arts while secretly instructing the pupils into the seven degrees of spiritual initiation modelled on the ancient Egyptian Temple mysteries.[22] Thus the masters of Chartres were able to continue the initiatory tradition of the ma'madot right under the noses of the unsuspecting church authorities.

During Fulbertus time as bishop, fire destroyed the cathedral. He soon had it rebuilt with the aid and support of the secret families. The long list of donors and supporters includes, among others, King Robert of France, the Rex Deus nobility of northern France and William Duke of Aquitaine.[23] Eight years after the death of Fulbertus, his successor, Thierry of Chartres dedicated the new cathedral in 1037. Thierry was in his turn, succeeded by Bernardus, another member of the families and one of the greatest scholars in the school.[24] Continuing the initiatory teaching, Bernardus based it on the work of Jesus' star pupil, St John the Divine. It was Bernadus who proclaimed 'the reason we can see so far is that we are dwarfs seated on the shoulders of giants.' It was in this manner that Rex Deus teaching began to spread its influence throughout Europe in a far wider manner than the relatively small number of those families might suggest. From the school at Chartres ultimately arose the first University in Paris and that was based on the model of the University of Cordova in Moorish Spain.

Bernard de Fontaine

Fulbertus was not the last Rex Deus member to join the church in an attempt to reform it, the abberant antics within one such family provides a graphic illustration of the volatile behaviour and disputes that could arise under such circumstances. A young nobleman from the County of Champagne, Bernard de Fontaine, better known to history as 'Bernard of Clairvaux,' expressed his intention of joining the relatively new and struggling order known as the Cistercians. The rest of his family were horrified at first but, under the persuasive influence of this charismatic man did a complete 'about turn.' Not only did opposition to his entering the church evaporate at the speed of light but also, more amazing still, many among his family and friends decided to join with him. It is a matter of record that thirty-two relatives and friends became novices with him when he joined the order in 1112.[25]

Bernard was not merely well connected but intellectually brilliant and he rose to a position of considerable prominence and power within the church. He never rose to be any higher than the Abbot of Clairvaux monastery, but that relatively lowly rank masked his very considerable influence and importance. He became the teacher of more than one pope, and the personal advisor to one of them. His influence extended far beyond the boundaries of the church hierarchy and he acted as an advisor to kings, emperors and the nobility. Bernard's deep and abiding commitment to initiatory teaching can be seen even today in the series of one hundred and twenty sermons he preached based on the *Song of Songs* by King Solomon.[26] While there is no documentary evidence that explains his family's collective charge to join the church, certain later events may give us an indication as to what was really afoot. With the gift of hindsight it would now appear that Bernard and his Rex Deus colleagues conspired to achieve an important common aim that has left its mark on European history. This conspiracy was wide ranging, took years of planning and involved a large number of people including his cousin, who became Patriarch of Jerusalem, his uncle Andre de Montbard, another knight from Champagne, Hughes de Payens, the St Clairs, the Setons, the Royal House of Flanders and one of the most powerful and important noblemen of his time Count Hughes I of Champagne.

Hughes I, Count of Champagne.

Hughes I, Count of Champagne, ruled a large and prosperous area that lay to the east of Paris. He owed allegiance to King Philippe I of France who was also his godfather. He also owed allegiance to the Duke of Burgundy and to the Holy Roman Emperor. The Counts of Champagne, the Blois family, were related by blood and marriage to the St Clairs,[27] the Capetian Kings of France, the Duke of Burgundy, the Duke of Normandy and both the Norman and Plantagenet Kings of England. Hughes' administrative centre, the city of Troyes became a centre of scholarship attracting savants and intellectuals of the highest repute. The tolerance of the Rex Deus families for the Jews was always significant and in Troyes, under Hughes' patronage, a Yeshiva was founded which soon gained international renown. One Jewish family who had migrated to Troyes from southern Europe had a son who is second only to the great Moses Maimonides in Jewish intellectual life. One of the most important Jewish Biblical scholars of all time, Rabbi Solomon ben Isaac, otherwise known as Raschi.

Although born in Troyes, Raschi attended Yeshivot in both Worms and Mainz before returning and setting up his own school in the city of his birth.[28] A frequent and regular visitor to the Count's court, Raschi attained heights of biblical scholarship that have never been equalled. It is only as a philosopher that he takes second place to Maimonides. Under the tolerant protection of the Count, Raschi was able to set up a Kabbalistic school of considerable fame in Troyes. The protection of the Counts of Champagne towards the Jews long outlasted the reign of Hughes I. In the later part of the 12th century when the Jews were expelled from France, they remained safe and securely in Champagne.

In 1104, Hughes of Champagne met members of other Rex Deus families in conditions of secrecy. The meeting included members of the families of Brienne, De Joinville, Chaumont and Anjou. A short time after this meeting, Hughes left for the Holy Land returning in 1108. He went back again in 1114 and, after his return, donated a tract of land to the Cistercian Order at Clairvaux where the monks promptly built an abbey. Its first Abbot was Bernard de Fontaine. These repeated visits to the Holy Land were the prelude to concerted public action by members of the Rex Deus families who founded an order whose name evokes tales of mystery, heresy, courage and intrigue on a grand scale—*The Poor Knights of Christ and the Temple of Solomon* more commonly known as The Knights Templar.

CHAPTER 13

THE KNIGHTS TEMPLAR AND BERNARD OF CLAIRVAUX

Bernard of Clairvaux rose to prominence and influence both in the medieval church and in the world of temporal politics, not only because of his useful family connections, but also as a result of his immerse energy. In spite of suffering from ill health throughout his life, he oversaw the foundation of at least sixty-eight Cistercian houses from his base in Clairvaux. His personal example and spiritual convictions had such a profound influence on the Cistercian order that he is sometimes called its second founder. His ventures into other branches of the initiatory tradition was wide-ranging. Situated in the principality of Seborga in northern Italy is one of the many Cistercian houses founded by Bernard. Local tradition would have us believe that it was established in 1113 to protect "a great secret."[1] Under the guidance of its abbot, Edouard, were two men, Gondemar and Rossal, who had been knights before they became monks. In the archives at Seborga a document claims that, in February 1117, Bernard arrived at the abbey with seven companions, released Gondemar and Rossal from their vows, and gave a solemn blessing to the entire group, which departed for Jerusalem in 1118. The document denotes that, before their departure, Bernard nominated Hughes de Payen as Grand Master of "the Poor Militia of Christ," and that Abbot Edouard consecrated him in that rank.[2]

The Foundation of the Order and Hughes de Champagne

An account written by Guillaume de Tyre, over seventy years after the events it describes, places the foundation of the order that became to be known as the Knights Templar in Jerusalem in 1118.[3] King Baldwin II granted them quarters on the Temple Mount within a few weeks of his accession to the throne,[4] they took the name of the "Poor Fellow-Soldiers of Jesus Christ" and were recognised as "the Knighthood of the Temple of Solomon."[5] Its first Grand Master was Hughes de Payen and the other founding members of the order were André de Montbard, Geoffroi de St. Omer, Payen de Montdidier, Achambaud de St.-Amand, Geoffroi Bisol, Godfroi, Gondemar, and Rossal.[6]

This group of supposedly random knights, apparently united only in their common religious purpose was, in fact, a tightly knit group of kinsmen who belonged to the Rex Deus families, and were closely associated with Count Hughes I of Champagne. As previously mentioned, Hughes made several visits to the Holy Land prior to the foundation of the Templars. Upon his return to the East in 1114, Ivo, the Bishop of Chartres, wrote to him rebuking him for abandoning his wife and vowing to himself to the "knighthood of Christ" in order to take up "that gospel knighthood by which two thousand may fight securely against him who rushes to attack us with two hundred thousand.[7]" This is not the only perplexing mention of the order prior to the generally accepted date of its foundation. What can only be reasonably inferred from this confusion, however, is the long-standing nature of the conspiracy and planning that supported the creation of the Templars. There is another peculiarity concerning Hughes de Champagne. Records disclose that, in 1125, he returned to the Holy Land and joined the Order of the Knights Templar, thereby swearing unquestioning obedience to its first Grand Master, previously his own vassal, Hughes de Payens.

Founding Members of the Order

Hughes de Payens was born on or about 1070 at the De Payen chateau on the banks of the Seine, one of the principal castles defending the County of Champagne.[8] He received the fiefdom of Montigny near Lagesse in the county of Champagne sometime between 1085 and 1090.[9] Hughes was the relative of two of Europe's most powerful men, Bernard of Clairvaux[10] and the Count of Champagne, who was also his overlord.[11] Because of his lineal descent from the Prophet Muhammad, he was also known as Hughes the Moor, which of course indicates that he was not only Rex Deus, but one of the Desposyni, a descendant of one of the brothers of Jesus.

It has often been claimed that Hughes de Payens was married to a certain Catherine de St. Clair, a marriage to which Tim had given some credence in earlier works. After having searched through countless archives however, Tim admits to not having found any valid documents confirming or even inferring any matrimonial alliance between Hughes and the wider St. Clair family. Thierry Leroy, a French author, has found documents confirming that Hughes de Payen was indeed married, but to a lady called Elizabeth, and that the marriage took place sometime between 1108 and 1114.[12] Despite various claims that Hughes died childless, he did, in fact, father at least one son, Thibaud de Payen, who was eventually elected abbot of the monastery of Sainte-Colombe in 1139. Recorded in one of the contemporary chronicles, the following words are used to describe the new abbot: "Theo Aldus de Pahens, filius Hugonis primi magistri temple Jerosolymitani," which translate as "Thibaud de Payen, son of Hughes, first master of the Temple of Jerusalem." One of Hughes' closest associates in the new knightly enterprise, André de Montbard, was the uncle of Bernard of Clairvaux,[13] a kinsman of the Duke of Burgundy, and yet another vassal of the house of Champagne. Geoffroi de St. Omer was the son of a noted Flemish nobleman, Hughes de St. Omer.[14] Closely related to the Royal House of Flanders were both Payen de Montdidier and Achambaud de St.-Amand, and the sons of the House of Flanders, Godfroi de Boullion and his younger brother Baudoin of Brittany, later became the rulers of the kingdom of Jerusalem—Godfroi as protector of the Holy Sepulchre and, after his death, Baudoin as King Baldwin I.

Recognition of the Order

In 1120 the Knights Templar received recognition from the patriarch of Jerusalem at the Council of Nablus.[15] Another distant cousin of Bernard of Clairvaux, the patriarch, gave the order its first insignia—a red two-barred cross that later developed into the Cross of Lorraine. General de Gaulle would later use this as a symbol of Free French forces during the Second World War. Writing in the Norman monastery of St. Évroul between 1075-c. and 1141,

Orderic Vitalis recorded that, in the 1120s, Count Fulk V of Anjou joined the "knights of the Temple" for a period of time during his pilgrimage to Jerusalem. Following his return to Europe, he continued to pay thirty pounds of Anjou for their support. The Templars were described by Orderic as *venerandi mitlites*, knights who should be held in great respect or admiration, and wrote that they devoted their lives to the physical and spiritual service of God, despised all worldly things, and faced martyrdom daily.[16]

The specified purpose of the new warrior monks was the protection of pilgrims en route from the Mediterranean coastal port of Jaffa to Jerusalem. Taking into consideration the fact that Hughes de Payens and the other eight members of the order weren't exactly in their first bloom of youth, how were they going to manage a task of this immense scale? It is certainly hard to envision nine middle age knights providing protection in such difficult terrain. When studying their main action during the first nine years of the order's existence this would present a problem that would render there stated objective unmanageable. Rather than patrolling the bandit-infested roads, they spent their time excavating beneath the Temple Mount, directly under their headquarters.[17]

During the latter part of the 19th century and the early years of the 20th, Lieutenant Warren of the Royal Engineers excavated the eighty-foot vertical shaft that they dug and the system of radiating tunnels to which it led. A variety of Templar artefacts were discovered by Warren in these tunnels that included a spur, the remains of lance, a small Templar cross, and the major part of a Templar sword. These intriguing relics rested, until his death, with their archivist, Robert Brydon, in Edinburgh, along with a letter from Captain Parker who accompanied Warren on his explorations. In 1912 Parker wrote to Brydon's grandfather and gave the finds to him for safekeeping.

With the discovery of these tunnels many questions come to mind: Were the excavations the chief reason behind the founding of the Order? Exactly what were they seeking? And most importantly, why were they immediately granted quarters above their chosen site of excavation? It is impossible to answer most of these questions with any certainty, however, it is reasonable to speculate on the probable answers to some of them based upon a foundation of fact.

A possible clue may be found carved on one of the pillars in the north porch of Chartres Cathedral, the doorway known as the Portal of the Initiates. Depicted on the carving is the Ark of the Covenant being transported upon a wheeled cart.[18] Legends originating with the early Israelites recounts that the Ark of the Covenant was buried deep beneath the temple in Jerusalem long before the Babylonian invasion. A well-established esoteric legend within Europe claims that Hughes de Payens was chosen to retrieve and bring it back to Europe.[19] The legend further claims that on its arrival to Europe, it was first hidden beneath the crypt of Chartres Cathedral, which was at the time, under the control of the Chartres masters. The English authors, Knight and Lomas, claimed that it was later moved for safekeeping and hidden beneath Rosslyn Chapel,[20] but advanced no supporting evidence of this intriguing theory.

It is also alleged that along with the Ark a vast quantity of ancient documents were uncovered. Throughout the years, there has been considerable speculation as to the nature of these documents and a reasonable consensus has emerged that they probably contained, among other things, copies of the Dead Sea Scrolls material found at Qumran, and treatises on sacred geometry, ancient science, and other aspects of the Hebraic/Egyptian gnostic tradition. Confirming this is the translation of the Copper Scrolls found at Qumran, as it lists a variety of sites where temple treasure and items of sacred import were hidden immediately prior to the destruction of the temple in 70 CE On the mid-20th century, John Allegro, the Dead Sea Scrolls scholar, excavated many of the other sites listed in the Copper Scroll. He found in several of these artefacts relating to the 12th—century Knights Templar, but nothing whatsoever from the era of the Temple's destruction by the Romans.

Ostensibly, it would appear that the only logic behind these bizarre circumstances is that the secret knowledge of these hiding places had been passed down through the generations for over 1,000 years via the oral traditions of the Rex Deus families. It is quite apparent that King Baldwin was a part of the conspiracy in light of the account that he granted them quarters over the precise site they wanted to excavate, and, it is indicative of this that the order first "went public" within a few weeks of his ascension. Up until that point, despite several visits to the Holy Land by both Hughes de Champagne and Hughes de Payens during the reigns of Godfroi de Boullion and his brother Baldwin I, no attempt had been made to found the order.

The Return to Europe and the Templar Holdings

King Baldwin II, at the new Grand Master's request, wrote to Bernard of Clairvaux asking him to intercede with pope for formal recognition of the order, for Bernard was, at that time not only advisor to Pope Honorius II, but also his former teacher.[21] Hughes de Payens along with his fellow cofounders set sail for Provence, then Normandy where he met with the English King Stephen, who gave him permission to travel through England and on to Scotland, where he stayed with the St. Clairs of Roslin.

A donation of land at Ballantrodoch was given to the Templars by King David of Scotland and it became the headquarters of the order there and has since been renamed Temple. With this land bordering on the St. Clair estates communication between the ancient family and the Knights Templar could be easily maintained. As a result of these travels, the order was immediately granted estates not only Scotland but also in England, Champagne, and Provence. Up to this day, there is still considerable dispute as to which of these was the first to be given. The most probable conclusion is that the lands around Les Arcs-sur-Argens in Provence were first, Temple Cressing in England shortly after, Ballantrodoch third, and Troyes fourth. The circumstance is complicated, as the gifts were first communicated orally and were only later confirmed in writing long after the knights had actually taken possession of their new properties. In actual fact, these first donations of land had been long planned and were soon followed by a veritable cascade of gifts, of castles, towns, farms, and villages throughout Christian Europe. An even larger number of donations of property and money followed the pope's official recognition of the order and the award of its first "rule."

The Templar Rule

Acting in response to King Baldwin's letter, Bernard of Clairvaux did bring the order to the attention of the pope, who willing gave his blessing to the warrior monks and commanded his papal legate in France, Cardinal Matthew d'Albano, to call a council of Church and temporal dignitaries to legalize the new order and give the knights their first religious rule. On 14 January 1128 the council opened at Troyes under the direction and presidency of Cardinal d'Albano. Attending were the archbishops of Rheims and Sens, and the bishops of Orleans, Paris, Soissons, Auxerre, Meaux, Chalons, Laon, and Samur. Also in attendance were the abbots of Vezelay, Citeaux, Pontigny, Trois-Fontaines, Saint-Remy de Rheims, Dijon, Molesmes, and, according to other accounts, the abbot of Clairvaux.[22] There is some debate in the records as to whether Bernard actually attended in person for all or even part of the council in view of his ill health. Nevertheless, the entire event was certainly influenced by his thinking. Secular authority was also well represented by the Count of Champagne, Thibauld IV, William II, the Count of Nevers, and another nobleman, André de Baudemant.

The Grand Master Hughes de Payens and his fellow knights were called on 31 January 1128 to appear before the council to receive the new rule that had been written by Bernard of Clairvaux.[23] Ten years after the Council of Troyes, Pope Innocent II issued the papal bull *Omne datum optimum*, which made the Templars responsible, through their Grand Master, to the pope and the pope alone, thus freeing them from the authority of bishops, archbishops, kings, and emperors. Less than twenty years after the Templars' foundation this papal action made it wholly independent of all prelates and princes, and thereby the most independent religious order in the Christendom. Soon it was to become the most powerful, both in wealth and military might.

The Order Grows

In the course of the two years following the Council of Troyes the Knights Templar had acquired land in Portugal and established close connections with the rulers of that country. From the eastern side of Spain donations came more slowly, but followed a similar pattern. Soon after 1130 the Templars owned property in Aragon. Consequently, by the early 1140s, they had acquired enough land and recruited sufficient members to sustain military operations on two fronts—in the Holy Land and the Iberian Peninsula. The order fought in most of the King of Aragon's campaigns against the Moors and acted in an advisory capacity to him. Templar forces in these campaigns were never numerous, but they could mobilize quickly and remained in the field as long as required.[24] In reality, they were the first full-time professional, standing army in both Europe and the Holy Land since the fall of the Roman Empire.

In the early years after the Council of Troyes the grants of land, castles and other properties came in so fast that, in some cases, the order had to defer garrisoning their new lands for several years due to a shortage of manpower. Their chief focus was, however, the protection of the kingdom of Jerusalem. Both the early recruits, knights and all others who were capable of military service, were sent to the East as soon as possible. They followed their Grand Master's example, for Hughes was accompanied by 300 knights drawn from the noblest families in Europe who had rushed to become members of the order, when he returned to the Holy Land in 1129.[25] Keeping in mind the difficulties in communication that existed in Europe in the early years of the 12th century, to say nothing of the time it took to arm and equip these men, much less transport them to a rendezvous point within Europe, this massive influx of recruits and their rapid transportation to the Holy Land is yet another clear example of prolonged and efficient planning on a very large scale.

The large number of recruits and the increasing list of donations of land and property did not all originate directly from the Rex Deus families. Bernard of Clairvaux was, in current terminology, a master of the art of public relations and publicity. He composed a tract, *In Praise of the New Knighthood*, that extolled the virtues of the Knights Templar and delineated the immense spiritual benefits that would accrue to those who supported its aims with acts of personal service, donations of land, or good old-fashioned money. One mysterious paragraph toward the end of this document almost gives the game away, as to the true objective of this knightly order whose sworn purpose was to protect, not only the pilgrims to the Holy Land, but the Holy Land itself. Bernard recorded:

> Hail, land of promise, which, formerly flowing only with milk and honey for thy possessors, now stretchest forth the food of life and the means of salvationfor the entire world.[26]

The core tenet of Church dogma was the belief that, more than 1,100 years before, Jesus had died on the cross at Golgotha in the supreme sacrificial act of salvation. With his death, he had already redeemed mankind and saved us all from sin. The Abbot of Clairvaux, Bernard, was a senior member of the Church, the advisor to a series of popes, at least to two of whom had been his pupils, had supposedly dedicated his life to furthering mankind's understanding of this dogma that the Church regards as a fact. Then what did he mean when he wrote: "Now stretchest forth the food of life and the means of salvation for the entire world"? Or, as provided in an alternative interpretation: "from which will come salvation for the entire world"? Could Bernard be referring indirectly to the documents found under the Temple Mount and their translation? Or could it be that he was referring to the reappearance of the original teachings of Jesus that he hoped for in this era of Rex Deus resurgence? It is highly probable that we will never know, unless further documentary evidence comes to light. What is apparent is that, following the circulation of his tract, *In Praise of the New Knighthood*, recruits, gifts of land, and money flowed into the arms of the Templars. They were not only beneficiaries; the previously struggling Cistercian order, which had revived appreciably after Bernard and his companions joined its ranks, also underwent an extraordinary period of expansion. During Bernard's lifetime, they established over 300 new abbeys, the most rapid expansion on record of any monastic order before or since. Moreover, throughout his life at least, the Cistercians and the Knights Templar were widely regarded as two arms of the same body—one a contemplative monastic arm, the other the strong, swift, military arm.

The major centres of Templar influence and power were located in Europe with France, Provence, Champagne, Bar, England, Tuscany, and the area now known as Languedoc/Roussillon closely followed by Aragon, Gallicia, Portugal, Scotland, Normandy and the Holy Roman Empire. In a short period of time, their estates, castles, and churches stretched from the Baltic to the Mediterranean, and from the Atlantic coastline to the Holy Land. All means possible was devoted to one end, the defence of the Crusader Kingdom of Jerusalem and, in fulfilling this goal, the order left no stone unturned in its endeavour to maximize its profits and increase its efficiency and power.

The Templar Estates

The Templars held a vast amount of properties in Europe most of which were not great castles with the exception of Portugal and Spain, where these were necessity in their battles against the Moors. Instead they held farmhouses, mills, barns, small chapels, and commanderies—administrative centres usually combined with agricultural buildings. In the main cities, strongholds were constructed to act as secure places for treasures in transit or to hold troops en route to the Holy Land. The warrior knights needed servants, farriers for their horses, and armorers; the farms needed general labourers, blacksmiths, carpenters, and herdsmen; their ships needed crews, carpenters, sail-makers, oarsmen, and senior officers and navigators; their church had their own chaplains and, as we shall see later, they needed masons and craftsmen in stone. These 'warrior monks' owned land in every climatic region in Europe; they owned vineyards, farms, pasturage for cattle and sheep, quarries, mills, mines, smithies, and stud farms. Basically, they became the first multi-national conglomerate in history.

A modern consultant in business management, the American S.T. Bruno, described them in the following terms:

> The fact of the matter is that the Templars ran a "world wide" system of farms, shipping concerns and financial services. They pressed olives in the Jordan Valley, made wine in France and traded wool in Ireland. Agriculture was, of course, only one activity. They also shipped lumber from Edessa, and carried pilgrims across the Mediterranean from Lombardy to Acre. They even provided a medieval form of "travellers cheque" to pilgrims and loaned money to kings. Although one might envisage their primary military "product" as singularly focused on the conquest of the Holy Land, the resource branch of the order operated in a number of different markets.[27]

The organizational skill required to operate this enormous, international, multifaceted enterprise and keep a standing army in the field at the same time was overwhelming. Nevertheless, they accomplished this, yet despite this obvious fact, some of their clerical critics within the Modern Church call them "illiterates!" Bruno alleges that, for nearly 180 years, the Templars managed their organization in a manner consistent with some of the most sophisticated and best management practices understood today in the 21st century.[28]

Protecting the Holy Land and Long-Distance Trade

Prior to the time of the Templars' foundation, long-distance trade, primarily conducted by sea, centred on the northern Italian cities of Venice, Genoa, and Pisa. These cities were in a position to exploit their geographical position and prospered greatly from trade with both the Byzantine and Islamic empires to the east. In its turn, Northern Europe slowly but steadily improved its wealth and offered timber and woollen cloth in exchange for spices and silks from the East.

In the beginning, long-distance overland trade was hampered with difficulty, as local barons imposed heavy tolls on goods passing through their lands and all goods and money on transit were prey to bandits who infested the countryside. All this changed with the arrival of the Templars. With their estates spread throughout Europe as they were, it gave them the ideal bases from which to fulfil their primary function, which was to protect the pilgrimage routes. As a consequence, long-distance travel and trade became safer and far more feasible. Substantial regional markets began to spring up; this further stimulated mercantile activity. Sufficiently independent of their nominal overlords, the Kings of France and the Dukes of Burgundy, to ignore any royal restrictions on trade, the Counts of Champagne began to encourage merchants to bring business to Troyes. They encouraged a climate of security, stability, and freedom that facilitated the growth of this international market situated near the midpoint between the emerging trading centres of the Low Countries in the northwest and prosperous trading cities of Venice, Genoa, and Pisa in northern Italy. Soon other powerful nobles followed this example, and trade was further facilitated by Templar action.

Templars and the Creation of Modern Banking

Trade of this description cannot grow unless the financial infrastructure to sustain it is present,[29] and the warrior monks added another string to their bow. The Templars were accustomed to working in many currencies and organizing the safe transport of gold and money across Europe to finance their militaries activities in the Holy Land, and now they began to offer financial services to the emerging merchant classes. They organized themselves as bankers, using a device they had learned from the Sufis of Islam—namely the "note of hand"—to arrange financial transfers from one part of Europe to another. This gave further momentum to trade and led to more profitable business for them. They advanced money to merchants, the nobility, prelates, and princes, and all their financial dealings were backed by their reputation for integrity, accuracy, and safety. They soon became the wealthiest financial institution in the Christian world.

If the roads and trade routes were not effectively protected, travel and the transport of goods could not take place in safety. The Order of the Knights Templar achieved both functions and, as a consequence, played a significant part in creating the fundamental necessary conditions for the accumulation of capital. These conditions were already in existence in the trading centres of northern Italy and, thanks to the services and security provided by the Templars, they spread quickly throughout the main centres of population in Europe. The political results that stemmed from the commercial success of the trading cities of northern Europe—namely an increasing independence and autonomy from their nominal rulers in the Papal States or the Holy Roman Empire—were soon reflected in a sustained and cumulative shift in balance of power in the rest of Europe. A shift in power occurred from the feudal barons of old to the mercantile class in the towns and cities. In some regions under the Rex Deus nobility, this developed into an embryonic form of democracy, as city councils in one form or another began to flex their muscles and, at first, complement and, later, rival the power of their nominal overlords.

This unique combination of fearsome reputation as fighting men and renown as defenders of Christianity, their ownership of large estates in every corner of Europe along with their financial ingenuity and reliability, led to Templars being appointed as ambassadors, advisors to kings, popes, emperors, and positions of responsibility in nearly every kingdom in which they operated. On the whole, the Templars rose to positions of almost incalculable influence throughout the European continent. They exerted power and sway in military matters, in diplomacy, in international politics, and above all in financial matters. Therein the question arises, 'what made them so different from other religious orders of great reputation, many of which were of far greater antiquity?' In order to understand the possible answers to this question, we must examine their belief system.

CHAPTER 14
THE BELIEFS OF THE KNIGHTS TEMPLAR

The comparison between the impressive achievements of the Templars in their 180-year history and those of other orders, which were established long before them and who outlasted them by many centuries, is surprising. Still, the apparent lines of inquiry that could explain these differences are ignored or brushed under the academic carpet as irrelevant. At the beginning of the 14th century, the Templars were suppressed, disgracefully, following a controversial trial for heresy conducted by the French Inquisition at the behest of King Philippe le Bel of France. Their internal records were either stolen by the Inquisitors; hidden by the knights for safekeeping; or destroyed. This lack of information has had two detrimental effects: giving free reign to speculation, and providing academic historians with an excuse for ignoring the real cause of the Templars' immense growth.

The obvious information vacuum is not quite complete, as it may seem. In fact, the Templars have left us with a considerable legacy that can be used as a guide to their true beliefs. This exists with their involvement with a form of veneration that is almost perpetually associated with Templar activity—namely the Black Madonna. Other clues to their beliefs can be found hidden, although in allegorical form, within another example of Rex Deus activity that originated in the city of Troyes—a literary work still fascinates millions of people today, *The Search for the Holy Grail*. The Templars also left us a memorable guide to their main principles of belief, carved as three-dimensional teaching boards in the great Gothic cathedrals they built or financed during the explosion of creativity that one perceptive British author, William Anderson, called *The Rise of the Gothic*.

The Cult of the Black Madonna

With its true origins rooted in pagan worship of a variety of mother goddesses, the cult of Mariolatry received its main impetus from Chartres. For instance, Notre Dame Sous-Terre at Chartres Cathedral is a Christianized variation on the Ancient Druidic practice worshipping the fire-blackened figure of a virgin about to give birth, *Virginibus pariturae*, described by Julius Caesar in *de Bello Gallico*, book 4. There are many such assimilations occurring throughout Europe, which retained older pagan forms of worship and incorporated them into Catholic practice.

The veneration of the Black Madonna began in a similar fashion. Several important Black Madonna sites either predate the foundation of the Templar order or, are located geographically far beyond their reach. The peak years of this strange cult, however, coincide with the time of the order's power, and the majority of the effigies are located in areas of Templar influence. Moreover, the cult is intimately enmeshed with veneration of Mary Magdalene. While it has always been happy to rake in the financial benefits of pilgrimage to these sites, the Catholic Church has consistently felt uncomfortable with the cult of the Black Madonna. As Mariolatry plays such an important role in the Catholic faith, this obvious discomfort with the intense local, national, and sometimes international, veneration of Black Madonna seems difficult to understand. Why would this particular effigy cause the hierarchy so much embarrassment? Does it represent something that the Church would not have us know?

One clue to the acute unease felt by the Church in this matter is found in the words of Bernard of Clairvaux. During the time of the Council of Troyes, Bernard demanded a specific requirement for all the members of new knighthood "to make obedience to Bethany and the House of Mary and Martha"—in other words, obedience and loyalty to the dynasty founded by Mary Magdalene and Jesus. Numerous scholars of the esoteric have come to the conclusion that the great Notre Dame cathedrals built or financed by the Templars were dedicated, not to Mary the mother of Jesus, but to Mary Magdalene and the son of Jesus—an idea that, when viewed through the eyes of Church, is heretical. The

Templar veneration of the Magdalene in the guise of the Black Madonna was rampant throughout the lands they controlled. Ean Begg, a perceptive Scottish researcher, lists over fifty centres of veneration found in churches dedicated to Mary Magdalene.[1] The Magdalene is described in the European esoteric tradition, as "the symbol of divine wisdom" and, according to the Nazorean tradition, she was depicted dressed in black like the priestess Isis, surmounted by Sophia's crown of Stars; her infant wore the golden crown of royalty.[2] The 20th-century initiate, Rudolf Steiner claims that symbolism can be interpreted up to at least nine levels, depending on the perception and initiatory status of the viewer. There is no exception with the Black Madonna. The first exoteric level is simply the mother of Jesus with her only child; the second, she is Mary, the seat of wisdom. At a more profound level, as in ancient Egyptian symbolism, the colour black indicates wisdom, so the Templars were venerating the goddess of wisdom, Sophia, embodied in the form of the goddess Isis and the Horus child, which is then camouflaged as the Christian holy mother and the infant Jesus.[3] From another level of understanding, Isis was venerated as "the Initiate of Light,"[4] or enlightenment.

Reverting back to the Christianization of pagan deities, the Black Virgin can also be held to represent the Earth Mother, the Egyptian goddess Anna, who was always depicted in Egyptian tradition as black.[5] Ean Begg, who has devoted several years to the study the Black Madonna and hidden streams of spirituality within Christian Europe, claims that the study of history and legends of the Black Madonna may reveal a heretical sect with the power to shock and astonish even current post-Christian attitudes, and a secret involving political forces still influential in modern Europe.[6] His remark, when judged in the light of the Rex Deus tradition, is right on the mark![7]

The Search for the Holy Grail

At the time the first Grail romance was written, Europe was, in some respects, a police state; anyone perceived as spiritually or religiously different was liable to be burnt at the stake. In order to survive, the Rex Deus families had learned the art of dissembling and perfected it to a high degree. Thus, whereas the Grail sagas claim to describe an arduous and dangerous quest for the most holy of relics—the cup of Jesus—encoded within it is another, immensely different meaning. The Grail romances gives us a description of a long, gruelling search by a knight subjected to many temptations and physicals dangers—a rather romanticized story based on the well-known perils of prolonged pilgrimage. Set during the supreme age of the veneration of holy relics, what is so different about the quest for the Holy Grail? Beyond the standard description of the quest, one that is acceptable to the hierarchy of the time, lies another story. The Grail saga serves as an allegory for an alchemical quest,[8] a heretical guide to a spiritual pathway to enlightenment.

Anyone, during the 12th century, seeking salvation simple had to volunteer for duty in the Holy Land. The reward promised to them for this exercise in Christian virtue was absolution of all sins; both those already committed and any that might be committed in the future. If killed in battle, service in the Crusades ensured the warrior would bypass purgatory and immediately ascend to heaven. Then what is the purpose of seeking the Grail? One logical reason to question the basic overt message of the Grail sagas is that, by going to any church or cathedral, anyone could, by the miracle of transubstantiation, get direct access to the actual body and blood of Jesus through the simple act of communion—without great trial or danger, merely the mild embarrassment of making an act of confession.

Contradicting the monolithic power of the oppressive Church of that age, the original Grail romances carry coded clues to a heretical belief system. The Fisher King, the king of the Grail castle, is injured. As he is imperfect, he weakly serves his impoverished realm, just as the usurpers of the true teachings of Jesus, those who lead the Christian Church, despoil the spiritual lives of those they claim to serve. His wasted kingdom or his ill health will not be restored until there is someone pure enough to see the Grail. Therefore, when the true teachings of Jesus triumph over greed, lies, distortion, and hypocrisy, the realization of heaven on Earth will be made manifest.

As for the initiatory aspects hidden within the romances, Tim's first literary collaborator, the late Trevor Ravenscroft, composed his masterwork, *The Cup of Destiny*,[9] around just these themes. His ambition was to impart to the younger generation that, within their drama and symbolism, these sagas conceal clues to a unique path of initiation into the deepest mysteries of the true teachings of Jesus. He was not alone in this conclusion, for one of the world's leading mythologists, the late Professor Joseph Campbell, citing a passage from the *Gospel of Thomas*, wrote of the importance of the Grail: "He who drinks from my mouth will become as I am, and I shall become he."[10] The conclusion Campbell reached was that this represented the ultimate form of enlightenment that can arise from a successful Grail quest.[11]

The words, "Holy Grail," are proclaimed to be a corruption of the term "Holy Gradual"—gradual in the sense of a gradual spiritual ascent or ascending initiatory way leading to eventual enlightenment. Another meaning has been assigned to the term in the last two decades. As it is written in French—Sangraal—is claimed to be a disguised version of Sang Real, or Holy Blood.[12] In 1981 in the English-speaking world, this was brought to public attention with the publication of Holy Blood and the Holy Grail, which claims that Jesus, supposedly the celibate Son of God, was in fact, as mortal as we are, that he married and founded a dynasty.

Allegory and Myth

Using myth and legend to convey spiritual allegories and uncomfortable truths into the public consciousness in an acceptable manner is a stratagem as old as speech and memory. People who reject these cultural vehicles as some form of inspired fiction suitable for children or the credulous ignore the fact that every meaningful part of life—heroic deeds, family and national traditions, and all religions, including Christianity—had also created a colourful mythology of their own. Through the works of Joseph Campbell and others, the value that is attached to mythology has undergone significant change.[13]

Myths are similar to symbolism, and can be understood at different levels. Furthermore if viewed with discernment, they can be signposts to hidden truth. Campbell claims: "Mythology is the penultimate truth, because ultimate cannot be put into words."[14] The Indian scholar Ananda Coomeraswamy wrote: "Myth embodies the nearest approach to absolute truth that can be stated in words.[15]" Kathleen Raine, a poet, put a similar idea far more succinctly when she said: "Fact is not the truth of myth; myth is the truth of fact."[16] Nevertheless, to reach a reasonable understanding of Templar beliefs, we need not depend solely on cultic practices that have outlasted them, or allegorical literature, or even myth and legend, for we have a far more tangible and visible source—the architectural heritage that they created.

During the 12th century, there was a mysterious and sudden outburst of cathedral building that left us with those majestic and powerful "prayers in stone" that still adorn the European landscape. Some of the questions that arise in the mind of any tourist or pilgrim who sees them today are: What elicited this enormous expenditure of resources at this particular time? And where did the unfamiliar architectural skills that created the rise of the Gothic come from? In order to answer these questions, we turn to one of the Church's traditional enemies, the Rex Deus families and their offspring and associates, the Knights Templar and the craftmasons.

The Holy Grail Sagas and Rex Deus

Contrary to the belief that the existence of the Rex Deus families was a closely guarded secret not revealed until the latter part of the 20th century, Rex Deus beliefs, legends, and stories had been widely known for more than nine centuries without anyone recognizing their true origins. In their efforts to preserve the Rex Deus tradition, the masterstroke was the creation of the stories of the search for the Holy Grail. This literary genre was created deliberately and successfully to serve the purposes of the descendants of Jesus. The grail sagas of the 12th and 13th centuries are an ingenious combination of pre-Christian traditions with a Christian gloss, and containing a coded guide to the true teachings of Jesus.

The Grail has been variously described as a chalice, a cup, a stone that fell from heaven, a stone within a cup, or a magical bowl,[17] the Grail is believed to be capable of restoring life to the dead, or good health to the wounded or infirm. It is depicted by Pre-Christian and Celtic legends as a cauldron with similar magical qualities.[18] At the north door at Chartres Cathedral, the Portal of the Initiates is the Grail carved as the "stone within the cup" carried by Melchizedek in the carving of this priest-king that has prominent position.[19]

The Grail sagas obtained their pseudo-Christian gloss through the inspired works of two remarkable men—Chrétien de Troyes and Wolfram von Essenbach,[20] who spent some years in the Holy Land and is believed by some scholars to have been a Templar Knight. Their stories were a clever amalgam of pagan legend, Celtic folklore, Rex Deus tradition, Jewish mystical symbolism, and alchemical Kabbalistic nuance, masked by a thin veneer of mainstream Christian veneration for the holiest relic in the Christian tradition—the cup used at the Last Supper and supposedly used by Joseph of Arimathea to catch the blood of Jesus after the crucifixion.

Around 1190 in the form of an unfinished epic, *Perceval*, or *Le Conte del Graal*, written by Chrétien de Troyes,[21] the first Grail romance appeared on the European literary, religious, and chivalric scene. A relative of Hughes de

Payen,[22] Chrétien de Troyes had trained for the priesthood and became a noted translator and writer of remarkable repute. De Troyes dedicated three of his early works to Marie, Countess of Champagne, the daughter of King Louis VIII of France and Eleanor of Aquitaine.[23] There are claims by some that he originally intended to dedicate Le Conte del Graal to Marie. However, she retired from public life when her husband, Count Henry of Champagne, died shortly after returning from the Holy Land. Chrétien de Troyes promptly searched for a new patron among the ranks of Rex Deus, Phillipe d'Alsace, the Count of Flanders and a close relative of the early Christian kings of Jerusalem,[24] who was also the son of a cofounder of the Knights Templar, Payen de Montdidier.

Eighteen years after the foundation of the Knights Templar, a collection of legends written by Geoffrey Monmouth concerning King Arthur and those of the Holy Grail came to public attention in 1136. While separate and distinct to begin with, they soon became inextricably mixed. Both literary genres share similar ideals of chivalry and speak movingly of a spiritual search for perfection played out against a backdrop of brutal reality that was all too tangible and familiar to the enthralled listeners and readers.

In the opinion of many scholars, it is ironic that both the Arthurian and Grail traditions seem to share a common source which has long since been lost. There have been comparisons made between this alleged "common source" and its relationship to the resulting sagas, and the similar relationship between the Q document and the Synoptic Gospels. We are not in a position to disprove the theory that there might have been some common written source connecting these two chivalric legends—one that was perhaps known to both Chrétien and Wolfram. However, we know that both authors' works were indeed linked by another, far more important and lasting, common source—the teachings and traditions of Rex Deus. Malcolm Godwin, a Grail scholar, came remarkably close to identifying the linkage when he wrote:

> The Legend of the Grail, more than any other western myth, has retained the vital magic that marks it as a living legend capable of touching both imagination and the spirit. No other myth is so rich in symbolism, so diverse and often contradictory in meaning. And at its core there exists a secret which has sustained the mystical appeal of the Grail for at least nine hundred years, while other myths and legends have slipped into oblivion and been forgotten.[25]

The most frequent description of the Holy Grail depicts it as a relic, a cup used by Joseph of Arimathea to collect the blood of Jesus after the crucifixion. This story was apparently concocted by someone with no knowledge whatsoever of the Jewish burial practice at that time, for, apart from anything else, any man who handled a corpse would be obliged to under go a prolonged period of purification, which is hardly likely on the eve of Passover. In biblical times this story would have been absolutely incredible because of the Jewish aversion to men handling corpses, much less blood. Moreover, orthodox Jewish burial traditions of that era demand that the corpse be buried with the entire body and blood together in order to guarantee life in the hereafter. This tradition is practiced today among the Hassidim and would definitely be a bar against the taking of blood from any corpse.

The Medieval Craftmasons

Apparently initiatory orders had always existed among the craftsmen who built the churches, cathedrals, and castles of medieval Europe. Commonly known in England as the craftmasons, in France they went by a variety of names: The Children of Father Soubise, the Children of Master Jacques, and the Children of Solomon, whose heirs are known today as Les Compagnons des Devoirs du Tour de France, or the Compagnonage. These three brotherhoods held certain beliefs in common: they observed a moral tradition of chivalry within their craft, they had humility toward the work that must be done, and they were men who knew how to use a pair of compasses.[26]

Furthermore, according to Raoul Vergez, a companion-carpenter of the Duties who rebuilt most of the church spires in Brittany and Normandy after the Second World War,[27] they all shared the same bread. Sharing the same bread is one of the indications of a community or fraternity, and those who know how to use a pair of compasses are men who have been initiated into the secret knowledge of sacred geometry. Having this qualification admitted them to the status of mason. The English author Ian Dunlop described the divine order of their skills when he wrote: "It is not uncommon in the medieval illumination to find God the Father represented as the 'architectus elegans' holding a large pair of compasses.[28]"

The initiated masons obtained qualification into a hierarchy of three ascending degrees: apprentice, companion, and master mason. The apprentice learned in an itinerant manner, moving from yard to yard throughout the

A Templar Ritual Chalice
Photo by: Hamilton White

country in what was described as a Tour de France, receiving instruction from skilled and initiated men known as companions. They were then initiated by their masters, in secret conclaves known as *cayennes*, once the required degree of skill was attained. Centuries later the three fraternities that merged into one, had different duties, skills and traditions. Mainly building in the Romanesque style, the Children of Maitre Soubise were found at the heart of the Benedictine monastic system. Their "signatures," or masons' mark differ greatly from those of their brethren who built in the Gothic style, even when their work is contemporary. According to tradition, Master Jacques the son of Jacquin, was made a master craftmason after serving an apprenticeship in Greece, Egypt, and Jerusalem, supposedly founded the Compagnons Passants du Devoir, or the Children of Master Jacques. The same tradition states that he the made two pillars of the temple of Solomon, one called Boaz and the other Jacquin.

The Children of Solomon and La Langue Verte

The Children of Solomon, the third fraternity, are the most important in Tim's investigations into the great Gothic cathedrals. Chartres cathedral and most of the other Gothic Notre Dames were built by them, such as those at

Rheims and Amiens. These magnificent buildings are all marked with their signature, the *chrisme à l'epée*—a Celtic cross enclosed in a circle. They were taught the principles of sacred geometry by Cistercian monks and they were named after King Solomon, the prime mover behind the first temple in Jerusalem. Many churches were built in the south of France, in both the Languedoc and Provence, by another branch of the Compagnonnage. This was the Compagnonnage Tuscana, whose traditions and rituals traced their mysteries back to Egypt and biblical Israel via their Roman and Greek roots. The late Guy Jordan informed Tim that according to their secret traditions, they were part of a collegia of constructors known as Les Tignarii, reputedly founded by the Roman initiate Numa Pompilius.[29]

The exact nature of the relationship between the Children of Solomon and the Order of the Templars is far from clear. No one can determine whether the craftsmen were an integral part of the knightly order, affiliated with it in some unspecified way, or just associated with it by usage. Supported by Bernard of Clairvaux, the Templars gave a rule to this fraternity in March 1145 that was prefaced by the words:

> We the Knights of Christ and of the Temple follow the destiny that prepares us to die for Christ. We have the wish to give this rule of living, of work and of honour to the constructors of churches so that Christianity can spread throughout the earth not so that our name should be remembered, oh Lord, but that Your Name should Live.[30]

It is conceivable that this fraternity of skilled masons working in the Gothic style were in fact affiliated in some manner with the Order of the Templars. Being granted great privileges by the establishment of that time, they were given freedom from all taxes and protection against any form of prosecution by the constructors of other buildings. It is also useful to take into consideration that, at the time of the suppression of the Templars, the Children of Solomon lost all the privileges and immunities granted to them.

The Knights Templar and the Children of Solomon both were intimately involved in that fantastic and productive era of cathedral construction known as the Rise of the Gothic. The English architectural historian, Fred Gettings makes this point completely clear:

The Knights Templar who were founded ostensibly to protect the pilgrimage routes to the Holy Land, were almost openly involved in financing and lending moral support to the building of cathedrals throughout Europe.[31]

Both Fulcanelli, the early 20th-century initiate and Kenneth Rayner Johnson, his biographer, claim that Gothic architecture was the fruit of the Templar's knowledge of sacred geometry, and was not merely an example of beauty, but also a three-dimensional code that passed a hidden message in architectural form of a *la langue verte*—the green language, or the language of initiation. Neither was alone in this belief, because earlier, toward the end of the 19th-century, F. Colfs would write: "The language of stones spoken by this new art, [Gothic architecture] is at the same time clear and sublime, speaking alike to the humblest and to the most cultured heart."[32]

In order to mask the details of their conversations from casual eavesdroppers such as the Church, La langue verte emerged as a disguise. Consequently, the heretics could communicate using a verbal code, without putting their lives or freedom in jeopardy. This coded communication proved a useful defence against persecution and so became the language, not only for the initiates, but also equally for the poor and oppressed. It could be considered the medieval ancestor of cockney rhyming slang and the "hip hop" or "rap" of the American inner-city ghettoes.[33]

Sacred Geometry

A divinely inspired art form, sacred geometry involves skills of engineering, building, and design. It is claimed by its practitioners to be handed down from master to novice in an unbroken chain from the earliest of times until the fall of Jerusalem in 70 CE. This elaborate chain of communication preserved, enhanced, and transmitted the secret knowledge used by the Egyptians and biblical Israelites to construct their sacred buildings. The knowledge of sacred geometry was apparently lost after the fall of Jerusalem, until the Knights Templar returned to Europe from Jerusalem in 1128 after completing their excavations under the Temple Mount. Many interesting questions crop up from the curious juxtaposition of the Templars' return from the Holy Land and the sudden explosion of building in the Gothic style that was to follow. Did they find some type of master plan for this new style of building under the Temple mount? Were there other developments in the works in Jerusalem that can explain this innovative form of architecture? In Europe there is no discernable developmental stage between the prevailing form of Romanesque architecture and the new, tall, graceful form of the Gothic cathedrals. This Gothic Style was definitely an astounding new development, but where did it originate?

The Rise of the Gothic

In previous works, Tim has suggested one possible source for the Gothic architecture –namely documentation discovered under the Temple Mount. Since he has proposed this idea in the absence of evidence of any viable alternative, however, he has always had some reservations about it. These derive from the fact that architectural development at the time any such documents might have been buried would not have included arches of any kind. Both Egyptian and Hebraic architecture were based on transverse lintels, not arches. In actuality, the only influence that might have stimulated the creation of an arch at that time was Roman.

Gordon Strachan, a colleague of Tim's, has since proposed a far more credible theory. He is a long-time associate of Keith Critchlow, who has devoted most of his life to an in-depth study of sacred architecture. His research is not limited by faith, culture, or time. Strachan's reasoning has the merit of simplicity and credibility. Furthermore, it is completely consistent with what we know of the cultural interchange occurring at the time of the First Crusade and thereafter.

Strachan strongly believes that the pointed arch that is the foundation of the Gothic style came from outside Europe. Moreover, he concurs that the country from which it came was, indeed, the Holy Land. He further claims that it is the result from "a unique blending of indigenous building skills with the architectural genius of Islam."[34] During their initial nine-year residence in Jerusalem, the Templars met many Sufis; and at that time, Sufism itself was experiencing a revival.[35] As previously mentioned, the Sufis were devout believers in a form of interfaith pluralism and, like their Rex Deus counterparts in Europe, followed an initiatory spiritual pathway. Strachan maintains that it was from contact with Sufis that the Templars first became aware of the manner of designing the Islamic *mukhammas* pointed arch. In fact, before bringing this knowledge back to Europe, they used it in the Holy Land to build a three bayed doorway with pointed arches on the Temple Mount, arches that can still be seen today.[36] As a consequence, the knowledge of sacred geometry gained an immense boost from the contact between the initiatory orders of both faiths—the Templars and the Sufis. Presuming that Strachan is correct in his analysis, this interfaith architectural legacy bequeathed to us by the Templars can still be appreciated as they yet stand in the flowering of artistic and religious expressions of medieval Gothic cathedrals.

There are two other mystical writers who also noted the significance of Templar influence on these extraordinary buildings in the last century:

> The building of cathedrals was part of a colossal and cleverly devised plan which permitted the existence of entirely free philosophical and psychological schools in the rude, absurd, cruel, superstitious, bigoted and scholastic Middle Ages. These schools have left us an immense heritage, almost all of which we have already wasted without understanding its meaning and value.[37]

Fucanelli in his work, *Le Mystère des Cathèdrals*, wrote that a church or cathedral was not merely a place of worship or a sanctuary for the sick and deprived, but also a place of commercial activity, public theatre, and secular beliefs.

> The gothic cathedral, the sanctuary of the Tradition, Science and Art, should not be regarded as a work dedicated solely to the glory of Christianity, but rather as a vast concretion of ideas, of tendencies, of popular beliefs; a perfect whole to which we can refer to without fear, whenever we would penetrate the religious, secular, philosophic or social thoughts of out ancestors.[38]

He further describes the Gothic cathedral as a form of philosophical "stock exchange," where lingering pockets of arcana and heresy were flouted under the noses of an unsuspecting clergy.[39]

The Golden Book

A formidable example of this can be found at Chartres, where the cathedral is a superb statement of the truths that lead man closer to God. It stands as a hymn to gnostic initiatory spirituality—a melodic symphony in stone that is a visible celebration of divine harmony that reverberates the truths that are just as meaningful today as they were when it was first constructed. Every pilgrim or tourist, regardless of his or her faith or lack of it, leaves the awe-inspiring building spiritually uplifted, inspired, and transformed. This is certainly the true measure of the enduring magnetism of the cathedral, which is known as the Golden Book, for inspired sages have inscribed on her their wisdom, an everlasting legacy to all who seek spiritual truth.[40]

Built as an addition to Fulbertus' 11th century structure, the west front of Chartres houses the three main doors. Thirty-eight detailed scenes from the life of Jesus can be seen in a small, narrow frieze that runs just below the lintels of all three doors. However, in these depictions, there is a very important scene that is omitted and that is the crucifixion. As a matter of fact, there is not one single direct reference to the crucifixion that dates from the 12th century that can be found in the entire cathedral.[41] That would strike anyone that is biblically educated as extremely odd. The core teaching of Christianity is the life, death, and the resurrection of Jesus. Then, why is it excluded from the rest of the carvings? Was it merely an oversight? Not at all! This astonishing omission of any commemoration of the central tenet of Christian dogma is quite deliberate: it is a reflection of the Templar belief that Jesus came to reveal and not to redeem.

The captivating stained-glass windows with vivid hues of yellow, red, and blue transform the natural daylight into a shimmering haze of subtle colour that pervade the entire interior. Chartres' stained glass does not react like ordinary glass; it was made using scientific knowledge—true gnosis—brought back by the Templars from their contacts in the Middle East.[42] Scholars claim that this form of glass was deliberately created so that it would filter out light rays or luminous particles that were deemed harmful to humankind's innate capacity for spiritual activity. The selective filtering of cosmic rays, they maintain, creates a wavelength of light that can harmonize with the natural vibrations of human cellular tissue and maximize the effect of initiatory energy.[43]

Immediately below the huge rose window in the north transept in the central lancet, Saint Anne, the mother of the Virgin Mary, is depicted wearing a halo that is usually associated with the Magdalene. The windows lateral to it are all initiates: Melchizedek, the King of Righteousness, whose teaches inspired the Kibeiri and their spiritual heirs, the Druids and the Essenes; Aaron, the brother of Moses and a priest of the Egyptian temple mysteries; King

David and lastly, King Solomon, who was "wiser than Moses and full of the wisdom of Egypt."

Three Black Madonnas are found within Chartres. There is a modern replica of the medieval copy based upon the Druidic figure Virginibus Pariturae in the crypt, which the official guides states was used as an initiation chamber. Another can be found in the main cathedral—the Virgin of the Pillar, clothed according to tradition in heavy, ornate robes formally shaped in a triangle.[44] Directly in front of the statue is a tangible level of energy, a place of God-given power where the vibration is especially low and induces a fainting feeling indicating that this is a point of spiritual transformation.

Depicted in stained glass is the third initiatory Black Madonna. With a fire that destroyed Fulbertus' Romanesque cathedral, centuries of strife, the French Revolution, and two World Wars, the Notre Dame de la Belle Verrière miraculously survived it all so that we can admire and adore her. Inside the cathedral are many other points of telluric power that have the capacity to raise one to the point of etheric enhancement, to a true "state of grace"—a quality that was recognized, used, and enhanced by the craftsmen who created this glorious building. From the north Portal of Initiates, initiation is further commemorated by figures on either side of the entrance. A carving of Melchizedek holding a chalice—the Grail from which the stone protrudes is on the left. He is depicted handing the cup to Abraham. Then there is Moses, who received the two tablets of the Law that some claim is represented by the pillars of the temple of Solomon, Jacquin and Boaz.

The labyrinth—a circular design made of black-and-white flagstones occupying one-third of the floor of the nave is one of the most intriguing symbols in Chartres. Cyndi had an experience here, stating that she felt a tingling sensation that started in her feet and moved up her back and into her head. The labyrinth is not just a Christian symbol, as several Neolithic labyrinths of identical pattern have been found. A few days following a trip to Chartres, Tim visited a folk festival in Brittany and watched a dance that gave a clear indication of the initiatory nature of the labyrinth. The music was authentic North African Arab music—slow, reedy, rhythmic, and entrancing. Led by the mayor and his wife, the entire village danced with their arms linked so closely that their sides seemed to touch, shuffling sideways in a curving formal design that replicated the exact pattern of the labyrinth. Tim immediately recognised in their movements a variation of a Sufi dance designed to bring about a shift in consciousness. Respectively, Chartres Cathedral is clearly a hymn to the hidden streams of spirituality—an instruction book of initiation carved in stone and masked by an outward display of Christian worship.

Amiens Cathedral and the Veneration of John the Baptist

Amiens is the largest cathedral in France where there is a vault that soars 140 feet heavenward. Dominating the west front is a statue of Jesus known as the Beau Dieu of Amiens. Jesus is depicted in this carving with his feet resting on a lion and dragon. Here in a central commanding position, is a representation of Jesus and the *Wouivre*, the initiatory telluric energy of the Druids. Directly below this is a statue of that supreme adept of the Old Testament, King Solomon. Like those of Notre Dame de Paris, the walls leading into all three doors are decorated with quatrefoils depicting alchemical symbolism representing, not the transmutation of base metals into gold, but the spiritual transformation of base, leaden humanity into the pure gold of spiritual enlightenment.[45]

In the opinion of the French Mystical writer François Calí, in traveling from Chartres to Amiens one makes an almost imperceptible transition—"from the love of God to the love of Wisdom—which is in order, number and harmony—which can be equated with God, but which need not be."[46] Attributes of divine gnosis are order, number, and harmony, which were treasured by the Templar knights. Amiens cathedral, a wondrous, symphonic blend of space, stone, and light, was designed and constructed to celebrate the gnostic principal of Sophia, or sacred wisdom, and to house the Knights Templar's prize relic—the reliquary containing the severed head of John the Baptist. According to Tim's friend and colleague, the late Guy Jordan, a noted Provençal scholar of Templarism, this object of veneration is nothing less than *la vrai téte Baphometique Templier*– the true Baphometic head of the Templars.

There is a series of carved panels in the transept depicting the biblical story of John the Baptist, all coloured in the medieval fashion. To give emphasis to this idea, the outer wall of the choir is decorated with superbly sculpted bas-reliefs that depict his life and death, including one where the top of his severed head is being pierced by a knife. The implication of this piercing is not known, but its importance to the Templars can be seen in their burial practices. In Provence, one Templar church in Bargemon has had part of its floor replaced with transparent Perspex sheet, allowing a clear view of human remains in a crypt beneath. Each skull is pierced in the manner depicted at Amiens and a row of skulls and long bones can be seen. In a passage from the Gospel of Thomas, the importance of John the Baptist to the Templars can be discerned where Jesus is quoted as saying:

> Among those born of women, from Adam until John the Baptist, there is no one superior to John the Baptist that his eyes should not be lowered (before him).

Churches dedicated to John the Baptist exist in abundance throughout the Languedoc and Provence, in the lands once subject to Templar rule. In Trigance, Provence, there is an ingenious arrangement that allows a beam of light to illuminate the altar with a golden glow at dawn on the Baptist's feast day. Carvings of John the Baptist take precedence in most of the churches and chapels, yet contemporary carvings of the crucifixion are notable by their absence. These buildings are noted, in many cases, not only for their alchemical symbolism, but also as homes to the Black Madonna.

The Initiated Leaders

The Knights Templar, like the Rex Deus families from which they sprang, were from the very first, masters of dissembling. Beginning with their inception, as we have seen, they purported to be a devout and militant Christian order founded to protect pilgrims and the Holy Land. They were declared to be responsible, through their Grand Master, solely to the pope. Undoubtedly, the vast majority of the knights and all the sergeants, craftsmen, and auxiliary members were staunch followers of the Catholic faith. The founders and the real leaders from that time forward were the "heretics" and Gnostics. However, this was a matter of extreme secrecy. The French scholars Georges Caggar and Jean Robin claim:

> The Order of the Temple was indeed constituted of seven "exterior" circles dedicated to the minor mysteries, and of three "interior" circles corresponding to the initiation into the great mysteries. The nucleus was composed of seventy Templars. [47]

It would be conceivable to conclude from this that the devout Christian members of the order belonged to the exterior circles and would rarely be permitted to rise to a status that entitled them to join the inner ruling circles. Rex Deus restricted their membership of the secretive ruling clique to other known members of the family who had proved their worth, or who came from an impeccable background. Outsiders who had earned the trust and respect of their leaders might possibly have been accepted for admission. However, the nucleus would have been solely recruited from Rex Deus. The leaders of the Templar order were dedicated to the quest for gnostic enlightenment, whose fruits they used to improve the quality of the lives of all who lived in their territories.

CHAPTER 15

GENOCIDE IN THE NAME OF JESUS AND THE FOUNDATION OF THE INQUISITION

A truly amazing culture arose in the Midi in Southern France in the 12th and 13th centuries, imbued with the principles of love, democracy and religious toleration.[1] This scintillating culture developed under the tolerant rule and guidance of the local Rex Deus nobility who had held power there since their installation by Charlemagne, and who protected and guided the growth of a religious sect who encouraged economic stability and prosperity that was unequalled anywhere else in Christian Europe.[2] The largely autonomous nobles of the area allowed their rule to be moderated by a high degree of democratic control by the wealthy bourgeoisie in the prosperous towns and cities of the one-time Spanish Marches.[3] Throughout the area of Occitania, the present day departments of the Languedoc/Rousillion, the one dominant Catholic Church was rapidly losing its grip and was in a state of almost total decline.[4] The Rex Deus nobility had long tolerated and encouraged the large scale Jewish community of Septimania and those Jewish merchants who lived throughout their lands and now gave sanctuary, protection and encouragement to a heretical group known as the Cathars who claimed to follow the true teachings of Jesus.[5] The Cathar priesthood, known simply as the bonhommes or good men [6] followed an initiatory path and guided their flock who were called the 'hearers.' It was their critics within the Catholic Church who called them 'the Cathars' or 'pure ones'—a corruption of the Latin phrase *'hereticus perfectus[7]'.*

By the mid 12rh century the vast majority of the highly literate and sophisticated local nobility were predominantly anti-clerical and viewed the Cathars with considerable favour. Indeed, Raymond VI of Toulouse took a Cathar perfectus with him whenever he travelled. The Count of Foix was particularly indulgent towards the new sect and, indeed, his wife, after raising her family, became one of the perfecti herself.[8] Roger Trenceval, Count of Beziers and Carcassonne, was tutored by Cathar perfecti and later bacme a heroic defender of the Cathars, a crime for which he ultimately paid with his life. Indeed, according to one church historian, Guiraud, the minor nobility of the Lauragais, the densely populated country between Carcassonne and Toulouse were almost completely Cathar in belief. Another church apologist, Pierre des-Vaux-de-Chernay recorded that 'the lords of the Languedoc almost all protected and harboured the heretics… defending them against God and the Church.'[9]

The tolerance of the Rex Deus nobility for the Jews had supremely beneficial results for not only did the Jewish communities in Occitania enhance trade prospects but also they played an important role in Jewish religious life that soon impinged on Christian Europe. Along with the wider Jewish communities in Spain and Northern Italy they produced the first written form of the mystical tradition known as the Kabbala.[10] Thus under the influence of Jewish traders, prosperity grew steadily and the encouragement by the Cathars of creativity and skilled artisans on the fieds of leatherwork, textile manufacturing and paper making enhanced this trend and brought about an unparalleled level of prosperity.

Cathar Dualism

The Cathars were Gnostics with dualistic beliefs that probably originated in Zoroastrianism,[11] Pythagorean teachings, and Mithraism transformed by early Christian thinking. Some scholars suggest that it also owed a great deal to Manichaeism, the initiatory early Christian cult once followed by St Augustine of Hippo.[12] They believed that the earth and all that is in it were the creations of an evil God, only the human soul and spirit were created by the God of Love. The objective of their teaching was to reach a state of spiritual enlightenment that would free them from the cycle of re-incarnation. Their priests, the Perfecti were of both sexes, easily recognized by their distinctive robes, who lived in communities that betrayed no trace of the perfecti's original social status. They travelled the country in pairs, ministering to the needs of their flock, teaching and healing. In these healing duties they consciously replicated the habits of the disciples of Jesus and the Essenes using their deep knowledge of medicinal herbs moderated by spiritual insight. It is recorded in the *Gospel of Thomas* that Jesus told his disciples that they would become capable of doing everything he did and proof of this can be found in the manner in which the perfecti strove to continue his healing ministry. They lived simply and travelled by foot to tend to the needs of their people. They believed that Gnosis, or sacred knowledge, came as a gift from God to those who followed their initiatory path and was to be used to benefit the communities in which they lived. This Gnosis had been passed from Jesus to St John and thence to them, and their form of spiritual baptism, *the consolamentum*, was given to those who had undergone a three year novitiate and was deemed to be an outward sign of sacred enlightenment. It was by taking the consolamentum that a believer, or hearer, became a perfectus. This sacrament was also granted to believers on their deathbed.

As believers in reincarnation and the possible transmigration of souls into the bodies of animals, the perfecti ate no meat, but they did eat fish. They also abstained from all sexual activity. Hardly an attractive prospect for the more worldly in the community. Ordinary believers were completely exempt from this harsh regime and could eat meat, marry, have sex, go to war and engage in all normal activities. Holy Mother the Church used this freedom to accuse the Cathars of immorality. The believers role in life was to prepare themselves for the their spiritual baptism in their last hours of life, thus releasing their souls from further incarnations by immediate union with the Divine. Believers used a ritual form of greeting, known as the *melhorer*, to the perfecti that they encountered as they went about their business. The perfect would inevitably respond with a blessing.

By 1167 four dioceses had been established in Occitania, Agen, Albi, Carcassonne and Toulouse. Later a fifth was created at Razes. Further afield, another was established in the County of Champagne and yet another in France. There were six more in the Balkans and another six in the North of Italy, in Lombardy and Tuscany. Each diocese was led by a bishop assisted by a 'major son' and a 'minor son' elected from the perfecti. On the death of the Bishop, he was succeeded by the major son, the minor son rose in rank and a new minor son was elected. Ranked below these officials was a deaconate and the communities of the perfecti. The bestowing of the consolamentum signalled the start of an initiatory, life-long process in which they acquired deeper levels of enlightenment as they progressed. One teaching that they held in common with the Templars and the Rex Deus tradition was that they believed that Mary Magdelene was the wife of Jesus.[13]

The Cathar Heresy

One of the earliest references from the church to the Cathar heresy can be found in correspondence between Prior Eberwin of Steinfeld and Bernard of Clairvaux in which he refers to a group he called 'the Cologne Heretics' led by an apostate monk called Henry. The resulting pressure from church authorities caused Henry to move to the far more tolerant territory of Toulouse.[14] Henry was soon followed by Bernard of Clairvaux himself. Henry was under the protection of the Count of Toulouse so Bernard wrote to the count and described the state of affairs he had found in the count's domains:

> The churches are without congregations, congregations are without priests, priests are without proper reverence and, finally, Christians are without Christ.[15]

He continued in the same vein by writing 'he revels in all his fury among the flock of Christ.' Bernard encountered a vigorous tide of anti-clericalism in Occitania, especially among the nobility, but was forced to admit that the Cathars were a sect of simple and devout spirituality led by a gifted priesthood: he described the perfecti in the following terms 'No one's sermons are more spiritual.[16]' At this time the Pope in Rome was alerted by clergy in Liege that a new heresy had emerged that had 'overflowed into various regions of France. One so varied and so manifold that it seems impossible to characterize it under a single name.[17] This new heresy which had its own hierarchy of priests and prelates was followed by believers and was characterized by militant anti-clericalism and a distinct anti-Catholic bias. It had followers in the Low Countries, Lombardy and the Languedoc.[18] But where did it come from?

Cathar Origins?

There is a generally held consensus among scholars that Catharism may well have sprung from Balkan roots. In, or around, 930 CE, a priest known as Bogomil had preached a similar Gnostic and dualistic doctrine in Bulgaria.[19] There is a high degree of plausibility to this hypothesis as after the Crusades, the Empire of Byzantium had encouraged trade with the west and in consequence, there was now a viable route by which thinking could pass from east to west as well as trade goods. Thus the Crusades had inadvertently created the means by which, initiatory, dualistic Gnosticism could be transmitted. The so-called Cathar heresy was an initiatory form of Christianity based upon *The Gospel of Love*, the secret and original Gospel of John, which taught that Jesus had come not to redeem mankind from sin but to reveal the true 'Way' to reach enlightenment.[20] The Cathars knew that the true teachings of Jesus was the most effective route to attain real spiritual union with God. They also knew that this spiritual pathway had its origins in Ancient Egypt, had been transmitted through mystical Judaism, the Essenes, the teaching of John the Baptist and had reached its peak of perfection with the words of Jesus. For them the true parent of their own church was the first 'Church' in Jerusalem led by James the Righteous, the brother of Jesus.

With both the Catholic Church and the Cathars claiming to be founded on the teaching of Jesus, they held surprisingly different beliefs. The Cathars absolutely denied the validity of any of the Catholic sacraments, especially Holy Communion.[21] They denied that the church hierarchy, including the pope, had any authority at all and argued vehemently against the Catholic concept of 'grace' which was absolutely central to Church Dogma and belief.[22] Cathar refusal to venerate the cross was based on the simple and logical question 'Why should we worship the rack on which our teacher had died?' For the people of the Cathar faith, Jesus was not a redeemer but the divinely inspired teacher who had brought them the supreme gift of Gnosis.[23] The Inquisition later accused the Cathars of practicing some form of 'sorcery' on the feast day of St John the Baptist and repeated the same accusation against the Templars at their trial—which may indicate that the church hierarchy believed that there was some degree of commonality between the beliefs of both the Cathars and the Templars.

The Crusade Against Fellow Christians

The Cather religion had taken deep root in the Languedoc, and soon grew to be all-pervasive in strength and power while the Catholic Church was in severe decline. Holy Mother the Church which had never tolerated rival religions in its realms, reacted in its traditional manner, firstly they sent a preaching ministry led by a fanatical Spanish priest, Dominic Guzman,[24] whose glib sermons fell on very deaf ears. His final sermon was an ominous and brutal warning of what was to come:

> For years now I have brought you words of peace. I have preached and I have implored, I have wept. But, as the common people say in Spain, if a blessing will not work, then it must be the stick. Now we shall stir up princes and bishops against you, and they, alas, will call together nations and peoples and many will perish by the sword. Towers will be destroyed, walls overturned and you will be reduced to slavery. Thus force will prevail where gentleness has failed.[25]

The congregation who heard this terrifying speech was completely incapable of understanding the appalling reality it prophesied. The gentle and tolerant population of Occitania were peaceful folk who did not know and simply could not comprehend the brutal methodology that the church used to extirpate heresy. They soon found out when, in 1209, Pope Innocent III declared a religious war, or crusade, against the Cathars. By this call, every committed Christian who took part for forty days or more, would be granted remission from all their previous sins, and any they might commit during the Crusade.[26] Crusaders were also granted the right to seize the property of any heretic, irrespective of their rank, and were, in effect, granted a licence to kill, pillage, murder and rape in the name of Jesus who the church called 'the Prince of Peace.' Knights, nobles, landless younger sons of the nobility, peasants and foot soldiers flocked to wage war under the papal banner and fought with venemous cruelty. Along with this bloodthirsty and devout mob of fortune seekers came the clergy who treated any suspected heretic with torture and then sent them to the warm embrace of death by burning at the stake. Despite this malodorous military expedition being granted official recognition as a Crusade, neither the Knights Templr nor the Knights Hospitaller took any significant part in the war.[27] The

King of France also stood aside until much later when, in 1229, he seized the opportunity to annexe Occitania into his Kingdom.

In the month of July 1209, the crusading army laid siege to the prosperous city of Beziers. Its lord, Viscount Raimon-Roger Trenceval, knew that the city was virtually indefensible and withdrew to his other centre of power, the superbly fortified city of Carcassonne. Along with him went the entire large Jewish population of Beziers who knew only too well of the persecution their fellow Jews had suffered at the hands of the staunchly Catholic populations of the North. The people of Beziers were advised by their bishop to surrender but ignored that and prepared to defend their homes.[28] The siege was brief and, on the evening before the city fell, the leaders of the Crusade who were well aware that the vast majority of its inhabitants were Catholics, asked the papal legate how they should treat their co-religionists when the city fell. They were told 'Show mercy to neither age nor sex…Catholic or Cathar… kill them all… God will know his own when they get to him.'[29] A typically Catholic interpretation of the words of Jesus—'Love they neighbour as thyself.'

The crusaders followed these brutal instructions to the letter, twenty thousand people, men women and children, were slaughtered without mercy—seven thousand of them who had taken sanctuary in the Cathedral under the protection of their clergy, were mercilessly murdered in those holy precincts. Pierre des Vaux-de-Chernay claimed that this was a punishment for the sins of the Cathars and their blasphemy against Mary Magdalene on whose feast day the city fell, he wrote:

> Beziers was taken on St Mary Magdalene's day, Oh supreme justice of providence! …The heretics claimed that St Mary Magdalene was the concubine of Jesus Christ. …it was therefore with just cause that these disgusting dogs were taken and massacred during the feast day of the one they had insulted.[3-]

The massacre was a deliberate attempt to terrorise other towns and cities into submission and one important result was that Narbonne surrendered unconditionally and not only offered substantial material support to the crusaders but also handed over to the crusaders the perfecti living in the city as well as all the considerable Jewish property within the city walls.

After the massacre in Beziers and the surrender of Narbonne, the crusaders besieged the well-fortified city of Carcassonne. After the first week, Viscount Trenceval and eleven of his companions were offered safe passage if they left the city and all its occupants to the tender mercies of the crusading forces, an offer that was vehemently refused. By the end of the second week, water supplies within the city were running low and the crusaders blocked all access to the river. On the 15th day of August, Trenceval was offered a safe-passage to conduct negotiations for the surrender but despite this assurance he was immediately imprisoned[31] and any rights of succession by his son were denied. According to most histories of this event, the cause of his eventual death in prison, in November 1209, was undoubtedly murder. When Carcassonne did surrender, the lives of all its citizens were spared but they were forced to leave the city in their underwear and all their property and possessions were forfeited to the crusaders. One of the leaders of the invading army, a certain Simon de Montfort was awarded all the feudal rights, privileges and lands of the Trenceval family.[32]

Simon de Montfort became the undisputed leader of the Crusade from that point on. And, as he tightened his grip on the Languedoc, flesh fuelled flames from 'heretics' burning at the stake flickered skywards with appalling regularity. The first public burning took place at Castres; at Minerve one hundred and forty were burned; four hundred Cathars were incinerated after the fall of Lavaur; forty more at Les Casses;[33] five thousand men, women and children were hacked to death when Marmande fell in 1226 and after the year-long siege of Montsegur, the last Cathar stronghold, two hundred and twenty-five more were burnt alive.[34] That is just some of those immolated as heretics. Appalling acts of brutality and carnage punctuated the crusade, After Lavaur, the eighty knights who had so bravely defended the place, were sentenced to be hung, but the gallows collapsed and, as an act of 'mercy' De Montfort had their throats cut. The Chatelaine, Lady Giraude was handed over to the soldiers and repeatedly raped before being thrown down a well and stoned to death.[35] Following the fall of Bram, one hundred of the defenders were selected at random and had their lips, ears and noses cut off, ninety nine of them had their eyes gouged out and the one remaining was left with one eye so that he could lead this cruelly maimed procession to the Castle of Cabaret as a warning to its defenders of what would happen to them if they did not surrender, Cabaret neither surrendered nor fell. At the battle of Muret, the slaughter was far greater than at the siege of Beziers. In addition to this seemingly unending catalogue of butchery and brutality, a scorched earth policy was adopted to starve the population of Occitanie into submission. The crusaders justified this dreadful behaviour by stating that they were defending Holy Mother the Church against heretics who had no rights. In this they had the support of several popes and the local clergy who made profit from the acquisition of the property of the heretics. All done in the name of the loving Jesus!

The Templars and Hospitallers

Despite the fact that this brutal and genocidal campaign had been officially declared a Crusade, neither of the two main orders of warrior monks whose *raison d'etre* was to wage war against the enemies of Christendom, took any significant part in the war. We do not have any record of the views on their non-participation held by any of the popes concerned, but we do have records of the reasons the orders put forward to explain their behaviour. More than thirty percent of all Templar holdings in mainland Europe were in Occitania and this area was also liberally adorned with Knights Hospitaller properties. These two orders who rarely have agreed on anything were suspiciously united in their excuses. They both clamed that the deeds of donation of their properties in the Languedoc, expressly forbade them from being used them for warlike activities. They also claimed, loudly and repeatedly, that these holdings were purely commercial, unfortified, understaffed, not garrisoned in the military sense and therefore useless as military bases or strongpoints in time of war.[36] There were also unexplained links between the Templars and the Cathars that continue to puzzle historians. As the crusade reached its peak, it is a matter of record that the Templars gave sanctuary to knights who had defended the Cathars.[37] The bodies of such knights were later exhumed and burnt by the Inquisition.

The Holy Office of the Inquisition

A new Church organization, the Inquisition, was founded in 1233 to finally extirpate the Cathar heresy. Led and staffed by the new Dominican order, founded by Dominic Guzman mentioned earlier, its purpose was to eliminate Catharism for once and for all.[38] This new Christian gift of the peace soon proved to be just as terrifying as the recent war. Torture was a routine part of any interrogation and anyone accused of heresy was denied legal representation. Torture, harassment and burning at the stake were the means employed by the Dominican Inquisitors to implement Jesus' command 'to love thy ene-mies.[39]'

If those accused of heresy abjured their faith they would not necessarily be sentenced to death, their punishment could include life imprisonment, loss of property or having to wear a yellow cross on their clothes. The yellow cross was, in fact, a slow and lingering death sentence as anyone who gave food or shelter to one who wore it would, in turn, be hauled before the Inquisition on a charge of heresy. This ruthless and all pervading reign of terror became a last-ing part of Catholic repression and is still with us today. Now it is not called the Inquisition but survives under the innocuous title 'the Congregation of the Doctrine of the Faith' and was, until his election as pope, headed by Cardinal Ratzinger, who later became Pope Benedict. Yet, in its primary objective, the Inquisition failed, many Cathars fled to Tuscany or Scotland, others simply went underground, but as an organised religion, the Cathar faith seemed to vanish completely by the end of the 14th century. Some joined the Templars but that proved to be only a temporary refuge for that brave knightly order was soon to become yet another victim of the dreaded Inquisition.

CHAPTER 16

THE DECLINE AND FALL OF THE KNIGHTS TEMPLAR

Goethe once proclaimed that coming events cast their shadows before them. That is to say, significant occurrences do not rise out of a mythical vacuum, unheralded or out of the sky; they are rather the culmination of a series of apparently unrelated circumstances that serve to lay the foundations for the future. In retrospect, we can discern in the historical record a cumulative change of events that weakened the power of the Knights Templar, deprived them of their bases in the Holy Land and their reason for existence, and ultimately displayed their vulnerability to apparently weaker forces.

The renowned leader Salah-al-Din Yusif ibn Ayyub, or Saladin, who lead the Muslim armies to victory over the European Crusaders, was born in 1138. He was the son of a skilled general, Najm-al-Din Ayyup, the young Saladin excelled in learning before he took up a military career in the service of the Saracen leader, Nur-el-Din. Before the year ended in 1138, through diplomacy, political realism, and military prowess, he had united disparate factions of the Muslim world and was ready to act on his lifelong ambition—to wage *jihad*, or holy war, against the Christian forces of the kingdom of Jerusalem.

In 1187, Saladin's victory at the Horns of Hattin not only defeated the largest Christian army ever assembled in the Holy Land; it also set in motion the final decline of crusader power in that war-torn country. Notwithstanding that the Christian defeat was caused by the ill-tempered strategic incompetence of

Gerald de Ridefort, the Templar Grand Master, Saladin was meticulous with planning and had superb military skills. At the end of the battle, Saladin ordered the execution of all 230 surviving knights of both the Templar and the Hospitaller orders. He was noted as saying: "I wish to purify the lands of these two monstrous orders, whose practices are of no use, who will never renounce their hostility and will render no services as slaves."[1]

Saladin knew that both orders followed rules that forbade them from being ransomed. Therefore, after each man was offered the opportunity to convert to Islam, which predictably was rejected, he was handed over to the Sufis for beheading. Many people have speculated why the Sufis undertook such a gruesome task when their beliefs and those of the Templars had so much in common. The answer is quite simple: The Sufis believed that all warriors who died for their beliefs went straight to paradise. Moreover, the Knights Templar and the Hospitallers, as Christian martyrs, knew they would go straight to heaven, so death held no fear for them. Like the good soldiers they were, the Sufis obeyed orders, knowing that the victim's instant entry into paradise was a far more noble and merciful fate than a lifetime of slavery.

Saladin's conduct when Jerusalem fell to his army later that same year stood in marked contrast to the bloody day that the holy city was captured by the Christian armies in 1095. There had been a gruesome blood bath, with the crusaders killing everyone in sight—Christian, Jew, and Muslim—until the horses of the conquering knights waded up to their knees in blood. Once the forces of Islam recaptured the city, Saladin negotiated a peaceful surrender and its inhabitants were offered the chance to be ransomed and not massacred. Following the capture of Jerusalem, the remaining crusader states in the Holy Land lingered for over a century. They were picked off little by little, until, in 1291 with the fall of Acre, Beirut, and Sidon, the Christian forces lost their last viable foothold in that sacred blood-soaked country. After this event, the warrior monks lost the main justification for their existence.

Resentment Against the Templars

An establishment as large and powerful as the Templars that was backed by papal prestige, economic success, and popular esteem derived from its valorous actions in the Holy Land could not help but excite the envy of others. Their influence and independence tended to foster arrogance, and the degree of papal privilege they enjoyed caused lasting resentment among the episcopate and the secular clergy.[2] Much of this resentment arose from the fact that the Templars paid no tithes—a situation that resulted in a massive loss of revenue to the local church, for the tithes that had been paid into their coffers ceased once lands were donated to the order. For instance, it would usually have collected considerable income from burials. However, when associate members of the order or anyone who donated lands, money, or goods to the Templars—needed burial, they were interred on Templar lands by the order's own priests and not by the secular clergy. Likewise, others who were indebted to the Templars had their own axes to grind; there was hardly a crowned head in Europe who did not owe money to the warrior-monks.

Matters reached a climax with the election of a new Grand Master in 1293. There were allegations of irregularities in this election and it is documented that, for some inexplicable reason, the Grand Master of the Hospitallers was invited to guide and advise the chapter of their main rivals in this closely fought election.[3] The end result was that an elderly, and reputedly illiterate, knight from the north of France, Jacques de Molay, was elected as the 23rd Grand Master of the Templar Order. Most descriptions of this tragic figure agree that he was brave, strict, and none too bright.

Soon after the fall of Acre, Pope Nicholas IV died in Rome. His demise triggered one of the most distorted episodes in papal history. During that time, a succession of popes, all riddled with corruption, were elected improperly; forced abdications were followed by elections subject to bribery and violence. Eventually, accusations of murder, idolatry, simony, sodomy, and heresy were levelled against Pope Boniface VIII.[4] Following this, under the malign influence of a cunning and unscrupulous monarch, King Philippe le Bel of France, Bertrand de Goth, Archbishop of Bordeaux, who was not even a cardinal, was elected to fill the papal throne as Pope Clement V.

Clement became, in effect, a makeshift pope chosen as supposedly neutral candidate to prevent civil war between the two major contending families in Rome. In order to distance himself from the tense situation in the papal city, he resided in Avignon where he reigned in considerable splendour, ruling his flock at the behest of his puppet-master, King Philippe.

King Philippe Le Bel

In October 1285, Philippe IV succeeded to the throne of France. Even though he was of the Capetian line, the Rex Deus traditions had long since died within the royal Family of France. King Louis IX, Philippe's grandfather, had been a sincere and zealous Catholic and was canonized as St. Louis for his crusading activities. France was now a large kingdom, having gained Normandy, Anjou, Maine, Touraine, the county of Toulouse, and the entire Languedoc. However, despite its size, the kingdom was in the grip of acute financial difficulties exacerbated by the costs of various wars that Philippe had to wage.

During the last decade of the 13th century, Philippe levied a 10 per-cent tax on the Church and imposed punitive financial measures on Languedoc. At the time of the war with England from1294 to 1297, forced loans were frequently imposed, and, between 1295 and 1306, Philippe repeatedly debased the coinage.[5] Eventually, this provoked riots against the king, who was forced to seek refuge in the Paris temple, the headquarters of the Knights Templars.[6] He owed 800,000 livres tournois to Lombard bankers who were despoiled by these unpaid loans and their assets were seized. The corrupt king devised a scheme to cover himself by cancelling his debt and producing substantial income. The Lombard bankers, in the 1290s, were subject to seizures, fines, and expulsions, until, in 1311, all debts were appropriated and they were imprisoned.[7]

Another obvious target were the Jews of France. In 1295, Philippe had their "usurious profits" confiscated and they were forced to reveal details of all their financial affairs. During July and August of 1306, all Jewish property throughout France was seized and the penniless dispossessed owners expelled from the country.[8] The majority of Jewish families from the Languedoc fled for sanctuary to Moorish Spain; Jews from other parts of France fled to Alsace, Burgundy, and northern Italy. A sizable group emigrated to the Muslim-controlled Holy Land. No one was safe from the corruption of this desperate and destitute monarch, especially those to whom he owed large sums of money. Philippe extorted a high price from De Goth for ensuring his election to the papacy. In doing so, he included his right to keep the tithes collected by the Church in France for a period of five years and a promise that the new pope would reside in Avignon under his watchful eye. Twelve of the monarch's chosen clergy were made cardinals and, as reported by some sources, a secret condition was imposed that was never publicly disclosed.[9] In contemplation of an amalgamation between the Hospitallers and the Templars, Clement V wrote letters to the Grand Masters of both orders inviting them to France in 1306. They were advised to "travel as secretly as possible and with a very small train as you will find plenty of your knights on this side of the sea."[10] The Grand Master of the Hospitaller, William de Villart, declined this invitation, explaining that he was engaged in an assault on the Turkish stronghold of Rhodes. It is apparent that both the pope and the king were aware of this, as it was public knowledge. Jacques de Molay did not have a ready excuse, however, and, defying the explicit instructions from the pope, set sail for the Templar port of La Rochelle with a fleet of eighteen ships. On board the fleet were sixty senior knights of the order,[11] 150,000 gold florins, and so much silver bullion that it required twelve packhorses to carry it.[12] De Molay knew that he might have to use bribery if reasoned argument against the proposed merger failed. Therefore, a large train of knights, packhorses, and transport arrived at the temple in Paris, where the king welcomed them.[13] The Templar Grand Master had, so he believed, prepared his case against amalgamation with considerable skill. He was prepared to declare that, as both orders had rendered signal services to the Church and the cause of Christianity, there was no rational reason to initiate change. He also used a spiritual argument: as the members had chosen their respective orders under the guidance of God, it might be blasphemous to insist that they now join another. He was ready to point out, as each order owned substantial properties and wealth, any move to amalgamate them might well bring dispute in its train. What he could not reveal to either the pope or king was the central issue that the Order of the Knights Templar was the military creation of descendants of the high priests of the original temple in Jerusalem.

However, De Molay's preparations were futile, for the proposed amalgamation of the two orders was just an excuse used to tempt the Grand Master to exchange the safety of Cyprus for the danger of France. During the funeral of the king's sister-in-law, Catherine de Valois, on Thursday, 12 October 1307, De Molay occupied the seat of honour near the king.[14] Within twenty-four hours, he would find himself in a very different position.

The Demise of the Templars

At the break of dawn on Friday, 13 October 1307, the king's agents throughout France opened sealed orders that had been distributed nearly one month earlier, on 14 September.[15] Following the instructions within them, French soldiers invaded every Templar property within the kingdom, arresting the Templar Grand Master, the sixty knights of the inner circle, and all but twenty-four of the members of the order residing in France.[16] The preceptor of France, Gerard de Villiers, was the only leading Templar to escape.

In order to justify this massive wave of arrests, charges were levelled against the premier warrior order of Christianity that was described as:

> ...a bitter thing, a lamentable thing which is horrible to contemplate, terrible to hear of, a detestable crime, an execrable evil, an abominable work, a detestable disgrace, a thing almost inhuman, indeed set apart from all humanity.[17]

These warrior monks who had fought so valiantly in the name of Christianity were accused of causing Christ "injuries more terrible than those he endured on the cross,[18] a comment that echoed the charge against the Cathars that they were more evil than the Saracens. Indeed, if one studies the charges brought against heretics throughout European history, there is an appalling similarity about them—as if the accusers, having devoted such thought and effort to devising new methods of torment for their victims, ran out of ideas when it came to framing the charges and simply conformed to tired and formulaic phrases.

King Philippe le Bel was circumspect in his actions, and extremely careful to explain that he was only acting at the request of Guillaume de Paris[19] the chief Inquisitor, a deputy of the pope and the king's confessor. Nevertheless, with the king's firm grip on Clement V and his relationship with Guillaume, it is apparent that Philippe was the prime mover in the entire affair and that, in this case, the Inquisition was acting as an arm of the state and not at the behest of the pope. It is clear that, although Philippe and Clement may have discussed these matters prior to 13 October, the king had neither sought the pope's consent for the arrests nor informed him of them until after the event.[20]

Long before their first interrogation of the knights, the Inquisitors had subjected many of them to threats and acts of torture. The Inquisitors, if nothing else, were consistent with their own established, although dubious, standards in that, after each victim's deposition was taken it was duly recorded that the accused had "told the pure and entire truth for the safety of his soul" and not because he had been subjected to intimidation and torture.[21] From the 138 depositions taken from the hearings in Paris in October 1307, which included those of Jacques de Molay and his leading knights, only four record that men were able to withstand the horrors to which they were subjected.

In other parts of France, the results were comparable. The inquisitorial records reveal that, as usual, the Inquisitors were scrupulous in keeping within their papal policy of *ecclesia non novit sanguinem*—the Church shall not shed blood—and that, therefore, the tortures applied to the Templars were the standard ones that proved to be effective over the years. Despite the English authors Knight and Lomas' allegation that the Inquisition crucified Jacques de Molay, there is not one shred of credible evidence that the Inquisition ever used crucifixion on any of its victims at that time. The fanatical Dominicans would have considered the crucifixion of anyone the ultimate blasphemy.

The Terrible Twins

King Philippe had outwardly conformed to established procedures by using the Inquisition; nevertheless, Pope Clement V was outraged at this apparent usurpation of his own prerogative. It was especially vexatious for him, as the Templars were responsible to the pope and the pope alone. Clement, however, lacked both the power and the will to stop the proceedings. In a futile attempt to regain some semblance of control over the situation, he issued a papal directive, dated 22 November 1307, ordering all Christian rulers in Europe to arrest all the Templars[22] in their domains and confiscate their properties in the name of the pope.[23]

The missive did not receive universal acclamation or agreement. The King of England had already refused to give "easy credence" to the charges against the Templars and written as much to the pope. Likewise, he had written to the kings of Portugal, Castile, Aragon, and Naples in terms that left no doubt that he supported the maligned order. The terms of the papal directive, nevertheless, left him no choice, and he replied that he would initiate action against the order "in the quickest and best way."

His actions were to some extent different from those taken by the king of France, however, in that very few knights were arrested and imprisoned: most were allowed to stay in their preceptories and, as torture was forbidden under English law, no one confessed to heresy when interrogated. Therefore, proceedings in England were unproductive until June 1311, when one knight, Stephen de Stapelbrugge, confessed to denying Christ and claimed homosexuality had been encouraged within the order. This event occurred after papal pressure had resulted in full application of ecclesiastical law and the use of torture had at last been sanctioned, a situation that resulted in further confessions.[24]

The trial of the order, in Portugal, resulted in a verdict of not guilty, and in Scotland, the trial if the Templars, conducted by William de Lamberton, bishop of St. Andrews, brought in, under his explicit directions, the old Scottish verdict of, "not proven, despite the best efforts of the prosecutors."[25] Lamberton was a close colleague of Baron Henry St. Clair of Roslin, and the leader of a shadowy group responsible for organizing support for Robert the Bruce in his struggle to gain the throne of Scotland.

The archbishop of Santiago de Compostela wrote to the pope pleading that the Templars be acquitted, especially as their skills and resources were desperately needed in the wars against the Moorish forces in Spain.[26] The Rex Deus family of the House of Savoy, the rulers of Lombardy, ensured that most of the bishops in their realm supported the Templar cause and those bishops issued a statement claiming that they could find no incriminating evidence against the order. There were some who were less favourable, and did bring convictions; in Germany and in Greece the results were equally mixed. However, in France, the agony of the Templars continued until it reached its fiery finale in 1314.

The Death of the Last Templar Grand Master Jacques de Molay

The archbishop of Sens, on 18 March 1314, accompanied by three papal commissioners, took their place on a stage erected outside the west front of the cathedral of Notre Dame de Paris. The archbishop was hardly a disinterested participant, for he had already supervised the burning of fifty-four Templar knights in 1310.[28] The confessions that had been extracted from the knights under means of extreme torture were read out to the assembled crowd by the bishop of Alba and he pronounced their sentence to perpetual imprisonment.

At this stage, the inept and illiterate Jacques de Molay redeemed himself by an act of calculated bravery that will never be forgotten. The once-great warrior, now a tortured wreck, seventy years of age and physically and mentally scarred by seven years in the care of the Inquisition, indicated that he wished to speak to the people. The assembled bishops, presuming that De Molay wished to confess, graciously granted him leave to address the crowd. Then, the Grand

Master made a speech that assured his immortality:

> It is just that, in so terrible a day, and in the last moments of my life, I should discover all the iniquity of falsehood, and make the truth triumph. I declare, then, in the face of heaven and earth, and acknowledge, though to my eternal shame, that I have committed the greatest of crimes but…it has been the acknowledging of those which have been so foully charged on the order. I attest—and truth obliges me to attest—that it is innocent! I made the contrary declaration only to suspend the excessive pains of torture, and to mollify those who made me endure them. I know the punishments which have been inflicted on all the knights who had the courage to revoke a similar confession; but the dreadful spectacle which is presented to me is not able to make me confirm one lie by another. The life offered me on such infamous terms I abandon without regret.[28]

Jacques de Molay's refutation of his previous confession was greeted with roars of support from the crowd. Geoffroi de Charnay moved to stand next to his Grand Master as a sign of support for his statement and spoke in similar terms, declaring the sanctity of the Templar order. Furthermore, he also revoked his previous confession.[29]

Immediately, the clergy suspended the proceedings, cleared the square, and reported the entire account to the king. Philippe put an end to the matter once and for all by sentencing the two brave knights to a slow and lingering death. On the Isle des Javiaux, on the same day in the evening, the execution took place. Prepared for them was a slow, hot, and smokeless fire to ensure that that the Templars' agony would be prolonged as possible, and both Jacques de Molay and Geoffroi de Charnay were slowly cooked to death. Legend maintains that, before being placed on the fire, De Molay cursed Pope Clement V and King Philippe le Bel and called upon both of them to appear before God in heaven within the year.[30] If this legend holds any validity, then it must be said that both the accursed king and the pope heeded that prophetic call: Pope Clement, who had suffered from chronic ill health for many years, died on 20 April, and King Philippe IV of France followed him to the grave on 29 November the same year.

The Accusations

The list of formal accusations made against the Templars was extensive—denial of Christ and defiling the cross, ritual murder and a ritual kiss, adoration of an idol's head (Baphomet), wearing a cord of heretical significance, alteration of the Mass, an unorthodox form of absolution, homosexual aberration, and treachery to other Christian forces.[31] The fact was that the vast majority of Templars were devout Christians and these charges were mostly unsubstantiated. As for the inner circle of Rex Deus nobles who actually controlled the order, they were undoubtedly heretics in the true meaning of the word, the accusations, however, were largely fabricated. Whereas they believed Jesus came to reveal and not redeem, they were under obligation from their own secret traditions to follow the outward form of prevailing religion, namely Christianity. Considering this point, most of the charges brought against them were baseless. The last, nevertheless, may appear to be justified, although it probably resulted from strategic incompetence rather than any collusion with the Muslims. Some of the usually charges levelled against anyone accused of heresy were homosexuality and sexual immorality. The wearing of a cord of heretical significance does have some veracity, for the initiation ceremonies they used a cable-tow noose just as the modern craft of Freemasonry does today.

The most plausible charge against the order was that of idolatry—adoring the bearded head of the idol, Baphomet. Established beyond all doubt was their veneration of one bearded head in particular, for the cathedral of Amiens was founded to house one object of veneration that was of supreme importance to the Templars—the reliquary reputed to hold the head of St. John the Baptist. There have been other bearded heads found on Templar properties, such as the large painting of a head discovered at the English holding at Templecombe in Somerset.

French scholar J-A Durbec catalogues among the symbols that he claims are indicative of Templar influence the "Mandylion", a depiction of a bearded head on a cloth, much like the veil of Veronica or the Turin shroud.[32] Noel Currer-Briggs, an English scholar, suggest that there is a considerable body of evidence that the Shroud of Turin was the original used to design the head at Templecombe and that the inner circle of the Templar order used it.[33] This may yet prove to be a valid case, since an internationally renown microbiologist, Dr. Leonicio Garxa-Valdes, has now discredited the carbon dating of the Turin Shroud on purely scientific grounds.[34]

Ostensibly, the most nonsensical charge was that of ritual murder. It may, however, have some tenuous basis in Templar ritual. It is likely that the initiation ceremonies of the medieval Knights Templar had much in common with those of the Children of Solomon. Furthermore, it is not irrational to suggest that they included a re-enactment of the murder of Hiram Abif, much as the Freemasons use today. It quite possibly led to making of this otherwise inexplicable charge.

Papal Suppression of the Order

The Templars were never, as an organization, convicted of any of the charges, whether true or false, brought against them. Yet, on 22 March 1312, the decision to suppress the order was announced in a papal bull, *vox in excelso*. The wording of the document is revealing, in actuality, the pope suppressed the order without condemning it:

> ...considering, moreover, the grave scandal which has risen from among these things against the Order, which it did not seem could be checked while this Order remained in being... even without blame being attached to the brothers...not by judicial sentence, but by way of provisions, or apostolic ordinance, we abolish the aforesaid Order of the Temple...and we subject it to perpetual prohibition...Which if anyone acts against this, he will incur the sentence of excommunication *ipso facto*.[35]

Now that the order was officially dissolved, the next perplexing situation was what to do with the order's vast estates, financial assets, and other possessions. Pope Clement wanted to transfer all the Templar assets to the rival Order of the Knights Hospitaller, however, he was opposed by most of his own clergy. Ultimately, the pope got his own way and, in another papal bull, announced the confiscation and transfer. The few exceptions he allowed were Templar properties in the kingdoms of Castile, Aragon, Portugal, and Majorca. In France, however, before any transfer could take place, deductions were authorized in favour of King Philippe. These covered the cost of the provisional administration of the properties since the time of the original arrest, and the expenses incurred by the confinement and interrogation of the knights of the order. Thus, the Knights Templar were made to pay for their imprisonment and torture.

The fate of the Templar treasure that the Philippe saw during his stay in the Paris Temple and the substantial sums he observed being carried into the temple when Jacques de Molay and his large train arrived from La Rochelle is an unsolved mystery that still provokes intense speculation. After the initial arrests were made, the king's seneschals raided the temple, the treasure had vanished, and by the time his troops reached La Rochelle, the Templar's Atlantic fleet, along with the eighteen ships that had carried Jacques de Molay and his retinue from Cyprus, had disappeared, its destination unknown.

Several explanations have been proposed for the mysterious disappearance of both the Templar treasure and the fleet. One account, so far uncorroborated, claims that an unspecified sum was transported northward to Belgium in a cart covered by hay. Historians, Stephen Dafoe and Alan Butler maintain that much of the Templar treasure was secretly transported eastward to Switzerland, where the Templars owned considerable property. They propose that the Templars knights then went underground and used their assets and skills to found that country's banking system.[36] Did the advent of the Swiss banking owe its origin to the Knights Templar? No on can as yet can confirm this, but it is a question certainly worth following. These speculations are not mutually exclusive, nor do they negate the third hypothesis, which at least has the merit of plausibility and, more important perhaps, is substantiated by considerable circumstantial evidence. In order to understand this theory, however, we must first examine the fate of the surviving members of the newly suppressed order.

The Fate of the Survivors

After the dissolution of the order, individual Templar knights fled throughout Europe. Their fate is hardly mysterious and can be easily established, as many of them joined other warrior orders. Some were absorbed into the Teutonic Knights, who were carving out their own fief on the shores of the Baltic; many joined the Order of Calatrava in the kingdom of Aragon; others, equally interested in fighting the infidels, joined either the Knights of Alcantara or the Knights of Santiago and continued their service in Spain.

The Knights of the Sword, also known as the Knights of Santiago, became affiliated with the Knights Hospitaller to ensure their survival, proving that they had learned a lesson from the persecution of the Templars. They, also, became extremely powerful and, by the end of the 15th century, controlled over 200 commanderies throughout Spain.[37] The order changed its name to the Knights of Christ while in Portugal and continued to administer the old Templar properties. They also switched their allegiance and obedience from the pope to the Portuguese king and carried on much as before. Numerous knights that had fled joined this renamed order, but soon, the rule of the Order of the Knights of Christ was changed to accept only those born in Portugal.

Some of the knights, in England, were granted small pensions and others simply ended their days in other monastic orders. Many fled for sanctuary to Lombardy, where many Cathars had sought refuge before them. Lombardy was known not only for its tolerance, but also as a centre of banking that certainly enjoyed a measure of resurgence after the suppression of the Templars. Nevertheless, it would be prudent not to pay too much emphasis on Templar exiles as the source of this renewed activity for, with the suppression of the Templar order, the Lombard's main competitor's in financial services was destroyed. A certain number of Templars just seemed to vanish.[38]

Templars in Scotland

There was one refuge in Europe where the pope's writ simply did run— Scotland. Precipitated by a bitter conflict with the crown, the kingdom of the Scots was riven by civil war. Robert the Bruce, the main contender, was excommunicated for the ritual murder of one of his rivals, John Comyn, on Church premises. The nobles ignored the papal degree against Robert, and they were also excommunicated. This, too, was ignored and the pope, in an act of total desperation, excommunicated the entire country.

Many Templars fled by sea to this Celtic safe haven and, along with those who came on foot over the border from England and the Templars who were stationed in Scotland, offered their assistance to Robert the Bruce. During the battle of Bannockburn that finally secured the throne for the Bruce and completely vanquished the English invader, 432 Templar knights, including Sir Henry St. Clair, Baron of Roslyn, and his sons, William and Henry, took part in the final charge that routed the English army and preserved independence.[39] After Bannockburn, Rex Deus tradition recounts that, as an act of gratitude and recognition, King Robert the Bruce became the Sovereign Grand Master of the Templar Order.[40]

Above all, the king was pragmatic; he knew that, in order for his new realm to survive, he would have to live in the medieval world as it really was, and that meant making peace with the pope in Rome. Correspondingly, he warned the Templars in Scotland to go underground—a feat that, with the assistance of the Rex Deus and Templar families, was accomplished in a manner that ensured the long-term survival of Templar traditions. In Scotland, Templar properties were passed to the Knights Hospitallers. However, the manner in which those holdings were administered in Bruce's realm was very different from their administrations in the rest of Europe. Templar holdings, in most countries, were absorbed into the itineraries of the Hospitallers. They were accounted for separately in Scotland, as though they were "being held in trust" and might be restored to their rightful owners at some time in the future.

Everything else aside, what of the vanished Templar treasure? It cannot be established as fact, but the French Masonic tradition recounts that it was destined for Scotland. The leading Scottish family, the St. Clairs of Roslin, fortunes underwent a dramatic improvement from that time forward. Already wealthy, the St. Clairs suddenly became what, in modern jargon, we call "super-rich." William, a later St. Clair Baron of Roslyn who became the third Earl of Orkney, was renowned for his incredible wealth.[41] He was the architect and builder of Rosslyn Chapel, a unique library in stone of arcane symbolism, a superbly carved reliquary of the Holy Grail, a memorial of Templar beliefs, and the core church of Freemasonry. Earl William was also known as "one of the Illuminati" and had been initiated into some of the leading chivalric orders in Europe.

Chapter 17
The Shroud of Turin

Some years after the suppression of the Knights Templar, a controversial relic made its first appearance in Europe, the cloth known today as 'The Shroud of Turin.' It was controversial from the start, for shortly after its first exposition, Henry Bishop of Troyes wrote in the 1350's:

> Many theologians and otherwise persons [have stated] that this could not be the real Shroud of Our Lord having the Saviour's likeness thus imprinted upon it, since the holy Gospel made no mention of such an imprint, while, if it had been true, it is highly unlikely that the holy Evangelists would have omitted to record it, or that the fact should have remained hidden until the present time.[1]

Yet, the earliest reference to what could be the Shroud dates from some time earlier in 1203 when a certain French crusader, Robert de Clari described a relic he had seen in Constantinpole at the Church of My Lady Mary of Blachernae, '...where was kept the sydoine in which Our Lord had been wrapped which stood up straight every Friday so that the *figure* of Our Lord could plainly be seen there.' Varying translations of the word 'figure' have caused considerable dispute. Should the translation be in the French manner, meaning 'face', or the English meaning 'full figure or body.' Somewhat mysteriously de Clari added 'no one, either Greek or French, ever knew what became of this sydoine after the city was taken [in 1204][2]. Other scholars claim that the Shroud, folded and framed, may have been exhibited as the Mandylion, an alleged imprint of Jesus' face on a cloth sent to King Abgar of Edessa for safekeeping. Linking these two relics is the ages-old tradition that neither imprint was made by the hand of man.[3] It is, perhaps, simply a coincidence that the known history of the Mandylion can be completed, with one short gap, by the documented history of the Shroud? Are they one and the same? No one can tell with any degree of certainty, it all comes down to a matter of belief rather than one of fact.

Known Owners of the Shroud

The first person named as the owner of the Shroud in the 1350's in France was a certain Geoffrey de Charnay who died in 1356. When Jacques de Molay, last Grandmaster of the Knights Templar was burnt alive in Paris, his companion in pain and martyrdom was another Geoffroi de Charnay, therefore it is reasonable to assume that either the Templar order, or Templars of the de Charnay family, had brought the Shroud back from Constantinople. The British scholar, Noel Currer-Briggs, a Fellow of the Society of Genealogists and also a founder member of the Association of Genealogists and Record Agents, discovered proof that Geoffrey de Charnay who first exhibited the Shroud, was a nephew of the Templar martyr Geoffroi de Charnay.[4] As the Templars had only recently been suppressed after being hauled before the Inquisition on charges of heresy, it is hardly surprising that the owners were somewhat reluctant to discuss the relic's recent history. The family of Geoffroi de Charnay were linked by marriage to the families of Brienne, de Joinville and Burgunady so it is highly likely that Rex Deus had chosen to take part in the Shroud's preservation in the almost certain knowledge that it would play a significant role in proving that Jesus had come to reveal a spiritual pathway and had not died to redeem mankind from sin!

The last surviving member of the de Charnay line, the childless seventy-two year old Margueritte de Charnay was given the Chateau of Varanbon and the revenues of an estate at Mirbel by Duke Louis of Savoy in return for certain 'valuable services' which remained unspecified apart from her gift of the Shroud to the Duke. Both Geoffrey de Charnay II and Margueritte's second husband, Humbert de Villersexel had previously been made Knights of the Order of the Collar of Savoy by earlier dukes.[5] Again, not only were the de Charnays and the Villersexels Rex Deus but so also was the house of Savoy. By the 15th century members of the hierarchy of the Catholic Church had begun to refer to the Shroud as Jesus' 'burial shroud.' The theologian Francesco della Rovere recorded in 1464 that 'This [the Shroud] is now preserved with great devotion by the Dukes of Savoy and is coloured with the blood of Christ.'6 Five years later this theologian became Pope Sixtus IV. His treatise, de Sanguine Christi was published in 1468 and was thus recognised as genuine by the pope himself and was then given its own feast day, May 4th.7

Some time in the early 16th century, the Shroud was damaged in a bizarre manner, the English Shroud scholar, Ian Wilson, claims that it would seem as though it had been subjected to a 'trial by fire' ritual and indeed the damage to the Shroud is consistent with it being folded and then pierced by a red-hot poker. Then in 1532, it was damaged still further by fire in the building in which it was kept. One edge was quite severely burned on all forty-eight folds of the cloth before the fire on the Shroud was extinguished. Repairs were made by sewing on a series of patches made from an altar cloth and the Shroud was then backed by a simple piece of holland cloth.8

The Duke of Savoy ordered that the Shroud be brought to Turin in 1578 and it has rested there ever since. In the last few years of the 17th century a magnificent Cathedral in the Baroque style, designed by Guarino Guarini and dedicated to St John the Baptist, was built to house it. The Shroud was ritually installed in its new abode on June 1st 1694. It was carried reverently into the Cathedral and given the place of honour hidden behind a grill above the high altar only to be exposed to the public on high feast days, weddings of the family of the Dukes of Savoy and great Church celebrations.9

The Shroud Itself

The Shroud of Turin is a single piece of cloth that measures 4.35 m long [14 ft 3 inches] by 1.1 m wide [3 ft 7 inches] with an additional strip sewn on the left side that is 8.5 cm wide [3.5 inches]. In a faint sepia monochrome, rather like a stained shadow, there appears the outline of the front and back of a bearded man with long hair, laid out as if dead.10 The imagery is subtle, faint and difficult to discern, however when taken in conjunction with the bloodstains it is not hard to see why, to the devout at least, it was believed to be the burial shroud of Jesus.

This famous relic was eventually photographed during its 1898 exposition by, an amateur photographer, Secondo Pio. In his later account, Pio wrote of the concern he experienced as he waited for the plates to develop. To his delight and growing wonder he realized that he was not seeing the image he had expected, a negative version of the vague figure on the Shroud. Indeed what lay before him was an unmistakeable and highly detailed photographic likeness in which the contrast between the light and shade in it imparted an almost three-dimensional quality in which the blood-flows from the head, hands, feet and side manifested themselves with an almost magical realism.[11] Pio had the overwhelming impression that he was looking at the likeness of an impressively built, tall man with a strikingly life-like face. Publication of these photographs stimulated a worldwide sensation and provoked immense speculation and scientific investigation that has continued ever since. With the considerable advances made in the art of photography, the Shroud was re-photographed by a professional in 1931 with even more remarkable results and again in 1969 and 1973.

Scientific Examinations of the Shroud

The publication of the first photographs of the Shroud of Turin stimulated immense curiosity among the general public and the scientific community, particularly among forensic pathologists and anatomists. The first to comment was the Professor of Comparative Anatomy at the Sorbonne in Paris, Yves Delage, who gave a public lecture on the 21st April 1902 entitled 'The image of Christ visible on the Holy Shroud of Turin.' He had a large, attentive and highly curious audience. The professor told them that, from a medical point of view, the wounds and anatomical data imprinted on the Shroud were so accurate that it seemed to him to be impossible for any artist to depict such a figure in the form of a negative image. Furthermore, in his opinion, as there was no discernable trace of any pigment on the cloth, he was convinced that the image on the Shroud was that of Jesus created by some photo-chemical process that had taken place in the tomb.[12] The learned professor's lecture started a vicious controversy; Marcelin Berthelot, the secretary of the Academy, even refused to publish the text in full.

When the second set of professionally taken photographs were published, the probable authenticity of the Shroud began to gain ground among the med-

Rex Deus ✛ The Families of the Grail

ical profession. Dr Pierre Barber of St Joseph's Hospital in Paris wrote that the wounds depicted on the Shroud were genuinely those of a crucified man,[13] conclusions that were further confirmed by the Cologne radiologist, Professor Hermann Moedder[14] and Professor Cordiglia of the department of Forensic Medicine at the University of Milan.[15] In the USA study was made of the bloodstains by Dr Anthony Sava of Brooklyn but, most of the modern medical research in the USA on the Shroud, has been conducted by Dr Robert Bucklin of Michigan, who later moved to California. The British photographer Leo Vala made a three-dimensional model of the head from his photos of the figure on the Shroud. When these photographs were studied by the distinguished ethnologist, Professor Carlton S. Coon of Harvard, the Professor described the face as that of a typical type found among Sephardic Jews and noble Arabs.[16] The wound marks on the back of the figure, which occur in groups of three, have been described by doctors as being physiologically accurate marks of flogging. Professor Judica Cordilglia identified bruising on the shoulders as being consistent with carrying the crossbeam of a cross and the damage to the knees as being the result of repeated falls.[17] Furthermore the wounds shown on the head, in the opinion of Dr David Willis, cannot be described with any accuracy except as those produced by a crown of thorns described in the Gospel accounts.[18]

Signs of Crucifixion

The wounds seen on the figure depicted on the Shroud have, naturally, attracted considerable attention. The blood-flow depicted on the left wrist demonstrates that, at the time of bleeding, the arm had been raised at an angle of about 55 to 65 degrees from the vertical.[19] This is entirely consistent with what we know of crucifixion as the victim would have had to try and maintain his breathing by raising his body to maintain the airflow to his lungs. Furthermore, in direct contrast to most artistic representations of the crucifixion, the nail wounds are on the wrists and *not* on the hands. Nailing through the hands would not have supported the victim's body weight bur through the wrists it would. Dr Pierre Barber who studied these matters in the 1930's claimed that the soldiers who nailed victims to a cross in that era, knew their anatomy for it was a common punishment and was carried out frequently. Barber went further and experimented by driving nails through amputated arms and found that there was a point at the same place as the wounds on the Shroud, which was easy to locate, would take the weight and was known as 'the space of destot.'[20] There was one unexpected bonus that arose from Barber's experiments, namely that when the nail passed through the wrist it stimulated the median nerve causing the thumb to contract and, on the Shroud, no thumbs are visible. He then posed the question 'How could a forger have imagined this?' He did similar experiments on amputated legs imitating nailing on the feet as depicted on the Shroud. His nails passed easily between the second and third metatarsal bones exactly replicating the wounds depicted on the feet of the figure depicted on the Shroud.[21]

On the left hand side of the figure is a clear wound mark that lies between the fifth and sixth ribs—as the image is laterally inverted this would have been on the right hand side of the victim's body. The blood-flow from this wound is intermittent with clear spaces between various bloodstains and these, Barber believed, were consistent with the Gospel account of blood and water flowing from a spear thrust.[22] In the opinion of one German radiologist, Professor Moedder, this 'water' came from the pleural sac. Dr Anthony Sava wrote that the scourging would have caused pleural inflammation causing pleural fluid to accumulate resulting, ultimately, in asphyxiation the principal cause of death a victim of crucifixion.[23] Thus, in the opinion of a variety of medical experts, the figure on the Shroud is undoubtedly one of a victim of crucifixion.

The position of the body as shown in the image, supine with the hands crossed over the pelvis, is absolutely identical to that discovered by Fr. De Vaux of the Ecole Biblique when he excavated Essene burials at Qumran.[24] This confirmation of Jesus being buried according to Essene practice completely contradicts de Vuax's principal aim as a Dead Sea Scrolls scholar, namely denying any connection between Jesus and the Essemes. Furthermore, contrary to Jewish practice and the accounts in the Gospels, it is quite obvious that the body wrapped in the Shroud had not been washed but had been liberally anointed with large quantities of expensive ointment before being hurriedly wrapped for burial.

Forensic Examinations

A commission was established in June 1969 to study the Shroud and recommend what forensic tests should be performed on it in order to establish its true nature and provenance. It was convened in secret but when the news leaked out and reached the public, both the cardinals and the custodians of the Shroud were promptly accused of acting 'like thieves in the night.' This accusation, which perhaps may have had some substance, was made by a German researcher, Kert Berna, who believed that the Shroud proved that Jesus did not die on the cross. The commission report published on the 17th of June, noted that the Shroud was in good condition and recommended that certain test be performed upon it that would only require very small samples of the original cloth. There was a two-day exposition of the relic in late November and, secretly samples were taken on the 25th of that month. Seventeen samples of thread were carefully removed from the cloth taking care that they should not be contaminated in any way. Professor Gilbert Raes from the Ghent Institute of Textile Technology was given two samples from one side of the Shroud and two other threads to examine. One sample of 12 mm in length was taken from the weft and another of 13 mm taken from the warp. The weave of the cloth was a 3 to 1 herringbone twill that was common at the time of Jesus, but more often seen in silk than in linen. Microscopic examination of the threads under polarized light established that the cloth was, in fact, linen. This investigation also found several small traces of cotton and it was deduced that the cloth had been woven on a loom that was also used to weave cotton fabrics. The cotton proved to be of a variety known as *gossipium herbacium* that is principally found growing around the Eastern Mediterranean. Professor Raes concluded, therefore, that the cloth had been manufactured in the Middle East.[25]

Particles adhering to the Shroud were identified as being small particles of mineral origin, fragments of hair, plant fibres, bacterial spores, spores from mosses and fungi, and pollen grains from various flowering plants, and these were all identified by Professor Max Frei. Among them were pollens from desert growing plants such as *tamarix, suade* and *artemesia*, which grow almost exclusively around the Dead Sea.[26] According to Professor Frei:

> These plants are of great diagnostic value for our geographical studies as identical plants are missing in all the countries where the Shroud is believed to have been exposed to the open air. Consequently, a forgery produced in France in the Middle Ages, in a country lacking these typical halophytes could not contain such characteristic pollen grains from the deserts of Palestine.[27]

There are six distinct and different pollens on the surface of the Shroud that are undoubtedly and exclusively Palestinian in origin. Frei also stated that there were pollen samples from plants from Anatolia in Turkey and eight varieties of pollen from Mediterranean plants that are consistent with the relic's history of exposure in France and Italy.

In the USA, in March 1977, a scientific conference was held on research on the Turin Shroud. It was not only attended by a wide range of scientists including Dr Robert Bucklin, a pathologist, and Professor Joseph Gambescia, but also by clergy from several denominations. There were scientists attending from the US Atomic Energy Commission, the Pasadena Jet Propulsion Laboratory, the Alburquerque Sandia Laboratory and the spectroscopy division of the Los Alamos Laboratory. Among the clergy was a major sceptic, Bishop John Robinson of 'Honest to God' fame. The bishop was not only most impressed with the international standing of the scientists involved but also with the serious manner in which they approached the whole question of the authenticity of this famous relic. He later wrote: 'there is none in this thing who is being either gullible or just dismissive.[28]' A report by the physicist Dr John Jackson and the aerodynamicist Dr Eric Jumper stated that the image had not been created by direct contact but by some form of emanation from the body and that there was a precise relationship between the intensity of the image and the degree of separation between the cloth and the body it had contained.[29]

Dr Jackson then astounded the assembly by showing the results of placing a 7.5 cm by 12.5 cm transparency in an up-to-date Interpretations Systems VP-8 Image Analyser—this produced a remarkable three-dimensional figure for all to see. Truly remarkable in that when a standard photograph is treated in the same manner it does not contain sufficient information in respect of distance or proportion to create such an accurate image. However, there was one strange anomaly in the image shown by Dr Jackson, the area around eyes showed a distinct bulge as if something had been laid upon them. Dr Jackson then quoted an old Jewish burial practice of laying coins or a broken piece of pottery over the eyes of a corpse and said that this could account for the bulges on the image.[30]

At the end of the conference, even the hardened sceptic, Bishop John Robinson claimed that in the light of all the evidence now available, the burden of proof had shifted and that it was now up to those who doubted the Shroud's authenticity to prove their case, rather than the believers.[31] To both his, and the wider world's, surprise, that is what soon appeared to happen.

Carbon Dating the Shroud of Turin

When the ex-King of Italy, King Umberto, died in 1983 custody of the Shroud of Turin passed from the family of Savoy to the Vatican. After intense pressure and lobbying permission was granted to subject the Shroud to Carbon Dating tests. Three laboratories of international repute were engaged to perform these tests: the University of Arizona in Tucson; the Swiss Federal Institute of Technology in Zurich and lastly, the Oxford Research Laboratory. While the samples were taken under conditions of secrecy, representatives from all three laboratories were allowed to be present and the whole process was video-taped. One 7 cm sample was cut from one corner and then divided into three, one for each laboratory. Cardinal Anastasio Ballestrero of Turin announced the results on the 13th of October 1988 and those results were confirmed shortly afterwards by Professor Tite of the British Museum who had supervised the entire process. The results, which shocked the Christian world, were that it was 99.9% certain the Shroud of Turin had originated during the period between 1000 and 1500 CE and that it was 95% certain that it was between 1260 and 1390 CE.

The world's press, fantasists and conspiracy theorists had a field day when the results were announced. One senior cleric, Brother Bruno Bonnet-Eynard, a fundamentalist Catholic and a leading member of *La Contre-Reformé Catholique au XXme Siecle*, went so far as to accuse Professor Tite of switching the samples used for the test. He went on to accuse all the scientists of a deliberate attempt to discredit the Catholic Church.[32] When interviewed on television this extremely right wing cleric fell back on an old and time honoured defence, he said that the Carbon Dating results were the result of a Jewish/Freemasonic anti-Catholic plot. Two German authors claimed that the results had been rigged by the scientists acting in collusion with the church.[33] They further claimed that the reason for this was that the church acted in this manner as the evidence on the Shroud *disproved* that Jesus had died upon the cross. Other authors, who assumed that the Carbon Dating was correct, rushed like Gaderene swine to promote a host of highly specious theories as to how the image on the Shroud could have been forged or otherwise created. Two British authors even went so far as to claim that the Shroud had bee wrapped around the crucified body of the last Templar Grandmaster, Jacques de Molay. They had obviously not conducted any research whatsoever as to the means of torture used by the Inquisition in France in the early 14th century.

The Carbon Dating Results Invalidated

Sometime later, an American scientist of high repute found evidence that completely invalidated the Carbon Dating results. Such results can be subject to massive distortion by extremely minute amounts of contamination and that is why the samples had been cleansed thoroughly before testing. However, unbeknown to the laboratories that performed the tests with such care, the Shroud was contaminated in a manner that arose from the nature of the cloth itself.

Many commentators, such as Ian Wilson, had previously recorded that the Shroud had a 'damask like sheen' when viewed with the naked eye.[34] This shiny appearance of the cloth has been discovered to arise from a micro-biological organism that completely envelops each strand of the cloth and that was completely impervious to the cleaning methods used in the Carbon Dating tests. The contamination was such that what was being tested was 60% micro-biological organism and only 40% cloth, thus distorting the results beyond all reasonable limits. Furthermore, the cleansing process used in the tests have been found to dissolve part of the cellulose from the linen, thus adding a further distortion to the results.[35] So, as a consequence of this contamination, there was such a distortion of the results that the whole question of the age and authenticity of the relic is, once again, wide open to debate.

Similar microbiological contamination was previously found on the surface of pre-Columbian Mayan artefacts from Mesoamerica and on mummy wrappings from Ancient Egypt. The initial discoveries that led to this re-evaluation of the Carbon Dating tests on the Shroud. were made by the Professor of Microbiology at the Centre for Health Sciences at the University of Texas, Dr Leonicio Garza-Valdes. He discovered that many Mayan carvings had ben coated by bacteria that produced a pinkish pigment as well as by fungi which varied in colour from brown to black. The overall result was to impart a particular 'lustrous sheen' to the carvings in question. He called this form of contamination a 'bio plastic coating.'[36] He then examined two different sets of mummy wrappings, the first from a mummy of a thirteen year-old girl discovered by Flinders Petrie that is kept at Manchester University in Britain and the second from a mummified Ibis from his own private collection. Both the girl's mummy and her wrappings had earlier been Carbon Dated by Manchester University with bizarre results. The bones of the mummy were dated to 1510

BCE and the wrappings to 255 CE, a startling difference of over 1700 years between them.[37] In the case of the mummified Ibis the difference between the dating of the bone and wrapping was between 400 and 700 years. In January of 1996 Dr Garza-Valdes examined these cloths under an electron microscope and discovered that a bio plastic coating enveloped the fibres on both of them.

The original samples cut from the Shroud of Turin for Carbon Dating had been cut by Professor Giovani Riggi Numana, who showed small fragments of them to Dr Garza-Valdes along with pieces of Scotch tape that had been used to remove blood samples from the Shroud. The Professor removed one fibre from the original sample and passed it to Dr Garza-Valdes who examined it under the microscope. He immediately saw that it was completely covered by a bio plastic coating that enveloped the fibre.[38] He has cultured the bacteria from the sample and found that it is still alive and replicating. Thus, Dr Garza-Valdes believes that if the Shroud was re-subjected to Carbon Dating today, using exactly the same cleaning techniques, the results would indicate an even more recent date as the bio plastic coating is composed of living bacteria that have multiplied considerably since the date of the original test, and that would skew the results even more. He has also examined the blood samples taken from the back of the head of the figure on the Shroud.

There already had been other scientific reports on the bloodstains on the Shroud, One Italian scientist, Dr Bauma-Bollone had classified them as human blood of the blood group AB.[39] Drs Adler and Heller agreed with their Italian counterpart and stated that these were indeed human bloodstains.[40] Thus Dr Garza-Valdes findings, that these were human bloodstains, was confirmed from other sources. Furthermore, the Blood group AB is historically the most common blood group found within Sephardic Jews who had inhabited the Holy Land at the time of Jesus. He also established the blood sample he examined was ancient due to the degradation of the sample he examined.[41] In the scotch tape along with the blood sample he also found several microscopic tubules of wood that he was able to establish were oak,[42] visible indications of the cross that Jesus was crucified upon.

Dr Garza-Valdes published his results in an article he wrote in 1996 and included the results of DNA testing of the blood sample. The front cover of the magazine in which he published this article was the face of Jesus taken from the Shroud and his article was entitled 'Secrets of the Shroud—microbiologists discover how the Shroud of Turin hides its true age.' The article states that the Shroud is, indeed, many centuries older than the Carbon Dating suggests. The principal inventor of Carbon Dating techniques, Dr Harry Grove of Rochester University in the USA, has been quoted as saying 'This is not such a crazy idea.' Thanks to the painstaking work of Dr Garza-Valdes, the Carbon dating of the Shroud of Turin has been completely invalidated.

A Message Hidden Within the Shroud

Let us consider a brief resumé of the scientific evidence concerning the Shroud of Turin. Professor Yves Delage of Paris stared categorically in 1902 that the wounds and anatomical data recorded on the Shroud are so accurate that they could not be the work of any artist. Dr Pierre Barbet reported that the wounds recorded on the Shroud were undoubtedly those of a crucified man and this view as endorsed by Professor Herman Moedder of Cologne, Dr Judica-Cordiglia, Dr Anthony Sava, and Dr Robert Bucklin. Professor Coon of Harvard described the face on the image on the Shroud as 'a physical type found in modern times among Sephardic Jews and noble Arabs.' The experiments performed by Dr Pierre Barbet depicted details that could not have been known or guessed at by any artist. The weave of the cloth and the cotton contamination of it prove that the cloth was manufactured in the Middle East. Pollen found on the Shroud show, indisputably, that it had ben exposed in the area of the Dead Sea. The image processing results that had produced such an astounding image of the head depicted in the Shroud led the ever-sceptical Bishop John Robinson to say that it was now up to the doubters to prove their case. We believe that when all these facts and specialist opinions are taken into consideration, bearing in mind the invalidation of the Carbon Dating results, that, in all probability, the Shroud of Turin may well be the cloth in which Jesus' body was wrapped when it was taken down from the cross.

The importance of the Shroud to the Templars and the Rex Deus families, when studied in the light of forensic medicine, indicate strongly that the body originally wrapped in the Shroud was still alive, in complete contradiction to church teaching and belief. We mentioned above that, contrary to Jewish tradition and normal burial practice, the body wrapped within the Shroud had not been washed but had been anointed with copious quantities of very expensive ointments that included aloe. These, we respectfully submit, were to hasten recovery after the terrible ordeal Jesus had undergone before and during his crucifixion. The death of a man who has been crucified is due to a massive increase in the secretion of pleural fluid, causing pressure on the lungs and, ultimately, suffocation. The spear thrust to his side would have relieved that pressure and allowed Jesus to breathe.

In spite of the two thousand years of repression and the persecution of all those who differed from Church Doctrine, the legend that Jesus survived the crucifixion has endured and is now more credible than ever. Legends of his survival trace his movements from Jerusalem to Egypt and eventually to Kashmir. Thus long-standing esoteric tradition, Rex Deus teaching and the forensic analysis of the figure depicted on the Shroud unequivocally all point in the same direction and lead to a conclusion that completely refutes the central point of church teaching, that Jesus died to redeem us from sin. St Paul, the man who deified Jesus and who was the first to describe him as 'our Lord and Saviour' was, as we have mentioned earlier, not a true follower of Jesus, and was rightly described by the true disciples and apostles as 'the spouter of lies' and 'the distorter of the true teachings of Jesus.' Now after nearly two thousand years the real truth is beginning to emerge, Jesus came to reveal and *not* to redeem. Thus it is not surprising that when Dr Garza-Valdes presented his findings to the church authorities, they point blank refused to allow a re-test of the Carbon Dating of the Shroud of Turin.

CHAPTER 18

NEO-TEMPLAR and CHIVALRIC ORDERS

After the suppression of the Templars, Rex Deus continued to use chivalric orders to further its aims for the idea of having a disciplined and visible executive arm, one close to seat of political power had long since proved its worth. The new chivalric orders used or founded by Rex Deus were all smaller than the Templars, owned no property and derived no income from their own resources. They were created in a fashion that seemingly gave them no autonomy and were responsible to noblemen of high rank or individual monarchs. They nearly all gave the appearance of being simply orders conferring prestige rather than true military orders of power and substance; orders of royal patronage filled with courtiers rather than professional soldiers. There was one exception to this, and although based in France, it was truly Scottish in origin and personnel.

There was in Scotland a long-standing nucleus of powerful houses of the nobility that were Rex Deus to the core. They gave birth to an order that was probably the most neo-Templar of them all—The Scots Guard.[1] This became the premier regiment in the French Army. It was a vibrant child of an old Franco-Scots tradition that dated back to the days of 'the auld alliance' created between France and Scotland in the days of Robert the Bruce. Military co-operation between the two countries had started at the time of Robert the Bruce and continued on throughout the Hundred Years War. Sir John Stewart and the two Douglas bothers played a significant role in the Battle of Orleans and, it is claimed, that the famous White Banner that became a rallying point for the French army that day, was painted by a Scot.[2]

After that war, France was in a state of chaos and, in an attempt to restore order, King Charles VII, created a new, national army, the first of its kind since the fall of the Roman Empire.[3] This army was composed of fifteen companies of ordinance with 600 men in each and the elite regiment was *La Compagnie des Gendarmes Ecossais.* The foundation of this regiment marked over a century of brave and devoted service by the Scots to the Kingdom of France. Their courage, commitment and unswerving loyalty to France reached its peak in 1492 at the bloody battle of Verneuil when the Scots, led by John Stewart and assisted by the Earls of Buchan, Murray and Mar along with Alexander Lindsey and William Seton were virtually annihilated.

The Scots Guard

One of the direct results of this conspicuous act if heroism and gallantry and as a celebration of the long alliance between France and Scotland, a special unit of elite Scots military men was established to render personal service to the Royal Family of France. A company of thirteen knights supported by twenty archers and mustered in two sections, *Garde du Roi,* the King's Guard and *Garde du Corps du Roi,* all known under their collective name of the Scots Guard.[5] In 1445, when a new standing army was created, the Scots Guard was increased to a total of sixty-five men with twenty-five of their number and their commander in the King's personal bodyguard. The commander and every officer in the unit were made members of the Order of St Michael, a branch of which was later founded in Scotland.[6]

There are many chivalric orders of greater renown, such as the Order of the Garter or the Order of the Bath but, unlike them the Scots Guard was a military order that fulfilled important positions in the political and diplomatic fields as well as in battle, a highly skilled and professional, fighting force.[7] All knights who had joined the Templar Order had to be of proven nobility and knightly rank before they were inducted, the Scots Guard recruited its officers from the leading families among the Scots nobility, the Setons, the St Clairs, the Stewarts, the Montgomeries and the Hamiltons, all families of the Rex Deus group. The Scots Guard evolved into' …a special vehicle where they [the young Scottish noblemen] were initiated into martial skills, politics, court affairs, foreign manners and mores and, it would appear ritualistic rites as well.'[8]

The Scots Guard maintained their privileged position for nearly 150 years and their commander also held other positions in the diplomatic and political field. Officers were extremely well paid and a captain in the Guard received a salary of over 2,000 *livres tournois* per year, its modern day equivalent would be in the region of $180.000. Members of the Scots Guard had sworn allegiance to the Royal House of France, the Valois dynasty, but their right to rule came under threat from a powerful branch of the House of Lorraine known as the House of Guise.[9] The rivalry between these competing dynasties was truly murderous and five French Kings were alleged to have met violent ends or been poisoned and members of both the Houses of Lorraine and Guise were also subject to assassination. As the King's Bodyguard, the Scots Guard were now placed in an extremely ambivalent position for the House of Guise were Rex Deus and, in 1538, Mary of Guise[10] married King James V of Scotland[11] uniting two highly important families within Rex Deus. King Henry II of France gave a substantial rise in both pay and privileges to the Scots Guard in 1547; yet, from time to time they continued to act on behalf of the House of Guise. During a jousting tournament in June 1559, Captain Gabriel Montgomery of the Scots Guard accidentally brought about the death of King Henry II by piercing his eye with the splintered end of a broken lance. Certain authors, such as Baigent and Leigh, have alleged that this death was no accident but part of a plot.[12] Whatever the truth of that, the loyalty of the Scots Guard became more and more obviously aligned to the House of Guise and this began to cause consternation at court. King Henry III was so angry that he stopped the Guard's maintenance, and although this was soon reinstated, the regiment began to fade into oblivion and it became merely one regiment in the French Army among others. This troubled history did not disturb the Scots Guard's hidden agenda which was to act as a conduit for Rex Deus tradition and teaching on French soil that was to later contribute so magnificently to the rise of Freemasonry in France. It also acted in a reverse direction, carrying insights from the Houses of Lorraine, Guise, Savoy and Burgundy to Scotland.

Orders of Chivalry

There were many separate links in the chain of transmission of the Rex Deus tradition, for the families had learned only too well the dangers of putting all their eggs in one basket after the fall of the Knights Templar. One was the Order of the Coquille, perhaps better known as the Knights of Santiago[13] that had provided a haven of refuge for many Templar Knights seeking sanctuary after October 13th 1307. This renowned order acted as a vehicle for transmission of Rex Deus principles for several centuries and, over time, it slowly evolved into a purely chivalrous order that welcomed into its ranks Rex Deus members from all over Europe. The Order of Santiago was the perfect cover for the transmission of Rex Deus teaching, seemingly so respectable, owing allegiance to their most Catholic Majesties in Spain and playing such an important role in the Reconquista, the war to free Spain from the Moors, that it was completely above all taint of suspicion. The Templars of the inner circle of the order had been wholly Rex Deus, but the Order of Santiago drew its membership from a wide variety of impeccable, noble sources of which Rex Deus was merely one, and so was unlikely to be subject to the unwelcome attentions of the Inquisition.

There was one order that arose in Europe in 1430 CE that we suspect only drew its membership from the ranks of the Rex Deus families. A purely chivalric order of considerable renown the Order of the Golden Fleece was founded by Philip the Good Duke of Burgundy and membership was strictly restricted to 24 members only.[14] Pope Eugenius IV described these members as 'Maccabeans Resurrected' a description that was, perhaps, a little too close to the truth for comfort as it tends to reflect the true dynastic origins of the knights in question. The social and moral standing of this order was such that explosion from its ranks on account of any deviation from its high sense of purpose brought a permanent mark of shame on that entire family's record for all time. In a church in Bruges there is a black shield carved above the seat of the Count of Nevers proclaiming the eternal infamy that flowed from his expulsion from the Order.[15] Another order, founded earlier in 1408 by the King of Hungary also had a restricted membership of 24 knights who were sworn to practice 'true and pure fraternity' and their armorial bearings depicted a dragon within a circle decorated with a red cross. Some little time after the foundation of this order, its founder became Holy Roman Emperor and the order gained new prestige and importance and was now known as the 'Imperial and Royal Court of the Dragon.' It is claimed that this order later had branches on Bulgaria, Bosnia, Italy and France.

Renee D'Anjou, Count of Provence and titular King of Jerusalem is one of the pivotal figures within the ranks of Rex Deus during the 15th century. He had fought, as a young man, alongside Joan of Arc, and was known as 'Good King Renee' as he was king of the Two Sicilies as well as inheriting the empty title of Jerusalem. Seven distinct strands of Rex Deus descent unite in his family. He was not merely noble and rich, but talented and creative. He wrote and composed many motets that are still played today and was a scholar of international repute who corresponded with Earl William St Clair of Orkney who built Rosslyn Chapel. He amassed a collection of original and important manuscripts in Latin, Hebrew, Greek and Turkish. He was renowned as a scholar of scripture, philosophy, history, geography and physics. He founded his own chivalric order in 1448, The Order of the Croissant, at Angers. Entry was restricted to knights of unblemished character and proven noble birth. The aims of the order were to be the attainment of courtesy, charity and fraternal love. They were especially instructed to employ their best efforts in aiding the poor. Another order that obviously fell under considerable Rex Deus influence was the Order of the Collar of Savoy which awarded its honours to several members of the de Charnay family.

Hidden History

Society is moulded and formed by a complex set of circumstances that interact together, as a conflict of ideas, belief systems, philosophies and ideologies. History is simply one account of what happens, always written from the perspective of the ruling elite at that time and ignoring the harsh experience of ordinary people. However, behind the bland propaganda viewpoint of the official version lies 'the hidden hand of history' recording the experience of the underclasses, the hidden streams of spirituality, heresy and political dissent and it is the tensions that arise between the official version of history and the hidden hand of history that mould our reality. The 'hidden hand' displays itself in folk-lore, myth, legend, song, dance and ritual and in the vast majority of cases, the outward disguise as ritual or myth was effective and masked the true, hidden meaning from the ruling classes. The 'Green Man' for example is found in the vast majority of medieval churches built before the 1450's, it is rarely remarked upon but it signifies a form of spiritual rebirth that is an essential part of Rex Deus teaching and is regarded as a heresy by the church. Yet, to the authorities, rituals and dances celebrating the 'green man' every Mayday were deemed harmless.

At Roslin in Scotland, on lands owned by the Rex Deus family of the St Clairs, each year Gypsies were given the freedom to perform certain plays that were strictly against the law—the Robin Hood plays. What was the significance of this forbidden piece of drama?

Cathars fleeing from persecution in the Languedoc had sought sanctuary at Roslin under the benevolent eyes of the St Clairs, one of the leading Rex Deus families in Scotland. There is a common core in the chain of belief linking the Gypsies, the Cathars and the Rex Deus initiates that found a vivid form of expression in the Robin Hood plays. While the church preached about the redemptive sacrifice at Golgotha, it lived in constant fear that the truth about the descendants of Jesus would be made public. This is what lay at the heart of the Robin Hood plays, Cathar beliefs, Rex Deus tradition and the international Gypsy festivals that take place at Les Saintes Maries-de-la-Mer in the Camargue in the South of France every May.

CHAPTER 19

THE SPIRITUAL BELIEFS OF REX DEUS

O ver five centuries after their suppression, Pope Pius IX condemned the Templars as Gnostics from the beginning and followers of the Johannite Heresy.[1] Most heresies are described by the Catholic Church in great detail but there is a deafening silence on the part of the church about this particular alleged deviation. However, as the church acted as prosecutor, judge and jury in cases of heresy their views are always suspect anyway. Perhaps the works by A. E. Waite and Magus Eliphas Levi may give us some indication of the nature of this particular deviation from church doctrine. Both claim that Jesus was an initiate of the Egyptian cult of Osiris and a follower of the goddess Isis[2] which may well explain Templar veneration of Isis under the guise of the Black Madonna.[3]

Rex Deus nobility right across Europe were noted for the toleration they displayed towards dissident religious groups such as the Jews and the Cathars. The ouvert arm of Rex Deus, the Knights Templar shared the fruits of their spiritual wisdom and insight with all the communities within which they resided, irrespective of differing belief systems. However, neither any actions by the Templars, nor the accusations of heresy made against them before their demise, clarify or detail, their core belief structure. The disappearance or suppression of their own records obscure any real understanding of either their true motivation or religious belief. We have demonstrated how, in the eyes of Rex Deus members at least, Jesus was the supreme initiatory teacher who, gifted though he undoubtedly was, was a man like any other. Like the Jews of biblical Israel from which they sprang, they regarded his deification as a blasphemy against Almighty God. There is another matter of supreme importance to mention, they followed what they believed to be 'the true teachings of Jesus' and not the blasphemous and heretical teachings of St. Paul. When we first began to research the whole issue of Rex Deus, we could only speculate about the spiritual path followed by Rex Deus members and were more than somewhat baffled when trying to assess their true motives. Some years after Tim's first contact with Michael Monkton and after the publication of The Second Messiah by Knight and Lomas, other members contacted Tim and gave him information that enabled him to question Michael again in greater depth. Thus, slowly and erratically Tim began to gain a deeper understanding of the belief system of the Rex Deus families.

The Gospel and Liturgy of the Holy Twins

Jesus the Messiah had proclaimed a new form of 'New Covenant' Judaism that was taught, after the crucifixion, by his twin brother Judas Thomas and his other brother James the Just. Later, Judas Thomas became Patriarch of Edessa while James the Just became the leader of the Jesus group in Jerusalem. James, who is described in the Acts of the Apostles, as 'the first bishop of Jerusalem', along with those who had walked and talked with Jesus behaved in an inexplicable manner for people, who the Christians claim, were starting a new religion. It is recorded in the Acts of the Apostles 'And they, continuing daily with one accord in the Temple ...'[4] While this may pose problems for devout Christians it is, however, entirely consistent with James in his position as High Priest and his followers desire to initiate a new form of Judaism which is the foundation of the belief system of Rex Deus.

The beliefs and rituals of this new form of Judaism were contained in *The Liturgy and Gospel of the Holy Twins*, which includes several writings by disciples of Jesus including *The Gospel of Thomas* and John the Evangelist's *Gospel of Love* so revered by the Cathars many centuries later. *The Gospel of Thomas* was later suppressed by the church and, if it were not for the wisdom and foresight of the devout monk who buried it at *Nag Hammadi* in Egypt, and its later rediscovery in the mid-20th century we would not have it today. As we have never seen a written copy of *The Liturgy and Gospel of the Holy Twins*, our account is based on the conversations held with Michael Monkton at Tim's house in Totnes, England. It begins with *The Proclamation of the Book* that reads as follows:

> The Book of the Old Covenant is sealed with seven seals and is locked by seven keys. The Angel of God holds that book and it shall be opened no more.
>
> The Book of the New Covenant is opened at the first page and the Messiah has written:
>
> The oath.
>
> The Encryption.
>
> The Prayer of Abba Ra Heim.
>
> The Proclamation of the Law.
>
> The Proclamation concerning the poor.
>
> The Proclamation of Forgiveness.
>
> The Commemoration.

The seven-foldedness of the phrasing is reminiscent of The Revelation of St John where it is used repeatedly. Symbolic references to seven seals can be found in many churches associated with the hidden streams of spirituality such as at St Sulpice in Paris.

The Oath reads as follows:

> If the words that I spoke were not the words of God, but my own words and if those who heard my words believed that these words were the words of God and trusted in them [i.e. believed in the revised Law, the first two commandments— and relied upon the relaxing of the dietary laws, circumcision and travelling] then the sin of breaking the Law is not theirs but mine—may the blood of their sin be on my hands as I will answer for that sin when I stand before God at mine end. Therefore you can believe in my words as being the words of God.

The Messiah was, in effect, telling his flock that he was now taking full responsibility for the dramatic changes in the Holy Law and he, and not his flock, was responsible to God for them.

The prophet Abraham had encoded into the Torah, sacred principles that he had been taught by Almighty God under the guidance of his spiritual master, Melchizedek.[5] The vibrant and Divine origin of these principles were immediately recognizable and contributed to his warm reception by the Egyptian pharaoh.[6] This gnostic vision of the Divine was of a far more loving God than the seemingly vengeful, legalistic idea of God preached by Moses. The Law, as described in the books of Exodus and Leviticus, laid down a legalistic and demanding set of strictures that, with the best will in the world, would be almost impossible to obey in full detail—in fact it made the people of Israel feel like perpetual sinners. Nonetheless, even within these demands, there was hope, as the High Priest who acted as the spokesman for his people on his knees before God, made atonement for all their sins and sought their forgiveness.[7]

The Encryption that followed *The Oath*, defined many of the aspects of God and demonstrated the humility of Jesus in his relationship with the Divine, in complete and stark contrast to the Christian idea that Jesus was God.

The Encryption

God is God.
God is the Great God of the Universe.
God is the Alpha and the Omega.
God is the Creator.
God is the Destroyer.
God is Life.
God is the Lawgiver.
God is the Judge.
God is Mercy.
God is Love.
God is Knowledge.
God is Wisdom.

A man was sent from God.

He was the Star.

He was the Teacher.
He was of the House of David.
He was of the Line of Aaron.
He is the Prince of Peace.
He is the Learned Lamb.
He is Our King.
He is Our High Priest.
He is the Prince of the West.
He is the Messiah
His name is Jesus.

Few Jews in that era would have had any major problem with these pious statements and even fewer Muslims of later centuries would take issue with them Christians would be horrified and most modern Jews would undoubtedly take umbrage at the idea that Jesus was the Messiah. However, there is one section of the Liturgy and Gospel of the Holy Twins that is guaranteed to upset adherents of all the major monotheistic faiths, as it lays considerable emphasis on the early, Egyptian and polytheistic origins of Judaism.

Those who use the prayer of Abba Ra Heim in the Liturgy are described as 'The Children who are followers of the Sun God Ra' a phrase that clearly and unequivocally speaks of the polytheistic, initiatory roots not only of early Judaism but ultimately also of Christianity. The teachings of Jesus in the New Covenant as outlined in the Liturgy were there to revive the concept of a loving God that Abraham would have recognised in place of the legalistic, demanding, punishing God of post-exilic Judaism.

The Prayer of Abba Ra Heim

Our Heavenly Father,
Alleluja
May Your Heavenly Kingdom Come on Earth
Alleluja
May Your Heavenly Laws be Obeyed Upon Earth
Alleluja
May you protect us from chaos and grant us our needs
Alleluja
Amen.

The similarities between this prayer, and the Christian 'Lord's prayer' simply demonstrates that they were certainly used by the same people.

The New Covenant

At the time of Jesus, the 613 strictures of The Law were almost impossible to apply in everyday life. This multitude of prohibitions, instructions and injunctions were further complicated by a plethora of Talmudic and Rabbinic commentaries all written to try and explain the implications of the law, which, only made matters worse as they were often abstruse, opaque and almost impenetrable. Jesus' objective was to try and bring order out of this chaos and make The Law comprehensible to ordinary people and therefore attainable in real life. He thus tried to sweep away the Law of Moses and replace it with two simple, yet nonetheless demanding, precepts which, if followed could totally transform the life of all true believers. The Proclamation of the Law falls into two simple and clear parts:

1. You will love God your Heavenly Father.
You will Obey His Heavenly Commandments.
You will serve the Lord Your God all the days of your life.

2. You will love your brother as you love yourself.
You will love all the people of the earth.
As you love your brother you will bring heaven upon earth.

The Proclamation of the Law is one of the few teachings of Jesus that escaped being censored or altered by the followers of St Paul and crept into prominence within later Christian teaching. For example, in the Gospel According to St Matthew we find:

Master, which is the greatest commandment in the Law?

Jesus said unto him, Thou shalt Love the Lord Thy God with all thy heart and with all thy soul and with all thy mind. This is the first and greatest commandment. And the second is like unto it. Thou shalt love thy neighbour as thyself. On these two commandments hang all the Law and all the prophets.[8]

After his triumphal entry into Jerusalem, Jesus made service to the poor the central theme of a speech he made from the steps of the Temple. This was in the morning three days before the crucifixion. As Heir to throne in the line of David he was regarded as a high priest in his own right. These are the words he spoke:

> You shall not eat if the poor do not eat.
> You shall not have clothing if the poor do not have clothing.
> You shall not have an habitation if the poor do not have an habitation.
> You shall not have warmth or a fire in your grate
> If the poor do not have warmth or a fire in theirs.
> You shall not be cured of your illnesses
> If the poor are not cured of theirs.

The Ebionim

The group that Jesus led throughout his ministry were the Nazarenes or Nazoreans, an inner circle of the Essenes. Soon after the crucifixion they became known as the Ebionim, or 'the poor' and they continued with a hereditary leadership for at least a century after the crucifixion with their leaders all being drawn from the family of Jesus. The arch heretic, Saul of Tarsus, better known as St Paul, joined them for a short time before being expelled for preaching heresy. Even the staunchly Catholic historian of Christianity Paul Johnson admits that from that time on, the evangelical efforts of St Paul were rapidly and dramatically losing ground to evangelists accredited by James the Just in Jerusalem.[9]

Thus, 'The Way', the spiritual pathway taught by Jesus, is the route by which we can all bring about heaven on earth by following his precepts. The medieval Knights Templar were not, as it is commonly believed, sworn to poverty, but held its goods and possessions in common so that while an individual member might be without personal wealth, the order itself could prosper. It could then use its wealth for the benefit of the entire membership and the communities within which they moved. Thus the spiritual beliefs of the Templars enabled them to raise the standard of living in all their local communities as they implemented the precepts of the Proclamation of the Poor. Living their beliefs, the Templars were able to enhance the lives of the peasantry, the craftsmen and the merchants and their devotion to the Proclamation to the Poor had a transformative and uplifting effect on tens of thousands of people throughout Europe. They began to bring about social justice by acting on their core principles of compassion and mercy. However it must be clearly stated that the same principles were binding on all good Christians too, but it was the Templars who led the way by acting on them in a universal manner. So what is the reason for the readily apparent discrepancy between Christian actions and those of the Templars? That may well be found within the final two attributes of God described in the Encryption: God is Knowledge and God is Wisdom—a concept later encapsulated by Vincent de Beauvais in the phrase 'Man can encompass salvation by means of knowledge.'[10]

Church Doctrine

Rex Deus members, the inner circle of the Knights Templar and the Cathars were united around a common theme—they were all Gnostics. All three groups were following an initiatory spiritual path that led to enlightenment. The attainment of enlightenment, gnosis or sacred knowledge, was kept secret but the knowledge gained was used to benefit the communities within which they all moved. It was treasured, maintained and enhanced for the benefit of all to bring about heaven on earth.

Holy Mother the Church also claimed to be following the true teachings of Jesus, however the church view of Jesus was so dramatically different from the Rex Deus perspective that, hobbled by dogmatic distortion and, above all, the deification of Jesus by St Paul, they fell into the trap of believing that Jesus' death on the cross was a sacrifice that redeemed all mankind from sin—provided of course, that the individual sinner paid due reverence and appropriate tithes to the church. They never adequately explained how, in spite of Jesus' redemptive act for all mankind, sinners could spend all eternity in hell for the punishment of their sins. Church ritual and practice was supposedly designed to encourage each individual to atone for his or her sins and gain personal salvation. This is in direct contrast to the central Rex Deus life of action designed to render service to the community for the betterment of all mankind. Both of these opposing groups called Jesus 'The Prince of Peace' yet while Rex Deus interpreted this as an instruction to show toleration to those of different beliefs, the church would use it as an excuse to harry, persecute torture and kill all who had the temerity to hold a different view. Truly, 'by their fruits shall ye know them.'

St Augustine of Hippo gave the church one of its major weapons in its efforts to create and manipulate a fearful and guilt ridden subservient church membership—the Doctrine of Original Sin, for which there is no scriptural justification whatsoever.[11] The church used this dogmatic distortion ruthlessly to control the congregations it supposedly serves, control and exploit in such a corrupt and brutal manner that its real legacy can be found in the Crusade against the Cathars and the Inquisition that followed that shameful episode. The Lord's Prayer, that asks for us to be forgiven our sins as we forgive others, despite its allegedly 'Divine' origin, was deemed inadequate and insufficient unless the devout believer obeyed the church's dictats with blind and unquestioning obedience.

The Proclamation of Forgiveness

When it comes to forgiveness, there is again a subtle difference between Rex Deus teaching and Church Doctrine. Jesus made *The Proclamation of Forgiveness* shortly after giving his compassionate instructions regarding the poor: If a man sins against another, he shall seek forgiveness from that man.

If that man will not forgive the sinner, the sinner will turn to God, trusting in the words of the Messiah, and being sincere in his desire to be forgiven, ask God to forgive him his sins.

God has spoken through the Messiah and said that a man who sincerely desires to be forgiven, will be forgiven.

The teaching and practice of Christianity has empowered the church at the expense of its congregation and has damaged society as a whole. The sinner who has gone through the ritual of confession, penance and forgiveness is now at liberty to sin again and again. At no stage is the sinner instructed to ask forgiveness of his victim or make any amends towards them. This is hardly in the spirit of Jesus's words or actions. The Rex Deus practice of seeking forgiveness from the victim seems to us to be in better accord with both natural justice and the Divine will that the guilt inducing doctrine of the church.

Followers of 'The Way'

Rex Deus members as they dispersed after the fall of Jerusalem, were instructed to follow the outward beliefs and rituals of the prevailing religion of their time and place. In secret, they celebrate the final meal shared by the Messiah and his followers, the so-called 'Last Supper.' During this meal Jesus is said to have made this rather strange speech:

> My Royal Priesthood I condemn: the disciples are like little children who have been orphaned and who have found a walled garden left unattended by the owners. They have climbed over the wall and dwelt in the garden eating and drinking the fruits therein. The owners return and the children stand naked before them and are sent away with nothing.

He then recalled the first Passover, the liberation from Egypt and Moses standing before God on Mount Sinai. He asked all who were present and who believed that his words were the words of God, to commemorate this evening and make the Thursday evening family meal as a celebration of his coming as the Messiah and his teaching about the New Covenant. They were instructed never to forget his teaching that his oath absolved them from all sin that might result from following his words. The duty that was incumbent upon them all was to live according to his teaching and help bring about heaven on earth.

The ' Followers of the Way', the labourers in the Vineyard or the Garden were virtually interchangeable terms denoting those who were his disciples and, later, members of Rex Deus. The question then arose 'How were they to preserve the knowledge of 'The Way' for future generations.' They were to pass his teachings down through the generations in secret, marrying only other members from the Rex Deus group and outwardly conforming to the required religion of their time. After the demise of the Templars they became aware that the Templar Order had brought enormous strength and hope to the families eventual survival and that they now had a new and pressing duty—to promote their aims, objectives and beliefs to others of goodwill, outside the Rex Deus family network in order to fulfil their sacred obligation to create heaven on earth. They used existing chivalric orders to further this aim as well as creating some of their own. Orders that were either founded or controlled by leading families among their group, such as Renee D'Anjou, the Duke of Savoy and the Duke of Burgundy. These gained immense influence right across Europe that lasted for centuries, however their most lasting and important success was the role they played in transforming the old, long established, Craft mason's guilds into the worldwide brotherhood of Freemasonry.

CHAPTER 20
THE INSTITUTION OF FREEMASONRY
AND THE ST. CLAIRS OF ROSLIN

The Cathars and Knights Templar who escaped to Scotland found refuge and sanctuary mainly in the lands of the St. Clairs of Roslin, a dynasty whose continuous and unbroken record of service, loyalty and courage earned them the name of The Lordly Line of the High St. Clairs. William the Seemingly St. Clair was the first member of the family to come to Roslin; he arrived in Scotland in 1057 with the knight Bartholomew Ladislaus Leslyn, escorting Princess Margaret, who later married King Malcolm Canmore.[1] Henri de St. Clair, the first to be born in Scotland, fought under Godfroi de Bouillon in the Holy Land in 1096 and was present at the siege of Jerusalem,[2] accompanied by members of eleven other leading Scottish aristocratic families.

A representative from each of the twelve families met regularly prior to the crusade and continued to meet at Roslin up until the late 18th century by which time all hopes of a Stuart restoration had died. All the families were linked by marriage, which included the Stuarts, Montgomerys, Setons, Douglases, Dalhousies, Ramseys, Leslies, and Lindsays, as well as the Sinclairs; they all were involved with the Templars, shared common beliefs and continued to propagate Templar traditions after the order's suppression. The families all played a part in the foundation of Freemasonry in Scotland and supported the Stuart cause.

Rex Deus ✝ The Families of the Grail

Laurence Gardner validates one important aspect of Rex Deus in his book, *The Bloodline of the Holy Grail*, claiming that the Stuarts were descended from leading families among the hierarchy in biblical Israel at the time of Jesus—dynastic roots similar to those shared by the families who met regularly at Roslin.

Earl William St. Clair

During the 15th century, the figure that did the most to preserve and propagate Rex Deus traditions was Earl William St. Clair. Earl William was not only the Lord of Roslin, but also the third St. Clair Earl of Orkney. His portrayal as a Knight of the Cockle and Golden Fleece[3] indicates his membership in two different orders mentioned earlier—the Knights of Santiago,[4] represented by the Cockle, and the Order of the Golden Fleece, founded by the Duke of Burgundy. He was also described as "one of the illuminati, a nobleman with singular talents" and as "a man of exceptional talents much given to policy, such as buildings of Castles, Palaces, and Churches.[5]" Earl William was a patron of craft masonry throughout Europe, a "Grand Master an adept of the highest degree.[6]" Scottish documents confirmed that he was not only hereditary Grand Master of the craft masons, but also of all the hard and soft guilds in Scotland,[7] such as the shipwrights, papermakers, tanners, and foresters.[8]

A true son of the Renaissance, William lived at the same time as René de Anjou and corresponded with him. Similar to Cosimo de' Medici, he was an obsessive collector of original manuscripts and acquired a vast library that he housed at Roslin Castle. A family historian records the appreciation conferred to this collection by Earl William:

> About this time (1447) there was a fire in the square keep by occasion of which the occupants were forced to flee the building. The Prince's chaplain seeing this, and remembering all of his master's writings, passed to the head of the dungeon where they all were, and threw out four great trunks where they were. The news of the fire coming to the Prince through the lamentable cries of the ladies and gentlewomen, and the sight thereof coming to his view in the place where he stood upon College Hill, he was sorry for nothing but the loss of his Charters and other writings; but when his chaplain who had saved himself by coming down the bell rope tied to a beam, declared how

his Charters and Writs were all saved, he became cheerful and
went to recomfort his Princess and the Ladys.[9]

The significance of these documents bolsters the fact that spiritual knowledge
runs like a river through the history of the St. Clairs. In his own day, Earl William was described as one of the Iluminati, which gives strong indication of
the esteem in which he was held—for what are the qualities of "the enlighten
ones" except those of deep and abiding spiritual knowledge and perception?
In fact, according to Tessa Ransford, a director of the Scottish Poetry Library,
the name Roslin translates from Scottish Gaelic as "ancient knowledge passed
down from generations."[10] The Roslin St. Clairs were the custodians of the
divinely inspired gnosis that was a true treasure of the Knights Templar. By
encoding this knowledge within the carvings of Rosslyn Chapel, Earl William
preserved that heritage for all time.

The Mystical Shrine-Rosslyn Chapel

Earl William St. Clair is best known for his most enduring and enigmatic
legacy, the mystical shrine of Rosslyn Chapel. The chapel's foundations were
laid between 1446 and 1450 and it was originally planned as a large collegiate
church. To construct this church, Earl William brought skilled and experienced master masons from all over Europe[11] and considerably enlarged Roslin
village in order to accommodate them. Roslin increased at such a pace that it
began to rival Haddington and even Edinburgh in size; it was given its royal
charter in 1456 by King James II.

The master masons that help build the chapel were paid £40 per year, a
substantial amount for a time when ordinary masons drew only £10 per year.
Earl William, as architect, patron, and designer of the chapel, exercised total
control over every detail of its construction. He left nothing to chance and,
like patrons of the artists in Renaissance Italy; he outlined his instructions
with such precision that they became the stuff of legend. Prior to any carving
being made in stone, a model was carved in wood and submitted to the earl for
approval. Then and only then did the stone carving begin. Hence the essential,
symphonic harmony of the design in Rosslyn Chapel is the cumulative result
of several factors; a plan drawn up by a remarkable and supremely gifted man
who exerted absolute control over design, quality, and construction; a comparatively rapid rate of building that left no time for contamination of the original

conception; and a crew of highly skilled masons who worked continuously on the same project, a rare occurrence in church building in that era.

Trevor Ravenscroft denotes: "The sculptures of Rosslyn are magnificent manifestations of spiritual insight or vision, given substance in stone." Douglas Sutherland described the chapel, in an article published in 1982, as: "A medieval masterpiece of masonry, containing some of the most exquisite carvings ever fashioned in stone, Rosslyn Chapel may now be half-forgotten but it is still very memorable.[12] There can be no realistic analysis of the meaning of the spiritual and artistic content of the carvings in this unique building that can be made without studying it with due consideration of the family history and the complex character of its founder. Viewed on their own, the carvings are simply beautiful and mysterious manifestations of masonic art that are susceptible to gross interpretation. Part of the enigma of Rosslyn Chapel is that, in this late-medieval, supposedly Christian Church, we find a plethora of symbolic references in stone in every initiatory spiritual tradition that can found in the history of mankind before its construction: a carving of the head of Hermes Trismegistus, the reputed author of the Emerald Tablets who is often equated with the Egyptian god Thoth; prolific carvings of the green man that commemorate the principle of spiritual death and rebirth central to all initiatory

A View of Rosslyn Chapel from the North
Photo by Cyndi Wallace-Murphy

paths; carvings of rosettes and five-pointed stars that once decorated the temples dedicated to Ishtar and Tammuz in ancient Babylonia, 2,500 years before the birth of Jesus.

Templar Symbolism in Rosslyn Chapel

Also, found throughout the chapel is symbolism intimately connected with the Knights Templar. J-A Durbec, a French scholar, listed the signs and symbols that validate the Templar attribution of any building as follows:

1. Carvings of a five-pointed star, *L'étoile.*
2. Two brothers on one horse, *deux frères sur une seule cheval.*
3. The seal known as the Agnus Dei, also known as the Templar seal, *un agneau pascal (nimbé ou non) tenant une croix patté audessus de lui.*
4. A stylized representation of the head of Jesus, like that represented in the Shroud of Turin or the Veil of Veronica, known as the Mandylion.
5. A dove in flight carrying an olive branch. *Une colombe tenant en son bec une branche d'olivier.*
6. A form of oriental cross known as the floriated cross.[13]

Before making any attributions to the Templars, we must proceed with caution, however, for the symbols listed by Durbec are, of course, all well known items of standard Christian iconography. When two or more are found in combination, however, within the same building, this suggests strong Templar influence. If they are all found together prior to the suppression of the order, we know we have a genuine Templar edifice.[14] In the case of Rosslyn, which was built over a century after the suppression of the Templars, we have something of a mystery. Contained within its sacred geometrical architecture are all the signs of true Templar construction. Furthermore, within the iconography, indications of Templar influence are not restricted to the diagnostic symbols already listed; they occur in one form or another at almost every turn.

Located in the vault of each bay in the aisles and arching across the roof of the crypt are carvings of the engrailed cross of the St. Clairs. At the junction of the arms of each cross, faintly but distinctively delineated in each case, is a variant on the *croix patté* of the Knights Templar known as the cross of universal knowledge. Neither is it mere coincidence that the heraldic colours of the St. Clair family are argent and sable, the same as those sported by the Sforzas of Milan and proudly carried on the battle flag of the Templar order, the Beauseant.

Resting in the chapel crypt and adjoining a 17th century guild stone depicting the King of Terrors is a Templar burial stone from one of local graveyards, another can be found in the north aisle of the chapel, engraved with the name William de Sinncler and surmounted by a floriated cross. Found on a pillar on the north wall is the Templar seal known as Agnus Dei; a similar pillar on the south wall bears the Veil of Veronica. The magnificent carving of a dove carrying an olive branch in its beak adorns the western section of the roof in a sea of five-pointed stars. From the very beginning, the St. Clair family of Roslin was intimately connected to the Templar order. They were members of Rex Deus who established the order, and the family castle was the final destination of Hughes de Payens when he returned from the Holy Land in 1172. The grave-marker found within the chapel that is so beautifully carved—the floriated cross—is a memorial to the man who led the Templar charge at Bannockburn in 1314, the charge that preserved the independence of Scotland and secured the throne for Robert the Bruce.[15]

Observing the Templar symbolism within Rosslyn chapel in the light of St. Clair history leads to one inevitable conclusion: the chapel whose design and content was strictly supervised by Earl William, was created as a lasting memorial to the much-maligned heretical Order of the Knights Templar and as a means of transmission of their ideals and beliefs to future generations. That is why the earl used the skills of his Masonic colleagues to such good effect in celebrating every known initiatory spiritual pathway that contributed, in one way or another, to the sacred gnosis preserved at considerable cost by the descendants of the twenty-four ma'madot of Israel.

This form of enduring celebration was not the only means used by Earl William to ensure the preservation of these initiatory rites. In his plans for the future, there are, in fact, more clues and signposts located within the chapel. Central to the Rex Deus tradition, these symbolic representations of sacred principles have been used for over 500 years by a fraternity strongly influenced by Earl William, for he may have used the construction of this holy shrine as the first step in creating an organization that would treasure and guard these secrets, and pass them on to future generations throughout the world—the craft of Freemasonry. The members of this brotherhood have all used their spiritual insight to transcend the geographical, cultural, and religious barriers that normally interrupt the progress of man.

The Foundation of Freemasonry

The enigma that surrounds the establishment of Freemasonry has been further clouded by the secrecy adopted by the craft in its relationship with the general public. The initial craft guilds of medieval masons throughout Europe had their own, sometimes very different, foundation myths, traditions, and initiation rituals. By some means or another, both in Scotland and elsewhere, the Craft masons were transformed into the precursors of modern Freemasonry. The argument of how, when, and where this happened has been harsh and drawn-out. The customary habit of secrecy adopted by the early Masonic brethren has made it difficult for historians to document the exact development of Freemasonry, and has complicated the rational study of these particular questions.

The controversy over Masonic origins often degenerates into a modern version of *odium theologicum*, in which the character of the proponent is questioned more vigorously than his or her theories. Nevertheless, receptive researchers from both sides of the argument are pursuing their various theories in a manner that will eventually resolve the issue. We believe that one family above all others had the motive, means, and the opportunity to initiate a transformative effect on the medieval craft guilds of operative masons and used it to such good effect that they evolved into the modern craft of Speculative Freemasonry. This belief will not silence those who emphatically defend their pro- or anti-Templar theories of origin, but it will, ultimately, provide solutions that can resolve this historical mystery for all time.

In this, we will describe certain aspects of the history of craft masonry; demonstrate how diverse members of Masonic guilds were brought together in one place, and how, under the guidance of the St. Clairs of Roslin, they began their transformation into the modern speculative craft. Additional evidence of the Rex Deus inceptions of the craft can be inferred from certain ancient rituals.

The Genesis of a Craft and the Early Origins of Freemasonry

Freemasonry, according to English poet and mythologist Robert Graves, began as Sufi society. It first appeared in England during the reign of King Athelstan (924–939), and was later introduced into Scotland as a craft guild. Graves claimed that the Sufic origins of the craftmasons, were as important as the role played later by the Templars that eventually resulted in the transformation of the operative craft guilds into Freemasonry. Graves places the origins of the Sufis long before the foundation of Islam:

> An ancient freemasonry whose origins have never been traced or dated although the characteristic Sufi signature is found in widely dispersed literature from at least the second millennium BCE[16]

He also describes how their hidden wisdom was passed through the generations, from the master to the pupil, as in so many initiatory orders.[17] Graves emphasizes the role played by the Sufi masters in building Solomon's Temple. We realize that there is a strong connection with the Hebrew people, for the Sufis' legendary mystical teacher, *el Khidir* or the Verdant One, is an anagram of two prophetic figures of biblical Israel—Elijah and John the Baptist. Thus, the question arises: Where did they get their ancient knowledge? The answer can be found in ancient Egypt in the era of the Pyramid Texts defined as the First Time.

We have previously described the level of sophistication and insight achieved by the three main branches of the Campagnonnage in early medieval France. Similar craft guilds operated in Germany, Italy and Spain, and those who built in the Gothic style had an exceptionally close relationship with the Templar order. Therefore, when the historian John Robinson recounts how the fleeing Templar knights were aided in their escape by lodges of craftmasons, our only unanswered question is: Were these specific lodges that gave shelter and passage in this manner the Children of Master Jacques, who later acquired the name of *les Compagnons Passants*?

The refugees joined the Order of the Knights of Christ in Portugal; in the Baltic States they joined the Teutonic Knights; in Lombardy, aided by the Cathars who had preceded them, they used their skills to strengthen the emergent banking system. However, in Scotland, the story was extremely different.

When King Robert the Bruce warned them to go underground; the Templars, nonetheless, kept their traditions alive. We propose that, under the protection of the St. Clairs of Roslin, Templar tradition and the craftmasons gnosis were given an opportunity to merge, to the mutual benefit of both.

Spiritual Knowledge and Masonic Gnosis

The skilled and perceptive master masons that created Rosslyn Chapel assumed that their artwork should be beautiful. However, sheer beauty was not enough. There had to be meaning—not simply meaning in the storytelling sense, although this was often an essential component, but a deeper and far more spiritual meaning. Keep in mind that, for the medieval craft mason, *ars sina scienta nihil est*—art without knowledge is nothing. In this framework, the knowledge referred to is "gnosis"—spiritual knowledge or mystical insight.

People of the medieval and Renaissance eras for whom the artwork was designed would have found themselves more deeply moved and far more involved in the symbolism of the art than any modern observer, however well versed. In that creative period, carvings, paintings, and even buildings were deliberately designed for men and women for whom symbolism was the breath of spiritual life—a spiritual life, moreover, that was startlingly different from that taught by the Church.

> For occultist, or medieval men, symbols have a real meaning. A symbol that is merely a symbol, merely a copy or an image, has no meaning; there is only significance in that which can become reality, in what can become a vibrant force. If a symbol acts upon the spirit of humanity in such a way that intuitive forces are set free, then and only then are we dealing with a true symbol.[18]

Earl William had planned a new reality for the future generations, an organization of compatible men who, from its birth, were, trained to learn by means of ritual, symbolism, and allegory. For them, symbolism became the driving force of true inspiration. This method of progressive involvement in the spiritual world, achieved through ascending degrees of initiation, brought the gnostic realities preserved by the families of the hidden tradition to a far wider audience.

The Apprentice Pillar

Of all the mysteries and legends that surround Rosslyn Chapel, few are as well known as that surrounding the most puzzling and beautiful of its artistic gems—the Apprentice Pillar. The long-standing story of the murdered apprentice, with its apparent reference to the initiation rituals of both the medieval guilds of craftmasons and the far older legend of Hiram Abif, Master Mason at the building of King Solomon's Temple, has immense symbolic, spiritual, and ritual resonance for the worldwide brotherhood of Freemasonry. The pillar is a representation of the Tree of Life essential to the study of Kabbala; it is also representative of the Yggdrasil tree of Norse mythology—the World Ash that binds together heaven and hell. It is another illustration of artistic and spiritual ambivalence that can be understood by Christians, pagans, and Jewish Kabbalists in a manner that transcends all frivolous religious divisions.

The Apprentice Pillar is one of three that divide the retro-choir from the central body of the chapel. Beside it is the Journeyman's Pillar and, lastly, there is the magnificent carving of the Master Mason's Pillar. As claimed by Masonic tradition, three important pillars of profound symbolic significance must support every true lodge. The Master Mason's Pillar symbolizes 'Wisdom' or sacred gnosis; the Journeyman's Pillar represents 'Strength'; the Apprentice Pillar signifies 'Beauty.' In the architectural terms significant to Masonic tradition, wisdom constructs, strength supports, and beauty is designed to adorn. Moreover, wisdom is ordained to discover, strength is made to bear and sustain, while beauty is made to attract. Yet, it would all be for nothing unless these pillars are erected upon the same rock or foundation—the one named Truth and Justice. These standards reflect those aspired to by the humble initiate of any valid spiritual path:

> He who is wise as a Perfect Master will not be easily injured by his own actions. Hath a person the strength which a Senior Warden represents he will bear and overcome every obstacle in life. He who is adorned like a Junior Warden with humility of spirit approaches nearer to the similitude of God than any other.[19]

Rosslyn Chapel was established in 1446 and Freemasonry some centuries later. Still within the confines of the chapel, symbolic references to Masonic

The Master Mason's Pillar (left) and the Apprentice Pillar (right)

Photos by Tim Wallace-Murphy

ritual, belief, and practice exist in abundance—to such a degree that there are few Masons in the world today who do not regard this place of beauty and spiritual enlightenment as the unofficial core church of the worldwide craft. Within the chapel, there are symbolic references to the Hiram Abif legend; the maul-marked face of the murdered apprentice gazes fixedly across the chapel at the contorted features of the Master Mason who supposedly killed him.

A strange anomaly emerged when plaster casts of the carvings were taken some years ago as an aid to the restoration process. It was determined that the head of the apprentice had been considerably altered—at one time, his faced had sported a full beard that had later been chiseled off. We have cause to believe that this alteration came about because Earl William had gone too far in his depiction of heresy, and that the two bearded faces were originally designed to show the heresy of the holy twins and the secret legend of the two Jesuses. Located nearby, on the south wall of the clerestory, is the carved face of the grieving widow and the phrase: "Who will come to the aid of the son of a widow?" This is one phrase that has held significant resonance for members of the Masonic crafts and guilds from the times of ancient Egypt down to the present. *Memento mori* proliferate, possibly the finest example being the exquisite carving of *la danse macabre*, the dance of death, on the ribbed vaulting of the retro-choir.

At some time, long before the foundation of Rosslyn Chapel and acting under the guidance of the St. Clairs, certain members of the inner circle of the Templar order were carefully selected from operative guilds for instruction in sacred knowledge. Included in the subjects of instruction were science, geometry, philosophy, and the contents of the documents recovered by the Templars during their excavation under the temple in Jerusalem.[20] The resulting effect was that, after the suppression of the Templars, Scotland in general and Midlothian in particular became beacons of enlightenment. This new brotherhood of speculative "free" masons formed charitable institutions to support the poorer members of society, and their respective guilds also set money aside for the benefits of their less fortunate neighbours. In Prince Michael of Albany's opinion, these were the only charitable institutions to be established in Scotland that were outside the control of the Church, they may well have been the first such organizations anywhere in the world.[21]

The establishment of Rosslyn Chapel, the assemblage of such a large group of highly skilled and influential masons from every corner of Europe, and the creation of their own community to house them gave Earl William the opportunity to extend and develop this type of organization. He was well aware that he was taking enormous risks, for the days of persecution and burning at the stake were far from over. In creating this recondite library in stone that is Rosslyn Chapel, however, and in stimulating and strengthening the new speculative "free" Masonic orders, he left us a lasting legacy that ensured that he, like his distinguished grandfather, Earl Henry St. Clair, richly deserved the title of "worthy of immortal memory."

Rosslyn Chapel's Retro Choir
Photo by Tim Wallace-Murphy

Earl William with his status as hereditary Grand Master of all the hard and soft guilds in Scotland, his authority over the Masonic court at Kilwinning, his Templar antecedents, the Masonic symbolism within Rosslyn Chapel, and his position as a scholar of esotericism all combine to demonstrate that he had the means, motive, and the opportunity to play an active role in transforming the ancient craft guilds into the modern speculative fraternity. The new Freemasonry gave no credence to barriers of class and eventually included King James VI of Scotland, who was initiated into the craft at the Lodge of Perth and Scone in 1601.[22] Two years later, when he became King James I of England, he needed influential allies as a counterweight to the greed of the self-serving British aristocracy. James found them among the members of the trade and craft guilds of England and introduced them on an informal basis to Freemasonry;[23] the first documentary evidence of inductions into Freemasonry date from 1640 during the reign of James' son, Charles I. In this period of repression, bloodshed, and war fought in the name of religion, the new fraternity wisely decided to be secretive from the beginning.

This secrecy makes it increasingly difficult to gauge the entire spectrum of esoteric streams that coalesced to form the craft, and to understand the various circumstances in each country that influenced local and national developments. The craft had a democratic appeal from the start in Scotland, and has continued in this manner every since. The tradition of preserving the sacred knowledge in an ascending hierarchy of degrees was almost intact and developed a high degree of sophistication and complexity in Scotland. Ultimately, this led to the development of the Royal Arch degrees of Scottish Freemasonry and Scottish Rite Freemasonry, which is still preserved in a relatively unpolluted form in parts of Continental Europe and the United States. Freemasonry, in Europe, developed an innate anticlerical and anti-Catholic bias and, for the first two or three centuries, maintained close connections with its Scottish brethren, both those at home and those in exile.

This long-term association is documented in the Rite of Strict Observance, where we discover that Masons from operative lodges of the Compagnonnage in France visited a lodge in Aberdeen in 1361, beginning a relationship that lasted for several hundred years. Even to this day, French lodges take particular pains to preserve, as far as possible, the esoteric teachings of the craft. The anticlerical bias was not as pronounced in England, and English Freemasonry became an integral part of the church/state establishment. Following considerable alterations to its rituals and beliefs, it became a major supporter of the House of Hanover after the expulsion of the Stuart line.

The innate democratic traditions of the Scottish craft that were the chief influence on the development of American Freemasonry may explain the high quality of the achievements of members on the new continent. These influential and masterful men possessed great spiritual insight and moral force that left an enduring imprint on the emerging American nation, primarily in the form of the Constitution of the United States, a ringing endorsement of freedom, democracy, and the rights of man that is the lasting spiritual legacy of this branch of Freemasonry.[24] Many of those who created and signed the American Constitution were either Freemasons or Rosicrucians,[25] including such figures as George Washington, John Adams, Benjamin Franklin,, Thomas Jefferson, and Charles Thompson. Alchemical symbolism taken from the Medieval Ages were enshrined in the American way of life with symbols such as the eagle, olive branch, arrows, and the pentagram, while the truncated pyramid and the all-seeing eye that adorn American banknotes, buildings, and monuments all point to the influence of the mystical past of Freemasonry on American life.

Rex Deus in Masonic Ritual

The understanding of Freemasonry and its inner workings that is accessible in the public domain is limited to what has been published by the craft, and is further circumscribed by vows of secrecy taken by individual members. For this reason, what we reveal here is presented in the certain knowledge that it represents only one small aspect of a far larger spectrum of ideas. However, there are particular correspondences between Masonic ritual and Rex Deus tradition that are readily identifiable. As an example, the Rex Deus oath of secrecy, "Lest my throat be cut or my tongue cut out," has a parallel in the ritual of the first craft degree of Freemasonry:

> These several points I solemnly swear to observe, without evasion, equivocation or mental reservation of any kind under no less a penalty than to have my throat cut across, my tongue torn out by the root and my body buried in the rough sands of the sea at low water mark…

The expression, "Lest my heart be torn out of my chest," which is the second part of the penalty of the Rex Deus oath, has its equivalent in Freemasonry's second degree:

> ...under no less a penalty than to have my left breast cut open, my heart torn there from, and given to the ravenous birds of the air, or to the devouring beasts of the field as prey.

There also two other replications of the Rex Deus oath found in Masonic ritual: "Lest my eyes be plucked out" is rendered in the ritual of the Knight White Eagle as "...under the penalty of forever remaining in perpetual darkness." While the use of a knife as a threat in the oath is repeated in the penalties recorded for the Past Master degree.

> ...having my hands lopped off at the wrist and my arms struck from my body and both hung at my breast suspended at the neck as a sign of infamy till time and putridity consume the same.

The charge of a form of idolatry in the form of the worship of a head that was levelled at the Knights Templar, as well as their ritual use of skulls, also reverberates within the walls of Freemasonry. Lomas and Knight, Masonic historians, recounts that, "Freemasonry around the world probably possesses some 50,000 skulls!"

The Hanoverian dynasty received support of the English Freemasonry, which led to unusual attitude adopted by the United Grand Lodge of England that actively discourages serious investigation into the origins of the craft, as they wish to erase from the record any reference to Scottish origins and its earlier alliance with the Stuart cause. As a consequence, there was a thorough purging of Scottish rituals from English Masonic practice. Thanks to the dedicated work of the Masonic scholar Dimitrije Mitrinovic in the early years of the 20th century, however, we are able to trace a high level of Rex Deus influence in some of these purged rituals.

Mitrinovic's library includes one book that records the fourth degree—that of the Secret Master—is concerned with mourning someone who remains anonymous.[26] The ritual of this particular degree commemorates a time when the constructing of the temple was brought to a halt due to a tragedy. To perform this ceremony, the lodge is draped in black and white and illuminated by light of eighty-one candles. The jewel of the degree is engraved with the letter "z" that refers to Zadok.[27] The Dead Sea Scrolls documents that the sons of

Zadok were the descendants of the high priests of the temple who were known as the Righteous Seed and the Sons of Dawn. This link to James the Just, who succeeded Jesus in the position of the Zadok, or Teacher of Righteousness, is part of the ancient Jewish tradition of the hereditary transmission of holiness preserved by the Rex Deus families.

Hiram Abif

Freemasonic tradition and ritual profess that the craft emerged from the time of Hiram Abif, who was killed by a blow to the temple for his refusal to betray a secret. This produces an inescapable parallel with the documented details of the death of James the Just. Hiram Abif was killed immediately before the completion of Solomon's Temple and, nearly 1,000 years later, when work on the Herodian Temple was nearing completion, building was brought to a temporary standstill as a mark of respect for James, the brother of Jesus, who had been ritually murdered. Chris Knight and Robert Lomas conclude that the tradition concerning the death of Hiram Abif is used as an allegory to mask the ritual commemoration of the murder of James the Just. Therefore, when Freemasons celebrate the ritual death of Hiram, they are commemorating one of the founders of Rex Deus.[28]

Another of the suppressed degrees—that of the Perfect Master—allegedly commemorates the reburial of the corpse of Hiram Abif. During this ritual, the lodge is lit by four groups of four candles, each placed at the cardinal points of the compass. The ritual portrays that King Solomon ordered Adoniram to construct a tomb for Hiram Abif in the form of an obelisk of black-and-white marble. The entryway to the tomb, which was completed in nine days, was set between two pillars supporting a square lintel engraved with the letter "J" hence is the association between this degree and the death of James the Just made explicit. Within this degree, the lodge is draped in green; green and gold are the heraldic colours of the royal house of David. Again, we find green and gold occurring as part of the 15ᵗʰ degree—that of the Knight of the Sword and the Knight of the East—which celebrates the building of Zerubbabel's Temple. We have always been perplexed that, as Rosslyn, a place of extreme importance to Freemasonry, while the building of Zerubbabel's Temple is commemorated on a lintel near the retro-choir, there is no direct reference to Solomon's Temple, only individual carvings of Solomonic interest.

The establishing of the Knights Templar is documented in a suppressed degree of Masonic ritual, the Knight of the East and West. The ritual claims that the degree was first created in 1118 when eleven knights took vows of secrecy, fraternity, and discretion under the eagle eye of the patriarch of Jerusalem. These knights include all nine founding members of the Knights Templar, with the inclusion of Count Fulk d'Anjou and Count Hughes I of Champagne. In this ritual, the presiding officer is known as the Most Equitable Most Sovereign Prince Master, and the High Priest supports him. Knight and Lomas claim that the Most Equitable Sovereign Prince Master was originally King Baldwin II of Jerusalem, and that the High Priest was most likely the Grand Master of the Templar order.

We submit that it is far more likely that the High Priest in this ritual represents the patriarch of Jerusalem. In this ritual, a large Bible hung with seven seals is placed upon a pedestal. Accompanying it is a floor display consisting of a heptagon within a circle, in the centre of which is a figure of a white-bearded, white-cloaked man with a golden girdle around his waist. The figure's extended hand holds seven stars that represent friendship, union, submission, discretion, fidelity, prudence, and temperance. The strange figure has a halo around his head, a two- edged sword issuing from its mouth, and is surrounded by seven candlesticks.[29] The seven seals hanging from the Bible and the seven stars are part of the principle of seven-foldness located in the Revelation of St. John of the Divine, one of two St. John's adored by the Templars.

The 20th degree, another suppressed degree—that of Grand Master—depicts the terrible destruction of the second temple in Jerusalem by the Romans in 70 CE Its ritual gives an account of the grief experience by the brethren who were in the Holy Land and how they had to flee from their homeland with the intention of constructing a third temple that would be a spiritual rather than a physical edifice. The creation of this new spiritual temple of God on Earth became a sacred duty. The narrative depicts how they divided themselves into a number of lodges before scattering throughout the length and breadth of Europe. One of these lodges came to Scotland, set itself up at Kilwinning, and was charged with the sacred duty of keeping records of their order. Consequently, the distinct outline of the story of the original Rex Deus families is described in this degree. As we have seen, another documents the founding of the Knights Templar, while a third commemorates the death of James the Just.

Enshrining Rex Deus secrets in a variety of degrees within the complex symbolism of Freemasonry is comparable to a man on the run seeking refuge in a large and crowded city. It is similar to the strategy employed by Earl William in randomly hiding a plethora of Templar and Rex Deus symbolism among the crowded and deliberately confused collection of carvings in Rosslyn Chapel. In spite of the vigorous attempts of the Hanoverian censors, the rituals used in these degrees have been documented for posterity and may well be in use today in France and America.

The spiritual inspiration of Freemasonry not only gave us the gift of the American Constitution, but it also contributed a great deal to the establishment of the principles of *liberté, égalité, et fraternité* that inspired the French Revolution and, lastly, the transformation of despotism into democracy. Additionally, Freemasonry played a role in the campaign for reunification of Italy through its influence on the Carbonari; both of the principal leaders of this revolutionary movement, Garibaldi and Mazzini, were active Freemasons. Once their armies liberated Rome from the tyranny of the papacy and gave a vibrant new reality to the old Visconti dream of a united kingdom of Italy, Pope Pius IX, deprived of all temporal power, began his lifelong exile in his self-imposed prison of the Vatican.

The pope vigorously denounced the Freemasons as the true authors of his debasement and vituperated furiously against them a series of encyclicals, papal bulls, and allocutions. In contrast to many Masonic historians within the

George Washington Laying the Foundation Stone of the Capitol
Photo Courtesy of the Supreme Council, Scottish Rite

craft today, this elderly pope was under no illusions as to the true origins of the 'diabolic' organization that had stripped him of all his earthly power. Freemasonry, for him, derived directly from the heretical Order of the Knights Templar, whom he depicted as being gnostic from their inception and followers of the Johannite Heresy. Neither was the pope under any misconceptions as to the true purpose of the Masonic fraternity, for, he claims, their aim was to destroy Holy Mother the Church. For Pius, there was little difference between the true aim of the Rex Deus families—that of reforming the Church around what they knew to be the true teachings of Jesus—and the destruction of the Church that had propelled him to dizzy heights of the papacy. Is there reason for us to doubt his opinions? How can we?—for this was Pope Pius IX, who first proclaimed the doctrine of Papal infallibility.

CHAPTER 21
PREPARING FOR THE FUTURE

The 17th, 18th and 19th centuries were an era of massive and fundamental social change; colonies fought for their freedom; revolutions changed the social order across nations and continents and, as we mentioned earlier, the city states of Italy were united at last and the Papal States were reduced from a ruthless mini-empire to the pathetic few acres immediately surrounding the Vatican. Individual Freemasons and members of the Rex Deus families played an important role in all of these acts of political, social and spiritual transformation. Immediately after the Reformation certain initiates stared corresponding right across Europe under the guidance of Erasmus and became known as 'the third force.' Another group of ecumenical initiates acting in concert with the Dutch 'Family of Love' formed an 'Invisible College' of spiritually inspired scholars who all contributed to the intellectual and spiritual Renaissance that evolved and developed into the Enlightenment. Among their number were such important figures as Isaac Newton, one of the most important founding members of modern science. The famed discoverer of The Law of Gravity was also a life-long esotericist and alchemist who claimed that the Judaic heritage deriving from Old Testament times was a divinely blessed archive of divine wisdom or gnosis. Not at all religious in the accepted sense of the word, he was a deeply spiritual man who completely rejected the Doctrine of the Holy Trinity and the deification of Jesus. He was among the very first personages of note who admitted in public that the New Testament had been distorted by the church.

Freemasonry spread across the channel to France from England and, through the Stewart exiles, from Scotland. When the deposed Stewart King was exiled to France in 1691 he was accompanied by a large number of companions, friends and supporters. This massive influx of Scots exiles helped to spread Freemasonry right across the continent. However, in France, at first at least, Freemasonry seemed to be restricted mainly to exiled Scots as the French seemed somewhat reluctant to join a brotherhood that had evolved from working people. Thanks to one man, that was about to change dramatically. Andrew Michael Ramsey was a graduate of Edinburgh University who had arrived in France in 1710 and promptly converted to Catholicism. After serving the Duc de Chateau-Thierry and later the Prince de Turenne[1] he was initiated into the Order of St Lazarus. He worked as a tutor to Bonnie Prince Charlie in Italy before returning to France where he took an active role in promoting Freemasonry. As the one-time tutor to Prince Charles Edward Stewart, Chevalier of St Lazarus and Grand Chancellor of the Grand Paris Lodge of Freemasonry, he may not have any original documents to quote, but he did\ have authority and he used it to considerable effect. He declared, without fear of argument, that Freemasonry had its origins not among the medieval stonemasons but from the kings, princes and emperors of the crusading era. He claimed that the original crusading kings and nobles had combined in one fraternity to rebuild the Temple of God on earth in the Holy Land. On their return to Europe they founded lodges that were later neglected in every country except Scotland from whence it had now come back to France. Ramsey's oration was published in the *Almanac des Cocus* in 1741. It certainly rang bells for Ramsey's French audience for they were reluctant they to associate with people who had worked with their hands, but they flocked in their thousands to join a fraternity founded by kings, nobles and emperors. This popularization of Freemasonry gave Rex Deus families the opportunity to intervene effectively and create rites and rituals firmly based on Rex Deus beliefs. Chevalier Ramsey's acknowledgement that Freemasonry had deep roots in Scotland and the influence of exiled Scots led to the creation of Scottish Rite Freemasonry. The papacy were far from enthusiastic about this new development and issued a papal bull, *In Eminenti Apostolatus Specula*, the first in a long line of bitter denunciations of Freemasonry. Two years after that bull was published it became a capital offence for any resident of the papal states to become a Freemason.

The role of individual Freemasons and Rex Deus members in both the America War of Independence and the French Revolution was a form of behaviour that was frequently repeated. However, the Craft of Freemasonry never took part in any political action as a body, but individual members, inspired by the principles of the craft, played an important role in a variety of revolutionary movements that improved the lot of ordinary people right across the globe. Garibaldi along with Mazzini and the Carbonari who followed them, were responsible for the reunification of Italy and putting very severe limits indeed on the temporal authority of the pope. Leading Freemasons were instrumental in bringing about the French Revolution and creating the political climate wherein the ideas of Liberté, Egalité and Fraternité could flourish. This was after the French Freemason, Lafayette, had assisted his American counterparts led by George Washington to free their new country from colonial domination by Britain. While the actions of certain Freemasons in the fight for independence and liberty is well known, what is not such public knowledge is that such activity by Freemasons on the political right wing was also common. Freemasons were heavily supporting right wing and repressive regimes in Austria, Britain, Switzerland and even, from time to time, in France. There were Freemasons on both sides at the Battle of the Alamo. Truly Freemasonry is a brotherhood that spans all races, creeds, social classes and shades of political opinion. One of the many reasons it has survived and prospered is that, within the lodge, discussion of divisive matters such as politics and religion are forbidden.

The Esoteric Revival

Post revolutionary intellectual and spiritual freedom stimulated by Freemasonic activity created a ferment of debate and interest in France during the mid-19th century and provided a foundation for an ever-deepening interest in the occult, or hidden mysteries. This, in its turn, led to a massive esoteric revival that did not limit itself to France but spread across Europe, into Britain and on to the Americas. This movement was not limited to the studying the realm of Christian esotericism or the Knights Templar, but warmly embraced Eastern mysticism from Muslim, Hindu and Buddhist roots. Helen Petrovna Blavatsky (1831–1891) founded the Theosophical Society, which is still with us today, to promote interest in Eastern forms of spirituality and spread it throughout the English-speaking world. Europe's own pre-history began to be taken far more seriously with a renewed interest being taken in her many Neolithic sites.

One centre of esoteric studies that rose to prominence in France and exerted considerable influence in the French colony of Canada was the Compagnie du St-Sacrement founded in the early years of the 17th century whose leading light was a certain Jean-Jacques Olier. It has been compared by some scholars to the medieval Templars and by others to an early form of Freemasonry. Its headquarters was at the Church of St Sulpice in Paris and it soon spread all over France and only a select few knew the names of any of the leaders of the branches and chapters. Contemporaneous accounts at the time of its foundation refer to a 'mysterious secret' which is the centre of its power. While ostensibly devoted to charitable works, its real objective was to seek political power. One director, Vincent de Paul, rose to be confessor to King Louis XIII and the order itself played a mysterious and formative role in the founding of Montreal in Canada. Descriptions of this strange body vary widely, from right-wing and ultra Catholic on the one hand to heretical, on the other. Towards the end, names such as the Duke of Guise and the Viscount of Turin are mentioned in its annals. Suppressed in 1665, it allegedly recalled all its records and secreted them somewhere in Paris.

Rex Deus in the World of Islam

The European group of families known as Rex Deus are not the only hereditary caste who have secretly preserved what they believe are the true teachings of Jesus. Living in the remote mountain range known as the *Jebel Asaria* that joins northern Lebanon and the Turkish border, are a mysterious tribe or sect, known as the Nosairi. To preserve their own secret belief system, the tribe outwardly wear the prevailing religion of that region, namely Islam, as a garment to conceal their true faith. Within that faith there are Christian and pagan elements, the use of incense, celebration of certain Christian feasts, and the veneration of both St George and St Matthew. This strange melange of beliefs has, despite its apparent secrecy, given rise to some scholarly comment. One Frenchman, Massingnon, believes that, at heart, the sect is really Christian.[2] Another French scholar, René Dessaud, takes that line of thought even further and suggests that this sect grew directly out of the Nazorenes led by Jesus himself and that, therefore, the Nosairi are older than either the teachings of St Paul and the earliest forms of either Christianity or Islam.

A British army officer who lived among the Nosairi for some years during the Second World War, earned the complete trust of the tribal leaders. His name was Norman Birks. When they disclosed certain of their secret beliefs to him, he would have immediately recognised them as Rex Deus beliefs had he known about them at the time. Birks was informed that, in order to survive, the Nosairi wore a perpetual garment of dissembling and disguise to mask their true beliefs from all outsiders. Their real beliefs were only revealed to initiates under an oath of secrecy that promised death as the penalty for anyone who revealed their secrets to outsiders. In their rituals their two most important symbols are the light and the chalice and 'they drink to the light' from the chalice. When Birks introduced the subject of the Holy Grail, one of their leaders replied 'The Grail you speak of is a symbol and it stands for the doctrine that Jesus taught John the Beloved alone. We have it still.' Birks wrote later, 'Here preserved in these remote mountains is a precious relic, a living fragment of *the alternative tradition*.'[3]

Among the Nosairi there are direct parallels to Catharism in that there are divisions between the hearers and the initiated who are called 'the elect.' The Initiated members of the elect wear a particular girdle to denote their status, like the Cathars and the Templars. Among the Nosairi, the people know that Jesus was a divinely gifted man and not God, but that nonetheless he was a perfect vehicle for 'the Light.' The term 'The Word' as used in the Gospel of John is not a metaphor for a transcendent being but simply the expression of a transcendent quality in the universe, which is ultimately attainable by all who follow the Way. They regard Jesus as an exemplar who had achieved union with the Divine in a manner that all men of goodwill could follow. Therefore among the Nosairi we have found an almost exact replication of the Rex Deus tradition, but hidden in this case within the world of Islam and not within Christianity.

Baigent, Leigh and Lincoln published *The Holy Blood and the Holy Grail* in 1981 revealing to an astounded world that Jesus had founded a dynasty. In 1993, the insightful American author Margaret Starbird published *The Woman with the Alabaster Jar*, a book that proved that Jesus had been married and had children. Tim first met Michael Monkton in 1994 and commenced his investigations into what he then called 'the Rex Deus hypothesis.' Laurence Gardner published a book in 1996 under the title of 'The Bloodline of the Holy Grail' that touched on many aspects of the same story but from a slightly different perspective. Then came H.R.H. Prince Michael of Albany's first major book, *The Forgotten Monarchy of Scotland* that traced his claim to be the heir to the Stewart dynasty and a direct descendant of Jesus. Other books on similar and related themes have followed. Two thousand years after the birth of an obscure Jewish Rabbi, Jesus the Nazarene is the truth finally coming out despite two millennia of church repression?

CHAPTER 22
CONCLUSIONS

O ur investigation was triggered by the furore surrounding the launch of *The Holy Blood and the Holy Grail* and the first revelations of the Rex Deus traditions by Michael Monkton. These disclosures in their turn provoked us to examine the roots of all three of the major monotheistic faiths and gave us an understanding of the reality that lay behind their foundation. A reality that, more often than not, is completely at odds with the foundation myths that these religions promote as their 'true' origins.

No-one can prove that Moses came down Mount Sinai carrying two tablets of stone inscribed with the ten commandments; nor is there anyone who can prove that the crucifixion of Jesus was a redemptive act nor can it be proven that the Prophet Muhammad had his visions in a cave during Ramadan— these are all matters of faith and not of fact. None of this devalues the indelible marks on the historical record made by followers of all three great religions. History records the actions done by the faithful and demonstrates the intensity of the faith of those who have acted—however, they do not validate in any way, the foundation mythology of Judaism, Christianity or Islam. When we come to examine the historical record, this is as true for the Rex Deus hypothesis as it is for the great religions. While we have found strong indications that the story we were told has a considerable foundation in fact, that is, it could be true, we have no irrefutable proof. As to the Cohenite marital practices, while we have some degree of independent verification up to the fall of the Roman

Empire and a considerable degree more after the 10th century when record keeping became efficient, once again it is impossible to verify the whole story.

Tracing concerted actions by the Rex Deus families was somewhat easier, the foundation of the Knights Templar, the propagation of the Grail Sagas, the first public display of the Turin Shroud are all relatively well documented. Thus the idea that the Rex Deus traditions have been a long-term force for good is undeniable. The fog closes in again when we come to the foundation of Freemasonry, largely owing to the innate secrecy of its early members who came together at some risk to themselves when the era of repression was only just coming to an end. The continuity between Templar belief systems, as demonstrated by their symbolism, and those of Rex Deus, as recounted by Michael Monkton, is fairly obvious. So, what is the situation today? And what of the future?

The Mystery of Rennes-le-Chateau Today

When that masterly storyteller, Henry Lincoln, introduced the mystery of Rennes-le-Chateau to the British public in 1972, he, like everyone else, was blissfully unaware of the furore and controversy that was to follow from that day to this. A situation complicated by fraudsters, fantasists and, sometimes, outright lunacy. Yet when all the obfuscation, errors and fantasies are stripped away two major issues still remain vibrantly alive. Firstly, the genie is really out of the bottle, despite two thousand years of lies and dogmatism by the Church, we now know that Jesus did have a family and his descendants live among us today. Secondly, we are no nearer a solution to the puzzle of where did Saunière get his money from than we were forty-four years ago. Henry's work has stimulated the growth of a sustained pilgrimage and tourist business in the region that has brought employment to the Languedoc in a manageable manner. All who come here are captivated by the natural beauty of Occitania, and a substantial number find a high degree of spiritual solace just by being here. The spiritual and intellectual benefit that has accrued to people who were stimulated to re-examine their faith, or lack of it, because of the work of Henry Lincoln, would be almost impossible to assess. Because of the interest in the Rennes-le-Chateau story, and Henry's later work on Sacred Geometry, people's mental horizons have been expanded in a manner that would have been thought impossible a few short years ago. Interest in related fields such as the

Knights Templar, Freemasonry, the Hidden Streams of Spirituality, other sacred sites such as Chartres, Rosslyn, Rocamadour and the Mont St Michel, has soared. Above all, people have been encouraged to question all religious pronouncements rather than blindly accept them. What, if any, relevance has Rex Deus teaching brought to the 21st century and where does it fit into the so-called 'New Age' philosophy?

From The Occult Revival To The Present

The Occult revival of the late 19th century carried on through the 1920's and 1930's inspired by the works of Gurdjieff, Ouspensky and Dion Fortune. By the mid to late 1950's, esoteric thought, New Age philosophy and Alternative Medicine had established a firm base among the middle classes in both the United Kingdom and the USA. The 'Counter Culture' of the 1960's helped spread the message and began to create a worldwide constituency among young people. Investigating esoteric spirituality and seeking a change in consciousness were activities no longer restricted to elderly scholars but have now spread worldwide, recognising no limits set by social class, age, sex or culture. Then came the publication of *The Holy Blood and the Holy Grail* and this ever-growing search for sacred knowledge became a tidal wave of insatiable curiosity. Everything was up for grabs. In the 1980's and 1990's Eastern gurus were a 'dime a dozen' and, in the early days of the Internet, self appointed 'spiritual teachers' touted for business offering instant enlightenment for a price. In this welter of activity, where was Rex Deus? Keeping quiet but preserving the message as usual.

Tim was introduced to the Rex Deus tradition in 1994 and has spent a goodly part of the intervening years exploring what can be found out about this highly secretive group. Their recorded public activities have been described within the pages of this book and are, undoubtedly of a sustained and beneficial nature. Their 'official' public face is The Order of the Fleur de Lys, whose motto is "Honour above self, Duty above wealth, Justice above the law and Truth above all." And while that gives us some indication of their aspirations it tells us little about their present intentions. However, when we look back through the centuries they never gave any forewarning of what they were about to do, so why should we expect them to be any different today? Are there any pressing problems, other than 'Global Warming' that could possibly benefit from Rex Deus attention?

Paradigm Change

There is a general feeling pervading society that there is a need for a new vision that transcends so-called 'normal' limits of age, race, creed, colour, gender and social class. A subtle and all pervading 'shift in consciousness' is already underway that is tangible. A search for 'the old way of knowing' preserved by Rex Deus, the Medieval Christian mystics, the Cathars and all the other hidden streams of spirituality, has been going on for some decades now. The concept is to use this Divinely inspired Gnosis to change society and imbue it with compassion, respect for truth and justice. The need for such change is apparent to anyone who watches television with its harrowing pictures of famine, deprivation, wars and man's inhumanity to man that are shown on a daily basis.

There are certain basic conditions that must obtain before such a paradigm shift can take place. Most importantly, there has to be a growing and widespread dissatisfaction with the present system. That, in itself, is not enough and unless there is the creations of a concerted minority of opinion-formers worldwide who are dedicated to change, nothing will happen. Then, when a social, economic and political turbulence or natural catastrophe occurs, this can provoke and reinforce the move towards change. In seeking these objectives, the true teachings of Jesus that have been preserved despite two thousand years of persecution are reinforced by the basic principles of all valid spiritual paths. Rex Deus families may be silent at the moment, but their teaching is available worldwide through Freemasonry and the Grail Sagas. Who looking at the world as it really is today, can claim with any honesty that it does not need to apply the principles of Brotherhood based firmly on the foundations of Truth and Justice. Maybe there is a Freemasonic conspiracy and, if there is, it is truly a simple one—to make this world a better place to live in. And that, in a nutshell seems to have been the objective of Rex Deus tradition, the true teaching of Jesus and the fruits of all valid spiritual paths. The Rex Deus families never had a monopoly on truth, but preserve it and share it they did to the ultimate benefit of all. Who can tell what else is yet to come? Meanwhile we can draw from many and varied sources of other spiritual paths as described by Sheik Ragip Frager:

> Spirituality is a river that came to earth with Adam, may God grant
> him peace.

It was refreshed by the prophets Abraham, Moses, Elisha, John the Baptist and Jesus, may God grant them peace.

It was refreshed and strengthened anew by the Great Prophet Mohammed, May his name be blessed and may God grant him peace.

It knows no boundaries of space, or culture or time,

Yet, every creed, every race and every culture claims it for its own.

My brethren, it is always the same river.

May Peace and Blessings be upon you all.

End Notes

Introduction

[1]*Lost Treasure of Jerusalem*, broadcast in the 'Chronicle' series by the BBC in Feb1972.
[2]*The Priest, the Painter and the Devil*, a 'Chronicle' film broadcast by the BBC in 1974, and the, *The Shadow of the Templars* broadcast in 1979.
[3]First published by Jonathan Cape in 1982.
[4]Anthony Powell, *The Daily Telegraph*.
[5]Miron Grindea, *The Sunday Telegraph*.
[6]Gérard de Sède, *Le Tresor Maudit*.
[7]First Published by Jonathan Cape in 1986.
[8]The Timewatch programme *The History of a Mystery*, broadcast by the BBC.
[9]*The Tomb of God* by Richard Andrews and Paul Schellenberger.

Chapter 1

[1]Gérard de Sède, *Rennes-le Château, Les Impostures, Les Phantasmes, Les Hypothèses*, p 11.
[2]Gérard de Sède, *Rennes-le Château, Les Impostures, Les Phantasmes, Les Hypothèses*, p 11.
[3]Gérard de Sède, *Rennes-le Château, Les Impostures, Les Phantasmes, Les Hypothèses*, p 11.
[4]Baigent, Leigh, and Lincoln, *The Holy Blood and the Holy Grail*, p 12.
[5]Baigent, Leigh, and Lincoln, *The Holy Blood and the Holy Grail*, p 12.
[6]Baigent, Leigh, and Lincoln, *The Holy Blood and the Holy Grail*, p 12.
[7]Gérard de Sède, *Rennes-le Château, Les Impostures, Les Phantasmes, Les Hypothèses*, p. 87.

[8]*The Cambridge Illustrated History of the Middle Ages*, Vol. I, 350–950, Robert Fussier, ed. P 63 and Baigent, Leigh and Lincoln, *The Holy Blood and the Holy Grail, p12*.

[9]Baigent, Leigh and Lincoln, *The Holy Blood and the Holy Grail, p12*.

[10]Louis Fedie, *Le Comte de Razés et le Dicese d'Alet*.

[11]Wallace-Murphy and Hopkins, *Rosslyn-Guardian the Secrets of the Holy Grail*, p 123.

[12]George Serrus, *The Land of the Cathars* pp 3 and 16.

[13]Michael Aue (Alison Hebborn, trans.), *The Cathars*.

[14]George Serrus, *The Land of the Cathars* p 50.

[15]Raymonde Reznikov, *Cathares et Templières*, p 7.

[16]Raymonde Reznikov, *Cathares et Templières*, pp 7–8.

[17]Picknett and Prince, *The Templar Revelation*, p 87.

[18]Information supplied by the *Centre des etudes Recherches Templières*, based upon the research of the founder, George Kiess.

[19]Baigent, Leigh and Lincoln, *The Holy Blood and the Holy Grail*, p 5.

[20]Tim Wallace-Murphy, *The Templar Legacy and the Masonic Inheritance within Rosslyn Chapel*, p 19, And Wallace-Murphy and Hopkins, *Rosslyn Guardian of the Secret of the Holy Grail* pp 99- 100.

[21]Gérard de Sède, *Rennes-le Château, Les Impostures, Les Phantasmes, Les Hypothèses*, p. 91.

[22]George Serrus, *The Land of the Cathars* p 33.

[23]Gérard de Sède, *Rennes-le Château, Les Impostures, Les Phantasmes, Les Hypothèses*, p. 17.

[24]Gérard de Sède, *Rennes-le Château, Les Impostures, Les Phantasmes, Les Hypothèses*, p 19.

[25]Baigent, Leigh and Lincoln, *The Holy Blood and the Holy Grail*, p 4.

[26]Gérard de Sède, *Rennes-le Château, Les Impostures, Les Phantasmes, Les Hypothèses*, p 20.

[27]Baigent, Leigh and Lincoln, *The Holy Blood and the Holy Grail*, p 4.

[28]Gérard de Sède, *Rennes-le Château, Les Impostures, Les Phantasmes, Les Hypothèses*, p 20.

[29]Baigent, Leigh and Lincoln, *The Holy Blood and the Holy Grail*, p. 4.

[30]Baigent, Leigh and Lincoln, *The Holy Blood and the Holy Grail*, p. 5.

[31]Gérard de Sède, *Rennes-le Château, Les Impostures, Les Phantasmes, Les Hypothèses*, p 19.

[32]Baigent, Leigh and Lincoln, *The Holy Blood and the Holy Grail*, p. 5.

[33]Gérard de Sède, *Rennes-le Château, Les Impostures, Les Phantasmes, Les Hypothèses*, p 27.

[34]Confirmed in Hoffet's archives in Paris at the Villa Mozart, also cited Gérard de Sède,.

[35] Gérard de Sède, *Rennes-le Château, Les Impostures, Les Phantasmes, Les Hypothèses,* p 20.

[36] Baigent, Leigh and Lincoln, *The Holy Blood and the Holy Grail,* p. 29.

[37] Baigent, Leigh and Lincoln, *The Holy Blood and the Holy Grail,* p. 7.

[38] Gérard de Sède, *Rennes-le Château, Les Impostures, Les Phantasmes, Les Hypothèses,* pp 34–5.

[39] Baigent, Leigh and Lincoln, *The Holy Blood and the Holy Grail,* p. 8.

[40] Baigent, Leigh and Lincoln, *The Holy Blood and the Holy Grail,* p. 8.

[41] Baigent, Leigh and Lincoln, *The Holy Blood and the Holy Grail,* p. 8.

[42] Baigent, Leigh and Lincoln, *The Holy Blood and the Holy Grail,* p. 8.

[43] Baigent, Leigh and Lincoln, *The Holy Blood and the Holy Grail,* pp 8–9.

[44] *The Lost Gospel according to St Peter,* v. 10.

[45] Gérard de Sède, *Rennes-le Château, Les Impostures, Les Phantasmes, Les Hypothèses,* p. 41.

[46] Gérard de Sède, *Rennes-le Château, Les Impostures, Les Phantasmes, Les Hypothèses,* p. 41.

[47] Baigent, Leigh and Lincoln, *The Holy Blood and the Holy Grail,* p. 9.

[48] Gérard de Sède, *Rennes-le Château, Les Impostures, Les Phantasmes, Les Hypothèses,* p. 46.

[49] Gérard de Sède, *Rennes-le Château, Les Impostures, Les Phantasmes, Les Hypothèses,* p. 66.

[50] Gérard de Sède, *Rennes-le Château, Les Impostures, Les Phantasmes, Les Hypothèses,* p. 49.

[51] Baigent, Leigh and Lincoln, *The Holy Blood and the Holy Grail,* p. 9.

[52] Baigent, Leigh and Lincoln, *The Holy Blood and the Holy Grail,* p. 10.

[53] Baigent, Leigh and Lincoln, *The Holy Blood and the Holy Grail,* p. 10.

[54] Gérard de Sède, *Rennes-le Château, Les Impostures, Les Phantasmes, Les Hypothèses,* p. 77.

Chapter 2

[1] Baigent, Leigh and Lincoln, *The Holy Blood and the Holy Grail,* p xiii .

[2] Baigent, Leigh and Lincoln, *The Holy Blood and the Holy Grail,* p xiv.

[3] Baigent, Leigh and Lincoln, *The Holy Blood and the Holy Grail,* p 6.

[4] Baigent, Leigh and Lincoln, *The Holy Blood and the Holy Grail,* p 6.

[5] Baigent, Leigh and Lincoln, *The Holy Blood and the Holy Grail,* p xiv.

[6] Baigent, Leigh and Lincoln, *The Holy Blood and the Holy Grail,* pp xv-xvi.

[7] Baigent, Leigh and Lincoln, *The Holy Blood and the Holy Grail,* p 16 .

[8] Baigent, Leigh and Lincoln, *The Holy Blood and the Holy Grail,* pp 36–7.

[9]Ravenscroft & Wallace-Murphy, *The Mark of the Beast*, p 52.

[10]Wallace-Murphy & Hopkins, *Rosslyn Guardian of the Secrets of the Holy Grail*, p 97.

[11]Wallace-Murphy & Hopkins, *Rosslyn Guardian of the Secrets of the Holy Grail*, p 98.

[12]Baigent, Leigh and Lincoln, *The Holy Blood and the Holy Grail*, pp 76–7.

[13]Ravenscroft & Wallace-Murphy, *The Mark of the Beast*, p 52.

[14]Baigent, Leigh and Lincoln, *The Holy Blood and the Holy Grail*, pp 66 & fff.

[15]Baigent, Leigh and Lincoln, *The Holy Blood and the Holy Grail*, p. 60–70.

[16]Baigent, Leigh and Lincoln, *The Holy Blood and the Holy Grail*, Chapter 4.

[17]Baigent, Leigh and Lincoln, *The Holy Blood and the Holy Grail*, p. 71.

[18]Baigent, Leigh and Lincoln, *The Holy Blood and the Holy Grail*, p. 72.

[19]Baigent, Leigh and Lincoln, *The Holy Blood and the Holy Grail*, p. 76–7.

[20]Baigent, Leigh and Lincoln, *The Holy Blood and the Holy Grail*, p. 85.

[21]Baigent, Leigh and Lincoln, *The Holy Blood and the Holy Grail*, p. 92.

[22]Baigent, Leigh and Lincoln, *The Holy Blood and the Holy Grail*, p. 93.

[23]Baigent, Leigh and Lincoln, *The Holy Blood and the Holy Grail*, p. 97–9.

[24]Baigent, Leigh and Lincoln, *The Holy Blood and the Holy Grail*, p. 100.

[25]Baigent, Leigh and Lincoln, *The Holy Blood and the Holy Grail*, p. 101–2.

[26]T Wallace-Murphy, *The Templar Legacy and the Masonic Inheritance within Rosslyn Chapel*, p 18.

[27]Baigent, Leigh and Lincoln, *The Holy Blood and the Holy Grail*, p. 110.

[28]Baigent, Leigh and Lincoln, *The Holy Blood and the Holy Grail*, p 267.

[29]Baigent, Leigh and Lincoln, *The Holy Blood and the Holy Grail*, pp 368.

Chapter 3

[1]Richard Andrews and Paul Schellenberger, *The Tomb of God*.

Chapter 4

[1]John Dominic Crossan, *Jesus a Revolutionary Biography*, p 34.

[2]John E Taylor, *The Immerser, John the Baptist in Second Temple Judaism*. P 278.

[3]Colin Wilson, *From Atlantis to the Sphinx*, p 81.

[4]Robert Bauval & Adrian Gilbert, *The Orion Mystery*, p. 58.

[5]I. E. S. Edwards, *The Pyramids of Egypt*, p 150.

[6]J. H, Breasted, *Development of Religion and Thought in Ancient Egypt*, p 102.

[7]Bauval & Gilbert, *The Orion Mystery*, p 63.

[8]Bauval & Gilbert, *The Orion Mystery*, p 63.

[9]I. E. S. Edwards, *The Pyramids of Egypt*, p 151.

[10]R O Faulkner, *The Ancient Egyptian Pyramid Texts*, p. v.

[11]John Anthony West, *Serpent in the Sky*, p 1.

[12]M. Rice, *Egypt's Making: The Origins of Ancient Egypt 5000–2000 BCE*, p 33.

[13]Rohl, *Genesis of Civilisation*, p 316.

[14]D. E, Derry, 'The Dynastic Race in Egypt' *Journal of Egyptian Archaeology*, 42 (1956).

[15]H, Frankfort, *Kingship and the Gods*, p 101.

[16]H. Winkler, *Rock Drawings of Southern Upper Egypt*,.

[17]David Rohl, *Genesis of* Civilisation, p. 316.

[18]David Rohl, *Genesis of Civilisation*, p. 265.

[19]G ,Goyon, *Le Secret des Batisseurs des Grandes Pyramids*.

[20]Aristotle, *de Caelo II*.

[21]Proclus Diodachus *Commentaries on the Timaeus*.

[22]I. E. S. Edwards, *Pyramids of Egypt*, pps 284–286.

[23]Colin Wilson, From *Atlantis to the Sphinx*. p 21.

[24]Bauval & Hancock, *Keeper of Genesis*, p 228.

[25]E, A, E, Raymond, *Mythical Origins of the Egyptian Temple*, p 273.

[26]André Vanden Broek, *Al-Kemi*, .

[27]Colin Wilson, From *Atlantis to the Sphinx*. p 32.

[28]Rene Schwaller de Lubicz, *Sacred Science*, .

[29]Colin Wilson, From *Atlantis to the Sphinx*. p 14.

[30]Lewis Pauwells & Jacques Bergier, *The Dawn of Magic*, p 247.

[31]David Rohl, *Genesis of Civilisation*, p 381.

Chapter 5

[1]Genesis ch 13 v 16.

[2]Genesis ch 20 v 12.

[3]Raschi, *Pentatuque selon Raschi*, p 251.

[4]Genesis ch 11 v 27.

[5]*Sepher Hajashar* ch 26.

[6]Genesis, ch 21 v 21.

[7]Isadore Epstein, *The Babylonian Talmud*.

[8]Sura 21.72 also cited by Osman in *Out of Egypt*, p. 12 .

[9]E. Sellin, *Moses and His Significance for Israelite Jewish History*.

[10]Sigmund Freud, *Moses and Monotheism*.

[11]Ahmed Osman, *Stranger in the Valley of the Kings*.

[12]Genesis, ch 45 v 8.

[13]A. Weighall, *The Life and Times of Akenhaten*.

[14]Genesis ch 45 v 87.

[15]T. Davis, *The Tomb of Iouiya and Touiya*.

[16]Robert Feather, *The Copper Scroll Decoded*, p 34.

[17]Exodus, ch 1 v 8.

[18]A. Osman, *Stranger in the Valley of the Kings.*

[19]M. Cotterell, *The Tutenkhamun Prophecies,* p 335.

[20]S. Freud, *Moses and Monotheism.*

[21]Cited by Robert Feather in *The Copper Scroll Decoded,* p 36.

[22]Flinders Petrie, *The Religion of Ancient Egypt.*

[23]Deuteronomy ch 5 vs 6–9.

[24]M & R Sabbah, *Les Secrets de L'Exode,* p 99.

[25]A Osman, *Moses Pharaoh of Egypt,* pp 172–3.

[26]A. F. d'Olivier, *La Langue Hébraique restitué.*

[27]M & R Sabbah, *Les Secrets de L'Exode .*

[28]M & R Sabbah, *Les Secrets de L'Exode* p. 7.

[29]Freud, *Moses and Monotheism.*

[30]M & R Sabbah, *Les Secrets de L'Exode* p. 6.

[31]M & R Sabbah, *Les Secrets de L'Exode* p. 6.

[32]Exodus ch 3 vs 21–22.

[33]Robert Feather, *The Copper Scroll Decoded,* p. 123.

[34]M & R Sabbah, *Les Secrets de L'Exode* p. 112.

Chapter 6

[1]Sigmund Freud, *Moses and Monotheism.*

[2]J. M. Allegro, *The Dead Sea Scrolls and the Christian Myth,* p 65.

[3]N. Cantor, *The Sacred Chain—a History of the Jews,* p. 7.

[4]N. Cantor, *The Sacred Chain—a History of the Jews,* p. 11.

[5]P. Johnson, *A History of the Jews,* p 42.

[6]J. M. Allegro, *The Dead Sea Scrolls and the Christian Myth,* p 40.

[7]Exodus, ch 13 vs 21–22.

[8]Exodus ch 33 vs 9–11.

[9]Psalms 99: 7.

[10]Karen Armstrong, *A History of God,* p 82.

[11]Cantor, *The Sacred Chain,.*

[12]R. Lane Fox, *The Unauthorized Version: Truth and Fiction in the Bible,* pps 225–233.

[13]Ammon Ben Tor (ed) *The Archaeology of Ancient Israel.*

[14]P. Johnson, *A History of the Jews,* p. 43.

[15]Karen Armstrong, *A History of God,* p 19.

[16]P. Johnson, *A History of the Jews,* p. 45.

[17]Karen Armstrong, *A History of Jerusalem,* p 27.

[18]The Jerusalem bible which is translated from the Hebrew. Also cited by M. Zeitlin, *Ancient Judaism,* p 173.

[19]Samuel ch 8 v 17.

[20]Karen Armstrong, *A History of Jerusalem*, p 40.

[21]Exodus ch 6 vs 14–25.

[22]D. Ussishkin, 'King Solomon's Palaces' *Biblical Archaeologist*, 35, 1973.

[23]I Kings, ch 6 v 19.

[24]I Kings, ch 6 v 26.

[25]II Chronicles ch 3 vs 15–17.

[26]II Chronicles ch 4 v 2.

[27]I Kings ch 11 v 7.

[28]I Kings ch 8.

[29]I Chronicles chs 23 & 24.

[30]S. Sanmel, *Judaism and Christian Beginnings*, p 22 .

[31]Aristobulus, *Fragment 5*, cited by Eusabius in *Preparatio Evangelica*, 13.12.11.

[32]I Kings ch4 vs 29–30.

[33]II Chronicles ch 1 v 10.

[34]II Chronicles ch 9 v 1.

[35]E. A. Wallis Budge, *The Queen of Sheba and her only son Menelik being the Book of the glory of Kings (Kebra Nagast.)* .

[36]Graham Philips, *The Moses Legacy*, p 52.

Chapter 7

[1]Cited in *The Historical Atlas of the Jewish People*, p 22.

[2]II Kings ch 24 v 14.

[3]Paul Johnson, *A History of the Jews*, p 82.

[4]Isadore Epstein, *Judaism*, p 83.

[5]Dan Cohn Sherbok, *A Concise Encyclopedia of Judaism*, pp 61–2.

[6]Dan Cohn Sherbok, *A Concise Encyclopedia of Judaism*, pp 43–44.

[7]R. Lane Fox, *The Unauthorised Version*, p 72.

[8]Norman Cantor, *The Sacred Chain*, p 29 see also B. S. J. Isserlin, *The . Israelites*, p 204.

[9]Norman Cantor, *The Sacred Chain*, p 29.

[10]Karen Armstrong, *A History of Jerusalem*, p 86.

[11]Karen Armstrong, *A History of God*, p 75.

[12]Karen Armstrong, *A History of God*, p 96.

[13]Isadore Epstein, *Judaism*, p 85.

Chapter 8

[1]Josephus, *Antiquities of the Jews*, Bk 18, ch. 1–2(Edinburgh: Nimmo, 1868.

[2]Armstrong, *A History of Jerusalem* (London: Mandarin, 1994), p. 121.

[3]Josephus, *Antiquities,* bk. 18, ch.1, v 5.

[4]Josephus, *Antiquities,* bk. 18, ch.1, v 5.

[5]Epstein, *Judaism,* p. 112.

[6]Johnson, *A History of Christianity,* pp. 15–16.

[7]Epstein, *Judaism,* p. 97.

[8]Robert Eisenman, *The Dead Sea Scrolls and the First Christians,* p. 227.

[9]Epstein, *Judaism,* p. 97.

[10]Josephus, *Antiquities,* bk. 18, ch.1, v 6.

[11]Geza Vermes, *Jesus the Jew,* p. 79.

[12]Armstrong, *A History of Jerusalem,* p. 116.

[13]Eisenman, *James the Brother of Jesus,* p. 200.

[14]Eisenman, *James the Brother of Jesus,* p. 133.

[15]Ezekiel ch 18: vs17–21.

[16]Zohar 59b on "Noah.".

[17]Epstein, *Judaism,* p. 103.

[18]Epstein, *Judaism,* p. 105.

[19]*Jerusalem Talmud,* Sanhedrin, X, 5.

[20]Johnson, *A History of Christianity,* p. 10.

[21]Strabo, *Geographica,* 16.2.46.

[22]Peter Richardson, *Herod: King of the Jews and Friend of the Romans,* pp. 184–185.

[23]Josephus, *The Wars of the Jews,* bk 1, 4, 22; *Antiquities,* bk. 16, 1, 47.

[24]Josephus, *Wars,* bk 1, 4, 24; *Antiquities,* 16, 1, 47.

[25]Josephus, *Antiquities,* 12.2.59–65.

[26]Macrobius, *Saturnalia,* 2.4.1.

[27]Josephus, *Wars,* bk 1.6.48–55; *Antiquities,* 17.1.49–67.

[28]The Gospel According to Matthew ch 1 vs 21fff.

[29]Ravenscroft and Wallace-Murphy, *The Mark of the Beast,* p. 113.

[30]Epstein, *Judaism,* p. 106.

[31]Josephus, *Antiquities,* bk 17, ch. 10, 9; *Wars,* bk. 2, ch. 5,1.

[32]Josephus, *Antiquities,* bk 17, ch. 10, 10; *Wars,* bk. 2, ch. 5,2.

[33]Eisenman, *James the Brother of Jesus,* p. XXI.

[34]Josephus, *Wars,* 1.1.

[35]Mark Allen Powell, *The Jesus Debate* (London: Lion 1998), p. 30.

[36]Hugh Schonfield, *The Essene Odyssey,* p.39.

[37]Malachi ch 3: vs1–4.

[38]Malachi ch 4: vs 5–6.

[39]Johnson, *A History of Christianity,* pp. 19–20.

[40]The Gospel according to John ch 1: v 21 .

[41]Josephus, *Antiquities*, bk. 18. Ch. 5. v. 2.

[42]John Dominic Crossan, *Jesus: A Revolutionary Biography*, p. 34.

[43]Joan E. Taylor, *The Immerser: John the Baptist in Second Temple Judaism*, p. 278.

[44]A.N. Wilson, *Jesus*, (London: HarperCollins, 1993), p. xvi.

[45]Karen Armstrong, *A History of Jerusalem*, p. 145.

[46]The Acts of the Apostles ch 2 v 46.

[47]James Robinson (ed). "Gospel of Thomas," in *The Nag Hammadi Library* (London: HarperCollins, 1990), p. 108.

[48]Morton Smith, *The Secret Gospel* (Wellingborough, UK: Aquarian, Press, 1985).

[49]The Gospel According to Matthew ch 1 vs :5–6.

[50]The Gospel According to Matthew ch 29: vs19.

[51]See the Gospel according to Matthew ch 21: vs1–11; the Gospel According to Mark ch 11: vs 1–11; the Gospel According to Luke ch 19: vs 28–44 and the Gospel According to John ch 12: vs 12–19.

[52]The Gospel According to John ch 12: v 13.

[53]Maccabees ch 13: vs 50–51.

[54]See the Gospel According to Matthew 21:12; the Gospel According to Mark 11:15; the Gospel According to Luke 19:45.

[55]Philo of Alexandria, *De Legatione ad Gaium*, p. 301; Epstein, *Judaism*, p. 106; Wilson, *Paul: The Mind of the Apostle*, p. 56.

[56]Wilson, *Paul: The Mind of the Apostle*, p. 107.

[57]Tacitus, *Annals*, 15, 44.

Chapter 9

[1]James Robinson (ed), "Gospel of Thomas," v. 12 in *The Nag Hammadi Library*.

[2]*Pseudo-Clementine Recognitions*, 1,4.

[3]Epiphanius, *Against Heresies*, 78.7.7.

[4]The Acts of the Apostles ch12: v 17.

[5]Robert Eiseman, *James the Brother of Jesus*, p. xx.

[6]The Gospel According to Matthew ch13:v 55.

[7]Eusabius, *Ecclesiastical History*, 2, 234–235; Epiphanius, *Against Heresies*, 78, 14, 1–2.

[8]In a BBC radio broadcast on St Paul.

[9]A. N. Wilson, *Jesus*, p. 101.

[10]Fida Hassnain, *A Search for the Historical Jesus*, p. 84.

[11]The Gospel According to St John, ch 2: vs 1–5.

[12]Hassnain, *A Search for the Historical Jesus*, p. 84.

[13]The Gospel According to St. John ch 11:vs 20, 28–29.

[14]The Gospel According to St Luke ch 10: v 39.

[15]Published in Rochester, VT, by Bear & Co., 1993.

[16]See Gospel of Matthew 26:7; also described in the Gospel of Mark 14:3.

[17]Margaret Starbird, *The Woman with the Alabaster Jar,* p. 36.

[18]Andrew Wellburn, *The Beginning of Christianity,* p. 55.

[19]The Epistle to the Galatians ch 2:v 9 .

[20]Eisenman, *James the Brother of Jesus,* p. xix.

[21]Epiphanius, *Against Heresies,* A 29, 4.1.

[22]Eisenman, *James the Brother of Jesus,* p. 79.

[23]Eisenman, *The Dead Sea Scrolls,* p. 340.

[24]The Acts of the Apostles, ch 7: v 59.

[25]The Epistle to the Galatians ch 1: v17.

[26]The Acts of the Apostles ch 24: v14.

[27]The Acts of the Apostles ch 11.

[28]Eisenman, *The Dead Sea Scrolls,* p. 146.

[29]The Community Rule, viii, 20ff., from the Dead Sea Scrolls.

[30]The Epistle to the Galatians ch 2:vs 11–13.

[31]The Epistle to the Galatians ch 2:vs 15–16.

[32]II Corinthians ch 3:v 1.

[33]Johnson, *A History of Christianity,* p. 41.

[34]The Acts if the Apostles ch 16:v 1.

[35]The Acts of the Apostles ch 24:v 24).

[36]I Corinthians ch 9: v 1–2.

[37]Wallace-Murphy and Hopkins, *Rosslyn: Guardian of the Secrets of the Holy Grail* ,p. 67.

[38]Cited by Laurence Gardner in *The Bloodline of the Holy Grail,* p. 154.

[39]The Epistle to the Galatians ch 5:vs 1–4.

[40]I Corinthians ch 9:vs 24–26.

[41]Robert Eisenman, devotes an entire chapter to Paul's attack on James, citing a variety of sources in chapter 16, *James the Brother of Jesus.* See also *Pseudo-Clementine Recognitions.*

[42]A glossed-over account of this can be read in Acts 21:33.

[43]The Acts of the Apostles ch 23:vs 21–24.

[44]The Epistle to the Romans ch 16:vs 10–11.

[45]Wilson, Paul: *The Mind of the Apostle,* p.54.

[46]The Acts of the Apostles ch 24: vs1–27.

[47]The Acts of the Apostles ch 8: vs 9ff.

[48]Josephus, *Antiquities,* bk. 14, ch. 8,v. 3.

[49]Eisenman, *The Dead Sea Scrolls*, p. 230.

[50]Epistle to the Philippians ch 4:v 18.

[51]Epistle to the Philippians ch 4:v 21.

[52]B.N. San. 81b-82b in the *Mishna Sanhedrin*.

[53]Jerome, *Lives of Illustrious Men*, 2.

[54]Eisenman, *The Dead Sea Scrolls*, p. 262. .

[55]Armstrong, *A History of Jerusalem*, p. 151.

[56]Ute Ranke-Heinemann, *Putting Away Childish Things*, p. 173.

[57]Josephus, Wars, bk. 2, ch. 17 v 4.

[58]Josephus, Wars, bk. 2, ch. 20, .

Chapter 10

[1]Neil Faulkner, *Apocalypse: The Great Jewish Revolt Against Rome*. P 276.

[2]Robert Eisenman, *James the Brother of Jesus*, p xxi.

[3]Karen Armstrong, *A History of Jerusalem*, p. 156.

[4]Sifre on Leviticus, ch 19 v 8.

[5]Karen Armstrong, *A History of Jerusalem*, pp 168–169.

[6]Eusabius, *Ecclesiastical History*, IV, v.

[7]Eusabius, *Ecclesiastical Histories*, III, & Karen Armstrong, *A History of*. *Jerusalem*, p 153.

[8]Fida Hassnain, *A Search for the Historical Jesus*. Pp 55–60.

[9]Wallace-Murphy, Hopkins & Simmans, *Rex Deus*, p79.

[10]*Guidebook to Les Saintes Maries de la Mer*, p 3.

[11]cited by Andrew Welburn, *The Beginings of Christianity*, p 87.

[12]Karen Armstrong, *A History of Jerusalem*, p 155.

[13]Ralph Ellis, *Jesus: Last of the Pharaohs*, p 208.

[14]Mark Allen Powell, *The Jesus Debate*, p 41.

[15]Robert Eisenman, *James the Brother of Jesus*, p 54.

[16]Hugh Schonfield, *Those Incredible Christians*, p 56.

[17]Burton L Mack, *The Lost Gospel*, p 2.

[18]Burton L Mack, *The Lost Gospel*, p 4.

[19]Hugh Schonfield, *Those Incredible Christians*, p. 48.

Chapter 11

[1]Paul Johnson, *A History of Christianity*, pp 43,44 & 59.

[2]Hubert Jedin (ed.), *History of the Church*, vol. I—From the Apostolic Community to Constantine p. 356....

[3]Hubert Jedin (ed.), *History of the Church*, vol. I—From the Apostolic Community to Constantine p. 356....

[4]Wallace-Murphy and Hopkins, *Rosslyn Guardian of the Secrets of the Holy Grail*, p. 51.

[5]Paul Johnson, *A History of Christianity*, p. 73–4.

[6]Paul Johnson, *A History of Christianity*, pps 67, 76 & 82.

[7]Wallace-Murphy and Hopkins, *Rosslyn Guardian of the Secrets of the Holy Grail*, p. 71.

[8]L. David Moore, *The Christian Conspiracy*, p 61.

[9]Paul Johnson, *A History of Christianity*, p 67.

[10]Paul Johnson, *A History of Christianity*, p 76 and David Christie-Murray, *A History of Heresy*, p. 1.

[11]L. David Moore, *The Christian Conspiracy*, p 62.

[12]Paul Johnson, *A History of Christianity*, p 88.

[13]L. David Moore, *The Christian Conspiracy*, p 310.

[14]Robin Lane Fox, *Pagans and Christians*, p. 655.

[15]Eusebius, *Ecclesiastical History*, vol. x.

[16]Paul Johnson, *A History of Christianity*, p 88.

[17]L. David Moore, *The Christian Conspiracy*, p 62.

[18]Robin Lane Fox, *Pagans and Christians*, p. 655.

[19]L. David Moore, *The Christian Conspiracy*, p 63.

[20]L. David Moore, *The Christian Conspiracy*, p 63.

[21]L. David Moore, *The Christian Conspiracy*, p 63.

[22]Paul Johnson, *A History of Christianity*, p 92.

[23]Robin Lane Fox, *Pagans and Christians*, p. 656.

[24]Paul Johnson, *A History of Christianity*, p. 88.

[25]L. David Moore, *The Christian Conspiracy*, p. 310.

[26]Nag Hammadi *Codex* VII, 3,.

[27]Laurence Gardner, *Bloodline of the Holy* Grail, p. 159.

[28]Declaration of the Council of Hagia Sofia.

[29]Ravenscroft and Wallace-Murphy, *The Mark of the Beast*, pp. 123–4.

[30]Paul Johnson, *A History of Christianity*, p. 117.

[31]Bertrand Russell, *The Wisdom of the West*.

[32]Paul Johnson, *A History of Christianity*, pp 135–8.

[33]R I Moore, *The Formation of a Persecuting Society*, p. 12.

[34]Paul Johnson, *A History of Christianity*, p. 87 p 65–6.

[35]R I Moore, *The Formation of a Persecuting Society*, pp. 12–3.

Chapter 12

[1]Wallace-Murphy, Hopkins & Simmans, *Rex Deus*, p 105.

[2]Cecil Roth, *A Short History of the Jewish People*, pp 165–166.

[3]A. J. A. Zuckerman, *A Jewish Princedom in Feudal France 768–900*, p 37.

[4]Cecil Roth, *A Short History of the Jewish People*, p 165.

[5]A. J. A. Zuckerman, *A Jewish Princedom in Feudal France 768–900*, p 60.

[6]Chaim Beinhart, *Atlas of Medieval Jewish History*, p23 .

[7]M. N. Adler, *The Itinerary of Benjamin of Tudela* .

[8]Fossier, *The Middle Ages*, p 484.

[9]Fossier, *The Middle Ages*, p 426–7.

[10]Wallace-Murphy, *The Templar Legacy and Masonic Inheritance Within Rosslyn Chapel*, p 25.

[11]Wallace-Murphy & Hopkins, *Rosslyn Guardian of the Secrets of the Holy Grail*, p. 199.

[12]L-A de St Clair, *Histoire Genealogique de la Famille de St Clair.*

[13]L-A de St Clair, *Histoire Genealogique de la Famille de St Clair.*

[14]L-A de St Clair, *Histoire Genealogique de la Famille de St Clair. P. 8.*

[15]L-A de St Clair, *Histoire Genealogique de la Famille de St Clair. P. 9.*

[16]Wallace-Murphy, Hopkins & Simmans, *Rex Deus*, p 105.

[17]Wallace-Murphy, Hopkins & Simmans, *Rex Deus*, pp 107–108.

[18]L-A de St Clair, *Histoire Genealogique de la Famille de St Clair.*

[19]Emile Male, *Notre Dame de Chartres*, p 9.

[20]Colin Ward, *Chartres, the Making of a Miracle*, p 7.

[21]Gordon Strachan, *Chartres*, p 9.

[22]Ravenscroft & Wallace-Murphy, *The Mark of the Beast*, p 75.

[23]Colin Ward, *Chartres, the Making of a Miracle*, pp 8–9.

[24]Ravenscroft & Wallace-Murphy, *The Mark of the Beast*, pp 74–75 .

[25]Michael Kubler, Un Vie Pour Reformer l'Eglise, *Bernard de Clairvaux.*

[26]Michael Kubler, Un Vie Pour Reformer l'Eglise, *Bernard de Clairvaux.*

[27]L-A de St Clair, *Histoire Genealogique de la Famille de St Clair.*

[28]Barnavi, *A Historical Atlas of the Jewish People,.*

Chapter 13

[1]Hopkins, Simmons, Wallace-Murphy, *Rex Deus*, p. 113.

[2]Querido, *The Golden Age of Chartres*, p. 114.

[3]William of Tyre, lib xii, cap. 7.

[4]John J. Robinson, *Dungeon, Fire and Sword*, p. 31.

[5]Charles G. Addison, *The Knights Templar* (London: Black Books, 1995), p. 5.

[6]C. Knight and R. Lomas, *The Second Messiah*, p. 73.

[7]Helen Nicholson, *The Knights Templar*, p.22.

[8]Leroy Thierry, *Hughes de Payns, Chevalier Champeonis, Fondateur de L'Order des Templiers* , pp. 34–35.

[9] J. Laurent, (ed.), Cartulaire de Molésome, pp. 214.

[10] Robinson, Dungeon, Fire and Sword, p. 36.

[11] Gardner, The Bloodline of the Holy Grail, p. 256.

[12] Leroy Thierry, Hughes de Payns, Chevalier Champagnoise, pp. 107–108.

[13] Hopkins, Simmons, Wallace-Murphy, Rex Deus, p. 112.

[14] Hopkins, Simmons, Wallace-Murphy, Rex Deus.

[15] Nicholson, The Knights Templar, p. 22.

[16] Anon, Secret Societies of the Middle Ages, p. 190; & Nicholson, The Knights Templar, p. 26.

[17] Graham Hancock, The Sign and the Seal pp. 94, 99.

[18] Graham Hancock, The Sign and the Seal, pp. 49–51.

[19] Graham Hancock, The Sign and the Seal, p 52.

[20] Knight and Lomas, The Hiram Key.

[21] Robinson, Dungeon, Fire and Sword, p. 37.

[22] George Bordonove, La vie quotidenne des Templiers (Paris: Hatchette, 1975), p. 29.

[23] Anon, Secret Societies of the Middle Ages, p. 195.

[24] Nicholson, The Knights Templar, p. 96.

[25] Anon, Secret Societies of the Middle Ages, p. 199.

[26] liber ad milites Templi: De laude novae militiae.

[27] S.T. Bruno, Templar Organization (self-published), p. 65.

[28] Bruno, Templar Organization, p. 165.

[29] Peter Jay, Road to Riches , p. 118.

Chapter 14

[1] Ean Begg, The Cult of the Black Madonna, p. 103.

[2] Wallace-Murphy and Hopkins, Rosslyn Guardian of the Secrets of the Holy Grail, p 105.

[3] Wallace-Murphy and Hopkins, Rosslyn Guardian of the Secrets of the Holy Grail,.

[4] Wallace-Murphy and Hopkins, Rosslyn Guardian of the Secrets of the Holy Grail, p. 62.

[5] Wallace-Murphy and Hopkins, Rosslyn, Guardian of the Secrets of the Holy Grail pp. 181–182.

[6] Ean Begg, The Cult of the Black Madonna, p. 13.

[7] Malcolm Godwin, The Holy Grail, p. 14.

[8] Joseph Campbell and Bill Moyers, The Power of Myth, pp. 197–200.

[9] Published by Red Wheel/Weiser, Conari Press.

[10] John Robinson (ed), "The Gospel of Thomas," in The Nag Hammadi Library .

[11] Joseph Campbell and Bill Moyers, The Power of Myth, pp. 197–200.

[12] Baigent, Leigh, and Lincoln, Holy Blood, Holy Grail , pp. 262–268.

[13]Joseph Campbell and Bill Moyers, *The Power of Myth*, pp. 197–200.

[14]Joseph Campbell and Bill Moyers, *The Power of Myth*, pp. 197–200.

[15]Cited by Ted Roszak in *Where the Wasteland Ends*, p. 154.

[16]Cited by Ted Roszak in *Where the Wasteland Ends*, p. 154.

[17]Malcolm Godwin, *The Holy Grail*, p. 14.

[18]Godwin, *The Holy Grail*, p. 16.

[19]Emile Mâle, *Notre Dame de Chartres*, p. 141.

[20]Godwin, *The Holy Grail*, p. 12.

[21]Godwin, *The Holy Grail*, p. 18.

[22]Ravenscroft and Wallace-Murphy, *The Mark of the Beast*, p. 52.

[23]Andrew Sinclair, *The Discovery of the Grail*, p 27.

[24]Andrew Sinclair, *The Discovery of the Grail*, pp. 27–28.

[25]Godwin, *The Holy Grail*, p. 6.

[26]Louis Charpentier, *The Mysteries of Chartres Cathedral*, p. 145.

[27]Louis Charpentier, *The Mysteries of Chartres Cathedral*, p. 86.

[28]Ian Dunlop, *The Cathedral Crusades*, p.6.

[29]Information supplied by the Provencal Templar scholar, the late Guy Jordan.

[30]La *Régle de St Devoir de Dieu et de la Croissade* (the Rule of the Children of Solomon).

[31]Fred Gettings, *The Secret Zodiac*.

[32]J. F. Colfs, *La filiation généalogique de toutes les Écoles Gothiques* (cited by Fulcanelli in his *Le Mystère des Cathédrales*).

[33]Wallace-Murphy, *The Templar Legacy and the Masonic Inheritance Within Rosslyn Chapel*.

[34]Gordon Strachan, *Chartres*, p. 14.

[35]Idries Shah, *The Sufis*, pp. 166–193.

[36]Idries Shah, *The Sufis*, p. 29.

[37]P.D. Ouspensky, A *New Model of the Universe*, P. 345.

[38]Fulcanelli, *Le Mystère des Cathédrales*, p. 36.

[39]Fulcanelli, *Le Mystère des Cathédrales*, pp. 39–41.

[40]Louis Charpentier, *The Mysteries of Chartres Cathedral*, p. 81.

[41]Louis Charpentier, *The Mysteries of Chartres Cathedral*, p.165.

[42]Louis Charpentier, *The Mysteries of Chartres Cathedral*, p. 139.

[43]Blanche Mertz, *Points of Cosmic Energy*, p. 105.

[44]Y. Delaporte, *Les Trois Notre Dame de Chartes*, p.11.

[45]Fulcanelli, *Le Mystère des Cathédrales*, p.12.

[46]Wallace-Murphy and Hopkins, *Rosslyn Guardian of the Secrets of the Holy Grail*, p. 176.

[47]G. Quespel, "Gnosticism," *Man, Myth and Magic*, p.40,.

Chapter 15

[1] Michèle Aue, *The Cathars,* p 3.

[2] Yuri Stoyanov, *The Hidden Tradition in Europe,* p 159.

[3] Michael Costen, *The Cathars and the Albigensian Crusade,* pp 32–4.

[4] Michael Costen, *The Cathars and the Albigensian Crusade,* pp 37–8.

[5] Yuri Stoyanov, *The Hidden Tradition in Europe,* p 159.

[6] Michael Costen, *The Cathars and the Albigensian Crusade,* p. 59.

[7] Simon de Vries, *Cathars, Country, Customs and Castles,* p 2.

[8] Michèle Aue, *Cathar Country,* p 13.

[9] Guebin et Moisoineuve, *Histoire Albigeoise de Pierre des Vaux-de-Cerny.*

[10] Haim Beinhart, *Atlas of Medieval Jewish History,* p 53, see also Stoyanov *The Hidden Tradition in Europe,* p 160.

[11] Michèle Aue, *The Cathars,* p 3.

[12] Yuri Stoyanov, *The Hidden Tradition in Europe,* p 15.

[13] Lyn Picknett & Clive Prince, *The Templar Revelation,* p 88.

[14] Yuri Stoyanov, *The Hidden Tradition in Europe,* p 156.

[15] St Bernard's letter to Alphonse Jordan cited by Wakefield & Evans in *Heresies of the Middle Ages,* pp 122–4 .

[16] Yuri Stoyanov, *The Hidden Tradition in Europe,* p 156.

[17] Wakefield & Evans, *Heresies of the Middle Ages,* pp 140–1.

[18] Yuri Stoyanov, *The Hidden Tradition in Europe,* p 156.

[19] Michael Costen, *The Cathars and the Albigensian Crusade,* p 58.

[20] Simon de Vries, *Cathars, Country, Customs and Castles,* p 2.

[21] Michael Costen, *The Cathars and the Albigensian Crusade,* p 65.

[22] Michael Costen, *The Cathars and the Albigensian Crusade,* p 66.

[23] Georges Serrus, *The Land of the Cathars,* p 35.

[24] Michael Costen, *The Cathars and the Albigensian Crusade,* pp 112–14.

[25] Georges Serrus, *The Land of the Cathars,* p 15.

[26] Michèle Aue, *Cathar Country,* p 15.

[27] Yuri Stoyanov, *The Hidden Tradition in Europe,* p 173.

[28] Michael Costen, *The Cathars and the Albigensian Crusade* p. 123.

[29] Caesarius of Heisterbach, vol II pp 296–8.

[30] Guebin et Moisoineuve, *Histoire Albigeoise de Pierre des Vaux-de-Cerny.*

[31] Georges Serrus, *The Land of the Cathars,* p 20.

[32] Michael Costen, *The Cathars and the Albigensian Crusade* p. 128.

[33] Michèle Aue, *Cathar Country,* p 12.

[34] Michael Costen, *The Cathars and the Albigensian Crusade* p. 160.

[35] Michael Costen, *The Cathars and the Albigensian Crusade* p. 132.

[36]Raimonde Reznikov, *Cathars et Templiers*.

[37]Information supplied by Nicole Dawe of the Abraxus Templar Research Group.

[38]Yuri Stoyanov, *The Hidden Tradition in Europe*, p 178.

[39]Yuri Stoyanov, *The Hidden Tradition in Europe*, p 178–184.

Chapter 16

[1]Geoffrey Regan, *Lionhearts, Saladin and Richard I* (London: Constable Publishing, 1998), p. 91.

[2]Malcolm Barber, *The Trial of the Templars*, p. 11.

[3]Robinson, *Dungeon, Fire and Sword*, p. 405.

[4]Barber, *The Trial of the Templars*, p. 24.

[5]L. L. Borelli De Serres, *Les Variations monétaires sous Philippe le Bel* (Paris, 1902), pp.293–294.

[6]Ravenscroft and Wallace-Murphy, *The Mark of the Beast*, p. 52.

[7]Barber, *The Trial of the Templars*, p. 40.

[8]Haim Beinart, *Atlas of Medieval Jewish History*, p. 59.

[9]Chris Knight and Robert Lomas, *The Second Messiah*, pp. 127–128.

[10]Knight and Lomas, *The Second Messiah*, p.133.

[11]Noel Currer-Brigs, *The Shroud and the Grail* , p. 95.

[12]F. W. Bussell, *Religious Thought and Heresy in the Middle Ages*.

[13]Currer-Brigs, *The Shroud and the Grail*, p. 96.

[14]Barber, *The Trial of the Templars*, p. 47.

[15]Barber, *The Trial of the Templars*, p. 45.

[16]Baigent, Leigh, and Lincoln, *Holy Blood, Holy Grail*, p. 46.

[17]Lizerand, *Le Dossier de l'Affaire des Templiers* (Paris: Belles Lettres, 1989), p.16.

[18]Barber, *The Trial of the Templars*, p. 45.

[19]Barber, *The Trial of the Templars*, p. 47.

[20]Barber, *The Trial of the Templars*, pp. 47–48.

[21]Barber, *The Trial of the Templars*, p. 57.

[22]Papal Bull of Clement V, *Pastoralis Praeminentiae*.

[23]Barber, *The Trial of the Templars*, pp. 193–195.

[24]Barber, *The Trial of the Templars*, p. 200.

[25]Wallace-Murphy, *The Templar Legacy and the Masonic Inheritance within Rosslyn Chapel* p.22.

[26]Wallace-Murphy, *The Templar Legacy and the Masonic Inheritance within Rosslyn Chapel* p.22.

[27]Peter Partner, *The Knights Templar and their Myth*, p. 82.

[28]Hopkins, Simmans, and Wallace-Murphy, *Rex Deus*, p.172.

Rex Deus ✠ The Families of the Grail

[29]Partner, *The Knights Templar and their Myth*, p.82.

[30]Ravencroft and Wallace-Murphy, *The Mark of the Beast*, p. 53.

[31]Barber, *The Trial of the Templars*, pp. 178–193.

[32]"Les Templiers dans les Alpes Maritimes," *Nice Historique*, Jan.-Feb. 1938.

[33]Currier Briggs, *The Shroud and the Grail*.

[34]Garza-Valdes, *The DNA of God*.

[35]Papal Bull of Clement V *Vox in excelso*.

[36]Stephen Dafoe and Alan Butler, *The Warriors and the Bankers*.

[37]Wallace-Murphy & Hopkins, *Rosslyn: Guardian of the Secrets of the Holy Grail*, P. 106.

[38]Robinson, *Born in Blood*, pp. 164–166.

[39]HRH, Prince Michael of Albany, *The Forgotten Monarchy of Scotland* pp. 65 & 150.

[40]Wallace-Murphy, *The Templar Legacy and the Masonic Inheritance Within Rosslyn Chapel*, p. 22.

[41]Fr. Hay, *The Genealogie of the St. Clairs of Roslin* (Edinburgh: Maidenment, 1865.

Chapter 17

[1]*Memorandum of P. D'Arcis*, Herbert Thurston S,J. trans.

[2]Robert de Clari, *The Conquest of Constantinople*, E. H. Neal trans.

[3]David Sox, *The File On The Shroud*, p 394. Noel Currer-Briggs, *The Shroud and the Grail*, p 106.

[5]Ian Wilson, *Blood on the Shroud*, p 117.

[6]Pope Sixtus, *de Sanguine Christi* .

[7]Ian Wilson, *The Turin Shroud*, p 190.

[8]Ian Wilson, *Blood on the Shroud*, pp 64–7.

[9]Ian Wilson, *The Turin Shroud*, p 193.

[10]David Sox, *The File on the Shroud*, p 17.

[11]Ian Wilson, *The Turin Shroud*, pp 14–5.

[12]Ian Wilson, *The Turin Shroud*, pp 19–20.

[13]David Sox, *The File on the Shroud*, p 66.

[14]Ian Wilson, *The Turin Shroud*, p 21.

[15]Giovanni Judica-Cordiglia, *La Sidone*, 1961.

[16]Robert K Wilcox, *Shroud* P 136,

[17]Ian Wilson, *The Turin Shroud*, p. 24.

[18]Ian Wilson, *The Turin Shroud*, p. 23.

[19]Ian Wilson, *The Turin Shroud*, p. 24–5.

[20]Ian Wilson, *The Turin Shroud*, p. 25–6.

[21]Ian Wilson, *The Turin Shroud*, pp. 25–6.

[22]Ian Wilson, *The Turin Shroud*, pp26–7.

[23]Ian Wilson, *The Turin Shroud*, p. 29.

[24]Ian Wilson, *The Turin Shroud*, p. 30.

[25]Fr. Roland de Vaux, Foulille au Khirbet Qumran published in *Revue Biblique*, no 60 (1953).

[25]Ian Wilson, *The Turin Shroud*, pp 52–4.

[26]Ian Wilson, *The Turin Shroud*, pp 60–62.

[27]Ian Wilson, *The Turin Shroud*, p 62.

[28]Ian Wilson, *The Turin Shroud*, pp. 196–7.

[29]Ian Wilson, *The Turin Shroud*, p 197.

[30]David Sox, *The File on the Shroud*, p 102.

[31]Ian Wilson, *The Turin Shroud*, p 202.

[32]Ian Wilson, *The Turin Shroud*, p 8.

[33]Kersten & Gruber, *The Jesus Conspiracy*.

[34]Ian Wilson, *The Turin Shroud*, p 8.

[35]Ian Wilson, *Blood on the Shroud*, p 226.

[36]L. A, Garza-Valdez, *The D. N. A. of God*, pp 16–19.

[37]L. A, Garza-Valdez, *The D. N. A. of God*, p 69.

[38]L. A, Garza-Valdez, *The D. N. A. of God*, p 27.

[39]Pierleuigi Bauma-Bollone, Identification of Group of the Traces of Human Blood found on The Shroud, *Shroud Spectrum International*, 6th March 1983, pp 3–6.

[40]Ian Wilson, *Blood on the Shroud*, p 88.

[41]L. A, Garza-Valdez, *The D. N. A. of God*, p 39.

[42]L. A, Garza-Valdez, *The D. N. A. of God*, p 87.

Chapter 18

[1]Michael Baigent and Richard Leigh, *The Temple and the Lodge*, p. 135.

[2]Michael Baigent and Richard Leigh, *The Temple and the Lodge*, p. 148.

[3]Michael Baigent and Richard Leigh, *The Temple and the Lodge*, p. 149.

[4]H.R.H. Prince Michael of Albany, *The Forgotten Monarchy of Scotland*, p 125.

[5]H.R.H. Prince Michael of Albany, *The Forgotten Monarchy of Scotland*, p 125.

[6]Michael Baigent and Richard Leigh, *The Temple and the Lodge*, p. 150.

[7]Michael Baigent and Richard Leigh, *The Temple and the Lodge*, pp. 151–2.

[8]Michael Baigent and Richard Leigh, *The Temple and the Lodge*, p. 152.

[9]Michael Baigent and Richard Leigh, *The Temple and the Lodge* p. 152.

[10]Forbes-Leith, *The Scots Men at Arms and the Life Guards in France*, vol I, pp 11–2.

[11]Forbes-Leith, *The Scots Men at Arms and the Life Guards in France*, vol I, pp 11–2.

[12]Michael Baigent and Richard Leigh, *The Temple and the Lodge* p. 155.

[13]Hopkins & Wallace-Murphy, *Rosslyn Guardian of the Secrets of the Holy Grail*, p. 7.

[14]H.R.H. Prince Michael of Albany, *The Forgotten Monarchy of Scotland*, p 102.

[15]Michael Foss, *Chivalry*, p189.

Chapter 19

[1]*The Allocution Against Freemasons*, Pope Pius IX.

[2]Magnus Eliphas Levi, *Histoire de la Magie*, A. E. Waite (trans).

[3]Ean Begg, *The Cult of the Black Madonna*,.

[4]The Acts of the Apostles, ch2 v 46.

[5]Genesis ch 14 vs 18–20.

[6]Genesis ch 12 vs 16–20.

[7]*Epiphanus-Haeres*, lxxxviii.

[8]The Gospel According to S t Matthew, ch 22 vs 36–40.

[9]Paul Johnson, *A History of Christianity*, p 41.

[10]Louis Charpentier, *The Mysteries of Chartres Cathedral*.

[11]See Matthew Fox's masterwork *Original Blessing*.

Chapter 20

[1]Geoffrey Regan, *Lionheart, Saladin and Richard I*, p. 91.

[2]Malcolm Barber, *The Trial of the Templars*, p.11.

[3]John J. Robinson, *Dungeon, Fire and Sword*, p. 405.

[4]Barber, *The Trial of the Templars*, p.24.

[5]L. L. Borelli de Serres, *Les Variations monétaires sous Philippe le Bel* (Paris, 1902), pp. 293–294.

[6]Trevor Ravenscroft and Tim Wallace-Murphy, *The Mark of the Beast*, p. 52.

[7]Barber, *The Trial of the Templars*, p. 40.

[8]Haim Beinart, *Atlas of Medieval Jewish History*, p. 59.

[9]Chris Knight and Robert Lomas, *The Second Messiah* p. 59.

[10]Noel Currer-Brigs, *The Shroud and the Grail*, p. 95.

[11]Noel Currer-Brigs, *The Shroud and the Grail*, p. 95.

[12]F. W. Bussell, *Religious Thought and Heresy in the Middle Ages* (London: Robert Scott, 1998).

[13]Currer-Brigs, *The Shroud and the Grail*, p. 96.

[14]Barber, *The Trial of the Templars*, p. 45.

[15]Barber, *The Trial of the Templars*, p. 45.

[16]Robert Graves' introduction to the first edition of *The Sufis* by Idris Shah.

[17]Graves' introduction to the first edition of *The Sufis*.

[18]Rudolf Steiner, from a lecture given in Berlin, 2 Dec. 1904, published as *Die Tempellegende und die Goldene Legende no. 93*.

[19]Geddricke, 18th-century historian of Freemasonry.

[20]HRH, Prince Michael, *The Forgotten Monarchy*, p. 120.

[21]HRH, Prince Michael, *The Forgotten Monarchy*, p. 120.

[22]Masonic archives in Freemasons Hall, Edinburgh.

[23]Knight and Lomas, *The Second Messiah*, p. 53.

[24]Wallace-Murphy, *The Templar Legacy and the Masonic Inheritance Within Rosslyn Chapel, p. 31.*

[25]Wallace-Murphy, *The Templar Legacy and the Masonic Inheritance Within Rosslyn Chapel.*

[26]S. M Ward, *Freemasonry and the Ancient Gods*, (London: Simkin, Marshall, Hamilton, and Kent & Co. 1921).

[27]Knight and Lomas, *The Second Messiah*, p. 204.

[28]Knight and Lomas, *The Second Messiah*, p. 204.

[29]Knight and Lomas, *The Second Messiah*, pp. 207-209.

Chapter 21

[1]A E Waite, An Encylopaedia of Freemasonr pp 314–5.

[2]Cited in the Encylopaedia of Islam.

3.Epilogue to *The Treasure of Mont Segur*, by Norman Birks.

BIBLIOGRAPHY

Addison, Charles C, *The History of the Knights Templar*, London, Black Books, 1995.

Allegro, John M, *The Dead Sea Scrolls and the Christian Myth*, London 1981.

Allegro, John M. *The Dead Sea Scrolls*, London, 1964.

Allan, Grant, *The Evolution of the Idea of God*, London 1931.

Anon, *Secret Societies of the Middle Ages*, Whitefish MT, 2003.

Amberlain, Robert, *Jesu ou le Mortel Secret des Templiers*, Paris, 1970.

Anderson, William, *The Rise of the Gothic*, London 1985.

Armstrong, Karen, *Muhammad*, SF 1993.

   A History of God, London 1994.

   A History of Jerusalem, London 1996.

Ashe, Geoffrey, *The Ancient Wisdom*, London 1997.

Aue, Michele, *Cathar Country*, 1995.

Baigent, Leigh and Lincoln, *The Holy Blood and the Holy Grail*, London 1982.

Baigent & Leigh, *The Temple and the Lodge*, London 1992.

   The Inquisition, London 1999.

Barber, Malcolm, *The Trial of the Templars*, CUP 1994.

   The Cathars, Harlow, UK, 2000.

Baring & Cashford, *The Myth of the Goddess*, London 1993 .

Barnavi, Eli, *A Historical Atlas of the Jewish People*, London, 1992.

Bauval & Hancock, *The Keeper of Genesis*, London 1996.

Begg, Ean, *The Cult of the Black Madonna*, London 1985 .

Beinhart, Haim, *Atlas of Medieval Jewry*, NY 1970.

Birks & Gilbert, *The Treasure of Montsegur*, Wellingboro, 1990.

Bruno, S, *Templar Organisation,—Privately Published. .*

Burman, Edward, *The Templars, Knights of God*, Rochester VT, 1990.

The Inquisition, Wellingboro, 1998.

Bussel, F. *Religious Thought and Heresy in the Middle Ages,* London 1918.

Campbell, Joseph & Myers, Bill, *The Power of Myth,* NY 1990.

Cantor, N, *The Sacred Chain,* London 1996.

Charpentier, Louis, *The Mystery of Chartres Cathedral,* London 1993.

Christie-Murray, David, *A History of Heresy,* OUP 1989.

Costen, Michael, *The Cathars and the Albigensian Crusade,* MUP, 1997.

Crossan, John Dominic, *Jesus, a Revolutionary Biography,* SF, 1995.

Currer-Briggs, *The Shroud and the Grail,* London 1987.

Dafoe & Butler, *The Warrior Bankers,* Ontario, 1998.

De Clari, Robert, *The Conquest of Constantinople,* Toronto 1997.

Delaporte, Yves, *Les Trois Notres Dames de Chartres,* Chartres, .

Desgris, Alain, *L'Ordre de Templiers et la Chevalrie Macconique Templiere,* Paris 1996.

De Sede, Rennes-le-Chateau, *Les Impostures, Les Phantasmes, Les Hypotheses,* Paris 1998.

De Vries, Simon, *Cathars, Country, Customs and Castles,* Comtal 1993.

Dunlop, Ian, *The Cathedrals Crusade,* London 1982.

Eisenman, Robert, *James the Brother of Jesus,* London 1997.

  The Dead Sea Scrolls and the First Christians, Shaftsbury, 1996.

Epstein, Isadore, *Judaism,* Penguin, 1994.

Faulkner, Neal, *Apocalypse—the Great Jewish Revolt Against Rome, AD 66—73,* UK, 2002.

Feather, R. *The Copper Scroll Decoded,* London 1999.

Forbes-Leith, *The Scots Men-at-Arms and Life Guards in France,* Edinburgh 1882.

Foss, Micahel, *Chivalry,* London 1975.

Fox, Robin Lane, *The Unauthorised Version, Truth and Fiction in the Bible,* London 1991.

Freud, Sigmund, *Moses and Monotheism,* Paris 1939 .

Fulcanelli, *La Mystere des Cathedrals,* Uk 1977.

Gardner, Laurence, *Bloodline of the Holy Grail,* Shaftsbury, 1995.

  Genesis of the Grail Kings, London, 1999.

Garza-Valdes, Leonicio, *The DNA of God,* London 1998.

Gettings, Fred, *The Secret Zodiac,* London 1987.

Godwin, Malcolm, *The Holy Grail,* London 1884.

Gruber & Holsten, *The Original Jesus,* Shaftsbury, 1995.

Guebin & Moisoineuve, *Histoire Albigeoise de Pirre des Vaux-Chernay,* Paris 1951.

Hamil & Gilbert, *World Freemasonry,* Wellingboro, 1991.

Hamilton, B, *The Albigensian Crusade,* London, 1994.

Hancock, Graham., *The Sign and the Seal*, London 1993.

Hassnain, Fida, *A Search for the Historical Jesus*, Bath, 1994.

Hay, Fr, *The Genealogie of the St Clairs of Roslin*, Edinburgh, 1865.

Jackson, Keith, *Beyond the Craft*, Sheperton 1982.

James, Bruno S, *St Bernard of Clairvaux*, London1957.

Johnson, Paul, *A History of Christianity*, London 1978.

Johnson, Kenneth, Rayner, *The Fulcanelli Phenomenon*, London 1980 .

Josephus, *Wars and Antiquities*, Edinburgh 1869.

Kersten & Gruber, *The Jesus Conspiracy*, Shaftsbury, 1996.

Knight & Lomas, *The Second Messiah*, London, 1997 .

   The Hiram Key, London 1996.

Knoup, James, *The Genesis of Freemasonry*, MUP 1947.

Leroy, Thierry, *Hughes de Payen, Chevalier Champenois*, 1997.

Lionel, Frederic, *Mirrors of Truth*, Paris, 1991.

Lizerand, Georges, *Le Dossier de l'Affaire des Templiers*, Paris, 1923.

Lockhart, Douglas, *The Dark Side of God*, Shaftsbury, 1999.

Mackenzie, Kenneth, *The Royal Masonic Cyclopedia*, Wellingboro, 1987.

Mâle Émile, *Notre Dame de Chartres*, Flamarrion, 1983 .

Moore, L. David, *The Christian Conspiracy*, London 1983.

Moore, R. I. *The Formation of a Persecuting Society*, Blackwell, 1990.

Nicolson, Helen, *The Knights Templar*, Boydell, 2001 .

Oldenburg, Zoe, *Massacre at Montsegur*, London 1999.

O'Shea, Stephen, *The Perfect Heresy*, Profile, 2000.

Partner, Peter, *The Knights Templar and Their Myth*, Destiny Books, 1990.

Picknett & Prince, *The Templar Revelation*, London 1997.

Powell, Mark Allen, *The Jesus Debate*, Oxford, 1998.

Raschi, *Pentatuque Selon Raschi*, Paris, 1993.

Ravenscroft, Trevor, *The Spear of Destiny*, Weiser, 1982,.

   The Cup of Destiny, Weiser, 1982.

Ravenscroft & Wallace-Murphy, *The Mark of the Beast*, London 1990.

Regan, Geoffrey, *Lionhearts, Saladin and Richard I*, London 1998.

Reznikov, Raymonde, *Cathares et Templiers*, Loubatierres, 1993.

Robinson, James, M (ed) *The Nag Hammadi Library*, London 1990.

Robinson, John, *The Priority of John*, SCM Press, 1985.

Robinson, John, *Born in Blood*, Arrow, 1993.

   Dungeon, Fire and Sword, London 1999.

Rohl, David. *A Test of Time*, London 1995.

Roth, Cecil, *A Short History of the Jewish People*, London 1953.

Runciman, Stephen, *A History of the Crusades*, 3 vols, Pelican, 1971.

Sabbah, M & R, *Les Secrets de l'Exode*, Paris 2000.

Saige, G, *Les Juifs du Languedoc*, Franborough, 2000.

Serrus, Georges, *The Land of the Cathars*, Loubatierres, 1990.

Schonfield, Hugh, *The Passover Plot*, Shaftsbury 1985.

    The Pentecost Revolution, Shaftsbury, 1985.

    The Essene Odyssey, Shaftsbury 1990.

Shah, Idries, *The Sufis*, London 1969.

Sinclair, Andrew, *The Discovery of the Grail*, London 1998.

Smith, Morton, *The Secret Gospel*, Wellingboro, 1985.

Sox, David, *The File on the Shroud*, London, 1978.

Starbird, Margaret, *The Lady with the Alabaster Jar*, Bear & Co 1993.

Stevenson, David, *The First Freemasons*, Aberdeen UP, 1989.

Stoyanov, Yuri, *The Hidden Tradition in Europe*, Arkana, 1994.

Strachan, Gordon, *Chartres*, Edinburgh, 2003.

Taylor, Joan, *The Immerser: John the Baptist in Second Temple Judaism*, Cambridge, 1997.

Thurston, Herbert (trans), *Memorandum of Pierre D'Arcis*.

Upton-Ward, G. M. *The Rule of the Templars*, Boydell Press 1992.

Vermes, Geza, *Jesus the Jew*, London 1973.

Wakefield & Evans *Heresies of the Middle Ages*, Columbia UP, 1991.

Wallace-Murphy, T, *The Templar Legacy and the Masonic Inheritance Within Rosslyn Chapel*, London 1994 .

Wallace-Murphy T, *The Enigma of Freemasonry*, Ivy Press, 2006.

Wallace-Murphy & Hopkins, *Rosslyn Guardian Secrets of the Holy Grail*, Shaftsbury, 1999.

Wallace-Murphy & Hopkins, *Custodians of Truth*, RedWheel/Weiser/Conari Press, 2005.

Wallace-Murphy, Hopkins & Simmans, *Rex Deus*, Shaftsbury, 2000.

Welburn, Andrew, *The Beginnings of Christianity*, Floris 1981.

Wilson, Ian, *The Turin Shroud*, London, 1998.

    Blood on the Shroud, Book Club Associates, 1978.

Zuckerman A. J. *A Jewish Princedom in Feudal France 768–900*, Ny 1972.

About the Authors

Cynthia Wallace-Murphy is a Professional Registered Nurse specialising in cardiology. She is also a graduate of Marketing and Management. She has travelled extensively throughout Europe and spent some time in the Middle East. She has been researching Western Esoteric Spirituality with an emphasis on the Cathars, Knights Templar, Hermeticim, and Christianity. She returned to France in Languedoc-Rousillon in 2013 in order to study medieval cathedrals and the Cathar strongholds. Having an empathic feeling, a strong connection with Occitania, she decided to make it her permanent home where she currently resides with her husband Tim Wallace-Murphy in the foothills of the Midi Pyrènèes. She has published several articles on her experiences through travel in several books before embarking on a collaboration with her husband in their first joint book entitled *Rex Deus: The Families of the Grail*.

Tim Wallace-Murphy is an Irish born internationally known author and lecturer. Wallace-Murphy, is the author of thirteen published books, mostly about the history of a variety of heretical forms of spirituality. He once redefined heresy as:

The use of God's gift of Freewill in matters of Religion, Faith and Dogma.

Tim has appeared in some eight or nine TV documentaries and many of his interviews can be found on YouTube. He has given talks and lectures in a wide variety of venues, to Masonic Lodges, Spiritual groups, clubs and associations across the western world such as in Seattle and Long Beach on the West Coast of the USA, in Denver Colorado, in Santa Fe New Mexico. New York, New Jersey, Connecticut, in Montreal and the Eastern townships in Canada, all across England, Scotland and Ireland, in France, Italy, Spain and in Prague.

Eleven of his works describe historical aspects of spirituality and cover a variety of themes including the Knights Templar, the Cathars, Rosslyn Chapel and the Western Esoteric Tradition as well as the Grail genre. The other two, including the most recent are more modern mainstream historical works, namely What Islam did for Us a study of how Islamic scholarship laid the foundations of most of the more valued aspects of European culture, and his latest work *The Genesis of a Tragedy—A Brief History of the Palestinian People*. Tim was provoked to write this work as the Palestinian side of this conflict is rarely heard in either Western Europe or the United States and if this ongoing running sore in East West relations is ever to be solved, the pain on both sides needs to be understood.

He has acted as a tour guide in some of the most beautiful and inspiring sacred sites in Europe. including Rosslyn Chapel in Scotland, Avebury Stone Circle in England and Stonehenge. Tim has escorted people of all faiths and some of none around such fascinating and beautiful Cathedrals as Chartres, Notre Dame de Paris, Orleans and Amiens and the jewel in the crown in Paris, Sainte Chapelle.

Made in the USA
Middletown, DE
28 March 2016